Baseball's Heartland War,
1902–1903

ALSO BY DENNIS PAJOT

*The Rise of Milwaukee Baseball:
The Cream City from Midwestern Outpost
to the Major Leagues* (McFarland, 2009)

Baseball's Heartland War, 1902–1903

*The Western League
and American Association
Vie for Turf, Players and Profits*

DENNIS PAJOT

McFarland & Company, Inc., Publishers
Jefferson, North Carolina, and London

LIBRARY OF CONGRESS CATALOGUING-IN-PUBLICATION DATA

Pajot, Dennis.
    Baseball's heartland war, 1902–1903 : the Western League and American Association vie for turf, players and profits / Dennis Pajot.
        p.   cm.
    Includes bibliographical references and index.

    ISBN 978-0-7864-6337-4
    softcover : 50# alkaline paper ∞

    1. Baseball — United States — history — 20th century.
2. Minor league baseball — West (U.S.) — History — 20th century.   3. Western League (Baseball league) — history.
4. American Association (Baseball league) — History.   I. Title
GV863.A1P35   2011
796.357'64097309041— dc23   2011031514

BRITISH LIBRARY CATALOGUING DATA ARE AVAILABLE

© 2011 Dennis Pajot. All rights reserved

No part of this book may be reproduced or transmitted in any form or by any means, electronic or mechanical, including photocopying or recording, or by any information storage and retrieval system, without permission in writing from the publisher.

On the cover: Mordecai Brown, pitcher for the 1902 Omaha Indians (Library of Congress)

Manufactured in the United States of America

McFarland & Company, Inc., Publishers
  Box 611, Jefferson, North Carolina 28640
    www.mcfarlandpub.com

Table of Contents

Acknowledgments — vi
Preface — 1

ONE ♦ The War Begins — 3
TWO ♦ Filling Rosters and Jumping Contracts — 33
THREE ♦ The 1902 Playing Seasons — 57
FOUR ♦ Rowdyism and Umpiring in the Western League and American Association — 89
FIVE ♦ League Peace but Battle Continues in Two Cities — 108
SIX ♦ American Association Interlude — 131
SEVEN ♦ The 1903 Seasons — 144
EIGHT ♦ The War Ends — 177

Appendix A: American Association 1902 and 1903 Statistics — 191
Appendix B: Western League 1902 and 1903 Statistics — 197
Chapter Notes — 201
Bibliography — 209
Index — 211

Acknowledgments

In any undertaking of this size one needs help. To write a book about baseball events that occurred more than a hundred years ago, SABR members are always the most helpful people in the world. As projects take quite a while to complete, names and e-mails get lost in the scuffle. I apologize to those I inadvertently forget here, and openingly state all their help was very much appreciated. I would like to thank the many who helped out. Angelo Louisa copied and sent me the Omaha newspaper coverage of the Omaha-Milwaukee series that ended the 1902 season. Ralph J. Christian provided me with information on ballparks in Des Moines. Mark Fimoff helped with some picture identification. Rex Hamann was helpful with attendance information in St. Paul. Jeremy Krock took the time to find the news clipping of an alleged shooting incident in Peoria. Brian McKenna was very kind in sharing information on Roy Evans. Dan O'Brien provided numerous bits of information on varied subjects that helped fill gaps in my material. Ed Morton provided me with some useful articles on the Jake Weimer injunction. Michael Sekeres sent me an article on Thomas Hickey. Mike Welsh provided me with a Sanborn map of Kansas City to help locate the ballpark. Kevin Johnson did the same with a Denver Sanborn. Gord Brown shared information with me on the ballparks in Colorado.

A number of people proofread chapters for me, helping greatly in finding mistakes I made, pointing out unclear passages, and improving my weak grammar. These readers include David Anderson, Cliff Blau, Bob Buege, Dennis Degenhardt, Mark Dugo, Rex Hamann, Len Levin, Norman Macht, Mark Ruckhaus and Stuart Shea. All errors remaining are mine alone.

My family helped in a number of ways to bring this book together. As always, my wife, Angie, was very generous in giving me time to research, type out material, and simply stare at the computer screen for hours. My daughter-in-law, Lauren Pajot, spent a good amount of time helping me get the numerous pictures and images used in this book in the proper format, cleaned up, and in order.

Preface

Growing up in Milwaukee in the 1950s and 1960s, I heard many stories of old Borchert Field and the minor league Brewer teams that played there. My parents' and grandparents' generations talked of legendary Brewer stars and other players from the powerful American Association — a league almost equal to the major leagues in many of these folks' minds. Nicknames like the Brewers, Mud Hens, Millers, Blues and Colonels were as familiar as the Braves, Dodgers, Cubs, Phillies and Giants.

I had no idea this fabled American Association had a history that began with a baseball war, and had been an "outlaw league" in its inception. Like all events in my idealized idea of baseball, I thought everything happened according to carefully laid plans of the "organized baseball" legends I had read about.

The two-year battle of 1902 and 1903 between the newly formed American Association and the recently established Western League has never been fully explained to my knowledge. As with all wars — real wars between nations, wars between spouses, or baseball wars — there are always causes and background before the fighting begins. Wars do not simply happen. During any war there are battles, victories (and, of course, losses), turning points, setbacks and false endings. In all wars there are losers. And unfortunately these losers are not limited to the main participants. In addition to the soldiers, there is always collateral damage to the people living where the fighting occurs and to the economy of other regions, affecting the people in those areas. All of this occurred in the 1902–1903 war between the American Association and the Western League.

The story of this two-year struggle is more a story of baseball owners than players, more about baseball business strategy than baseball field strategy. The stars of the book are magnates and managers rather than home run hitters. The names of Thomas Hickey, Michael Sexton, George Tebeau, D.C. Packard and W.T. Van Brunt are not familiar to most readers of baseball history. The names Harry Quin and Charles Havenor are unknown in Milwaukee, even though without them the magnificent Brewers might not have existed and the legendary Borchert Field in which the Brewer teams played would have not stood tall in the minds of so many generations. No doubt Charles Strobel and Thomas Bryce have similar fates in Toledo and Columbus. But all these men played critical roles in the forming of the American Association, Western League and the history of minor league baseball.

The players who took the diamond in these two years were a different breed than the players of later generations. A few names will be familiar, and some even famous, but most are only a few lines of statistics at a baseball reference site. Some never made the major leagues, and a few are only known to us by their last name. But all these men played a role, not only in helping to form the American Association and Western League, but also in the formation of a minor league system that laid a solid foundation for the golden years of the minor leagues.

These men played a different type of baseball — now referred to as the "deadball era" — and played under a different code. As Chapter Four will show, fighting with teammates and fans was not uncommon. "Kicking," the term used at that time for arguing with the umpire, was an everyday occurrence. Physically fighting with the umpire was not a daily event, but hardly a week went by without such an incident. Umpires being punched, kicked, and worse were common stories in newspapers. And umpires fought back, with equal violence.

For those who think the controversy over the building of stadiums in cities was a later-twentieth century and beyond phenomenon, the struggles of locating and securing property for ballparks at the beginning of that period will be of interest. Many of the ballparks where teams in these two leagues played were only built after political and other struggles were overcome.

These two leagues endured many struggles to stay alive after a difficult birth and shaky infancy. As history shows, the American Association went on to a longer and more successful life. But this outcome was not a certainty in 1902 and 1903.

One of the hopes of my work on this book is that interest will be sparked in the early minor league history of the fourteen cities that held franchises in these two leagues. All these cities have a rich minor league history that deserves to be known by all, especially those lucky enough to call any of these towns their home.

ONE

◆ ◆ ◆ ◆

The War Begins

In 1900 the Western League formed with franchises in Omaha, Pueblo, Denver, St. Joseph, Des Moines and Sioux City. After a successful season, during which all teams made money, the Western League expanded to eight franchises for 1901, consisting of Colorado Springs, Denver, Des Moines, Kansas City, Minneapolis, Omaha, St. Joseph and St. Paul. Kansas City ended up winning the league championship by ten games. With a commanding lead throughout most of the season, there was little interest in a pennant race. The Western League's expansion movement for the 1901 season had not been as financially successful as hoped. The teams in Kansas City, St. Paul and Minneapolis were not patronized as well as expected, but these cities were still an improvement on the previous circuit, which laid the foundation for further expansion of the league. It was reported most of the clubs made some profit in the 1901 season.

With rumors of the Milwaukee American League franchise being transferred to St. Louis late in the 1901 season, word of changes regarding the minor Western League began to spread. In mid–September Western League president Thomas Hickey confirmed there would be changes in the cities in the league. Hickey said if the American League Brewers were transferred to St. Louis, it would be "more than probable" Milwaukee would have a team in the Western League. Two other cities being considered were Louisville and Indianapolis. Denver, Colorado Springs, Des Moines and St. Joseph were those in consideration of being dropped.[1] In October word had it that the Western League was thinking of expanding into a 10- or 12-team circuit, and would no doubt take in the cities of Louisville and Indianapolis, and possibly add Lincoln, Milwaukee, Columbus and Toledo. Columbus and Toledo had teams in the Western Association in 1901, and both had lost considerable money. There was also talk of invading Chicago, a move possible while the National League and American League were doing battle, and no National Agreement was in place with the minor leagues. Initial plans would supply this Chicago team with the best players from Colorado Springs and Denver, and then add some local talent. The rumored Chicago franchise was said to have secured backers and grounds. Two men interested in this Windy City club were Jimmy Ryan and Bill Everitt, both long-time Chicago National League favorites. *The Sporting News* thought a Western League team in Chicago would "not be unprofitable."[2] Later, Kansas City, St. Paul and Minneapolis were said to be dropped from the Western League. Rumors of which cities would be dropped and added continued well into November.

A future strongman in Western League affairs entered the scene in October 1901 when Thomas F. Burns purchased the Colorado Springs club from William Hulen for $5,000. Burns had a load of capital and was looking to make improvements in the local club. Burns was a native of Maine and a railroad engineer, working for the Rio Grande line for years. He came to Colorado around 1885, and teamed with his brother, James F. Burns, who was one of the locators and the president of the great Portland gold mine in Cripple Creek. Thomas became interested in the mining business, eventually owning a number of properties and making a fortune. A prominent Mason, Thomas Burns was also a member of the Pike's Peak Club, where he spent most of his leisure time. His passion centered on horse racing, but now he expected to have an equal passion for baseball.[3] Because of Burns' vast wealth, his Colorado Springs team would be known as "the Millionaires."[4]

Harry D. Quin and Charles S. Havenor, who had played roles in a short-lived American Association movement the previous year, were interested in keeping baseball in Milwaukee if the Brewers left for St. Louis. Havenor, a former Fourth Ward alderman, was owner of the Havenor & Bauman Tailoring store on Milwaukee's Grand Avenue. Quin owned a book and sporting goods store in the city. Charles Havenor was quoted as saying, "I would favor a league made up of central Western cities, for instance, Milwaukee, Detroit, Indianapolis, Kansas City, Louisville, Toledo, St. Paul and Minneapolis. That would make a pretty fair circuit, but it might be possible to improve it a bit. With such a circuit and a salary limit of $2,500 a month, the league could live and do a good business I am sure. I am ready to take a chance at it."[5]

As the transfer of Milwaukee to St. Louis stalled in November, so too did the plans of Hickey's Western League. However, other developments were occurring that would have an effect on the circuit.

The Western Association had been badly mismanaged and its president, William Meyer (who also acted as treasurer), had been arrested for embezzling about $5,000 from the league treasury. It was reported the club owners of the Western Association blamed Toledo owner Charles J. Strobel of negligence in not seeing that the bond Meyer secured had not been properly made out when the league accepted it.[6]

Strobel had had enough of the Western Association, and let off steam in an article in *The Sporting News* in November 1901:

> I made up my mind at the meeting of minor leagues in New York, when we were placed in class B — which allows a salary limit of $1,200 a month — that I would not fool around with any three-cent organization any more. I could not give Toledo people decent ball for $1,200 a month, and the people do not want an inferior article. The town has outgrown such a league as this Western Association, and if I am to manage a club next season it will not be in any league like that of this year. My salary list last summer was $2,100 a month, and I have reserved every man who played last year for next season. I would do well trying to get those fellows for $1,200 a month, wouldn't I? Toledo wants good, fast ball, I will give it to them if such a thing is possible. I have hopes of getting into this new league, and have been promised a franchise if the league comes this far east. But I am done with cheap leagues like the Western Association.[7]

Charles Strobel — Owner of the Toledo Mud Hens would later become involved in A.A.'s biggest contract dispute with the American League, involving Addie Joss (Toledo–Lucas County Public Library).

Strobel said the Western Association circuit received $3,500 more from him than his Toledo club garnered from other teams, and that Columbus brought in $2,500 less than it paid out.

Charles J. Strobel was born in 1864 in Kenton, Ohio. He later claimed to be of Swedish heritage, although he was generally thought to be German. He was managing at Tacoma in the Pacific League when an opportunity arose to purchase the Toledo franchise of the Interstate League. On July 24, 1896, Strobel purchased the club for $2,500; he would also serve as the team's manager.[8] Toledo was in the Interstate League until 1900, when the Western Association was formed. The same year Strobel purchased the Toledo franchise, it acquired the nickname "Mud Hens." According to the Toledo Mud Hens' official website, the team played at Bay View Park that year. The surrounding marshland near the park was frequented by an abundance of these strange birds with short wings and long legs, which brought about the nickname. Strobel was also an early promoter of aircraft racing. In his *New York Times* obituary in 1915, it was noted after his retirement from baseball, Strobel went into the airship business, backing a number of successful aviators.[9]

At the Western Association's November 8 meeting, Strobel and Thomas J. Bryce, president of the Columbus club stock company, suggested the Western Association be disbanded and then reorganized with some of the smaller cities replaced by larger cities. However, if the Western Association disbanded, even temporarily, this would result in the club owners losing all their protection rights and territorial rights under the National Agreement of the minor leagues. It was thought by some that Strobel and Bryce would then claim all these players and territory. The measure was voted down. Strobel and Bryce then resigned from that Western Association, citing the Association's low salary limit of $1,200. The resignations of Toledo and Columbus were accepted, but the territories were retained by the Western Association. The new head of the Western Association, Charles B. Power, wired the National Association of Professional Baseball Leagues and secured the territorial rights, franchise and players of Toledo for his league. A Toledo man, J.W. Gunnels, was offered the Western Association franchise and initially accepted but soon turned down the offer. For the moment, Strobel was without a baseball franchise, a ballpark and players. However, in the end the Western Association never put teams in either Toledo or Columbus against Strobel and Bryce. No doubt the Association knew these two men had the people of their hometowns on their side and decided not to challenge either.

Thomas Bryce — Clothing store owner and one of the wealthiest men in Ohio owned the Columbus Senators. He would die of a heart attack in the grandstand of his baseball park in 1908 (*St. Paul Globe*, December 27, 1903).

The 38-year-old Thomas Jefferson Bryce, who along with his brother, Alexander Chalmers Bryce, had founded Bryce Brothers clothing store in Columbus in 1896, was said to be one of the wealthiest men in that Ohio city. He also was backed by a stock company of 110 businessmen.[10] Bryce would be impossible to fight against in Columbus, not only because of his financial situation, but because of the respect he gathered in the community. When Bryce passed away only six years later, dying of a heart attack in the grandstand of his own ballpark and falling into the arms of John McGraw, *Sporting Life* would write that "his life was exemplary; his business activities were varied, great and honorable; and his base ball career was strikingly successful by reason of his honesty, his fair dealing, his clean methods, and his sincere love for the sport — a love which always abided with him and amounted almost to a passion. In all respects he was a model magnate, of whom base ball had a right to be proud. In life he was respected and loved and in death he will be sincerely mourned."[11]

Rumors of a re-organized Western League, being called the American Association, had been in the press for a month or more. President Thomas J. Hickey was not saying what cities he had in mind, preferring instead to wait until after he could meet with all the Western League owners. A report out of Chicago assured that city a franchise in the new league. It was said a company was being formed and that the team would be managed by Cap Anson. This Chicago team would play in the old West Side Grounds, providing competition to James Hart's National League team.

What Thomas Hickey envisioned were actually two leagues — a smaller Western League consisting of Denver, Colorado Springs, Omaha, St. Joseph, Lincoln and Sioux City — and a larger league including Kansas City, Columbus, Milwaukee, Toledo, Indianapolis, Minneapolis, St. Paul, and Chicago. However, Hickey soon ran into trouble with some owners of the Western League. On November 24 six of the Western League owners (A.B. Beall, Minneapolis; W.T. Van Brunt, St. Joseph; Frank

Thomas Hickey — Founder and first president of the American Association (*St. Paul Globe*, March 30, 1902).

Flynn, Des Moines; James Manning, Kansas City; Thomas F. Burns, Colorado Springs; William Rourke, Omaha) met at Council Bluffs, Iowa, to oppose Hickey's planned expansion and started discussions to oust him as president. The meeting was to be secret in order to prevent Hickey from moving first. However, Hickey caught wind of what was going on and gathered his supporters. Rourke and Beall, the owners from Omaha and Minneapolis, were also recruited and offered franchises in Hickey's planned league.

Thomas Jefferson Hickey was born in Sandwich, Illinois, on October 7, 1861. As a young boy the family moved to St. Louis where Thomas was introduced to baseball. Hickey became a professional roller skater and in the early 1880s built a skating rink in Lincoln, Nebraska. After his enterprise was destroyed by fire, the young man decided to organize an independent baseball club in Lincoln. He was involved in the formation of the Western Association in 1889, and operated the baseball team in Lincoln from 1893 to 1895. Hickey then moved to St. Joseph, was elected president of the Western Association, and served in that position until 1898, when the league suspended operations because of the Spanish-American War. In 1900 he helped organize a new Western League (the established Western League having changed its name to the American League), serving as president in 1900 and 1901. Hickey would remain as the American Association president until after the 1903 season, and then again from 1917 through 1935.[12]

Hickey announced his resignation from the Western League — and thus the National Association of Professional Baseball Leagues, in which he was chairman of the Arbitration Committee — stating he would become president of the new league. On November 29, 1901, this new independent American Association of Professional Baseball Clubs met at Chicago's Leland Hotel. The delegates present were: William H. Watkins and Charles Ruschaupt, Indianapolis; Harry D. Quin and Charles Havenor, Milwaukee; George Lennon, St. Paul; Thomas J. Bryce, Columbus; Charles Strobel, Toledo; A.B. Beall, Minneapolis; William A. Rourke, Omaha; and George Tebeau, Kansas City. Petitions to join the league from Chicago, Cincinnati and Louisville were turned down. It was said a Chicago franchise was decided against because Cap Anson would have to field a team so strong in that city in order to compete with the major league clubs that no team in the American Association would be able to compete with it. Thomas Hickey was elected president, secretary and treasury of the new league, with Harry Quin named vice president. Quin and Watkins were appointed to draw up a constitution and by-laws. Each club put up $500 cash, which guaranteed a 10-year position in the Association.

This new American Association declared a policy of absolute independence. It would not affiliate with the National League or with the new National

Association of Professional Baseball Leagues, an organization formed by a number of minor leagues to protect them from the major leagues — and themselves — in regard to player contracts and salaries. According to Thomas Hickey, this decision to go independent was not "taken in any spirit of defiance, but because the new organization considers itself out of the class of the minor leagues, although not ranking with the major organization."[13] Contracts would be respected, but not reserves. There was to be no salary limit (a $2,000-a-month limit on Class A leagues had been put in place by the National Association), although there was a tacit agreement to keep the expenses within the limit of the expected income.

George Tebeau of Kansas City explained the American Association had been formed because the collapse of the Western League was inevitable. When the Western League's expansion brought in St. Paul, Kansas City and Minneapolis, the league's expenses and salaries increased 40 percent. It was expected the increase for 1902 would be another 20 percent. He felt franchises in Des Moines, Sioux City, St. Joseph and Colorado Springs would not prosper under those increases, and ultimately would fail. Tebeau's Kansas City franchise, as well as St. Paul and Minneapolis, demanded to be classed with such clubs as they had been associated with in the past to be profitable. The Toledo correspondent to *Sporting Life* made it simple: "Toledo is thoroughly tired of horse and buggy leagues."[14]

Sporting Life had this to say about the American Association's independence and future:

> But doubtless the chief reason for independence — or to put it harshly, but more truly, outlawry — was compulsion. The insistence of the Western Association as regards the Toledo and Columbus territory, and the refusal of the Western League to surrender part of its territory made it impossible for the National Association to sanction the new league movement without ruinous self-stultification. Mr. Hickey and his co-laborers thus were compelled to chose between abandoning their scheme or going it alone, and they chose what to them seems the lesser of two evils.
>
> Nevertheless, in starting as free-booters and without salary limit the American Association magnates have started wrong, and they must know it as most of them are veterans in the minor league game. For this reason we believe that all has not yet been said or done. Fortunately the long winter is before them to evolve a more satisfactory basis of operation; but unfortunately so many things may be done before spring as to make affiliation with the National Association impossible — in which event the new American Association in particular, and minor league ball in general, will be the sufferer.[15]

The Sporting News was not as kind, especially to the American Association owners. The St. Louis weekly said the league's membership is of minor league proportions, but it is the ambition of its promoters to have it considered a major league, not quite up to the standard of the American or National, but many degrees above the ordinary minor organizations. Over half of the cities did not keep step with the Western League, from which the American evolved. Omaha, Toledo, Columbus and St. Paul were failures. Minneapolis was a good field one season and unproductive the next. Milwaukee managed to maintain its Western League entity, but its club was seldom a source of revenue to the owners or their partners. Indianapolis has never paid a large profit to the men behind the club, notwithstanding the uniformly good team it has held. Kansas City, under Manning, was a money maker, with Tebeau and a pennant winner, it was a decided disappointment.[16]

The Sporting News held its biggest slaps for the A.A. owners. Even though the American Association claimed neutrality in the ongoing major league war, *The Sporting News* believed it to be an ally of the National League. The National League had suspended the rules for drafting and purchasing players from the minor league months prior in its fight with the American League, forcing the minors to form a National Association for mutual protection. The majority of the owners now in the American Association had pledged allegiance to the minors' National Association, but now were violating the Association's territorial rights. "The deserters not only repudiated the obligations they owed to their 1901 partners, but left them stranded without the least prospect of going on in the base ball business without loss." The paper thought the men running the American Association did not have the baseball experience or intelligence to make it go. However, *The Sporting News* believed Thomas Hickey had executive talent and would, if unhampered, administer the affairs of the Association in a sound business manner. The weekly predicted: "When the days of disappointment that always come to a majority of the cities which have teams in a championship race, the men behind most of the clubs will not be traceable or resourceful."[17]

Doc Shively, a Kansas City newspaperman, saw George Tebeau as the real power in the American Association. He wrote in *The Sporting News* of December 14, 1901: "George Tebeau has been the real president of the Western League since its reorganization two years ago. Hickey, who had held the title, was merely a figurehead, a man Friday, for every one of the movements made by him has had to be sanctioned by the Kansas City magnate. They have had their heads together constantly, and Tebeau has been the originator of most of the schemes. In fact, his pull with the chief executive has been so strong that Hickey has often been designated vice-president by some writers."[18]

George Tebeau was born in St. Louis in 1861, three years before his baseball-playing brother Oliver "Patsy" Tebeau. George began his baseball career in his hometown with the amateur Shamrock club in 1884 as manager and pitcher. The next year he took charge of the Leavenworth team but soon signed with the Denver club of the Colorado State League, where he played two years. In 1887 he went to the big leagues, playing three years with Cincinnati of the American Association. Tebeau moved around the minors and majors for a number of years, serving as an outfielder and team captain. In 1900, with the help of a $100 advance from D.C. Packard, George assisted Thomas Hickey in organizing the new Western League, becoming part-owner of the Denver club. Tebeau's team won the pennant that year and made the most money in the league. For the 1901 season Tebeau established the Kansas City club in the Western League and again won the league championship. Tebeau's leadership and executive abilities showed him to be an unqualified success.[19] *Sporting Life* would later say of him: "There is no use denying the fact that George Tebeau is one of the greatest base ball men in the country. He is in the same class as Ban Johnson. No one is ahead of him. He has shown this to be true time and time again."[20]

On December 3, 1901, the Milwaukee American League franchise was transferred to St. Louis, temporarily giving the American Association a one-team show in the Wisconsin city. However, the Western League was not gone from the picture. At the Western League's December 4 meeting, James Whitfield of Kansas City was elected Hickey's successor as president of the league, with a raise in salary to $2,000 a year. The franchise situation was discussed, and it was decided to retain franchises in Minneapolis, St. Paul, Omaha and Kansas City, regardless of the actions of the American Association. The Western League claimed all the territory it had occupied the previous year under its five-year league contract. George Tebeau's rights to the Denver franchise, which he owned with D.C. Packard, were taken from him. Several parties applied for the Denver franchise, one being Otto Floto, sports editor of the *Denver Post*, who was representing the proprietors of that newspaper. Another was Charles J. Reilly, a big league veteran who had played for Los Angeles of the California League in 1901 after toiling in Denver the previous year. At this time the Western League consisted of only Kansas City, Omaha, Colorado Springs, St. Joseph and Des Moines.

The National Association of Minor Leagues immediately declared it supported the Western League in its fight against the American Association and expelled Thomas Hickey from its body. George Tebeau declared it would be "war to the death" in Kansas City. As Tebeau already had the grounds and was well liked, and James Manning's popularity had slipped after leaving K.C. for Washington, D.C., *Sporting Life* appeared to give Tebeau the edge in Kansas City.[21] However, *The Sporting News* saw things just the opposite. The paper stated Western League president James Whitfield was a fixture in K.C., having worked at the *Kansas City Star* since 1884 and becoming the paper's sporting editor. Whitfield had been involved in Kansas City baseball since the 1880s, serving as the Kansas City National League club's secretary in 1886, in addition to being instrumental in securing an American Association franchise in 1888. Manning was "deservingly popular" in the city, and the new field manager, Charles "Kid" Nichols, was just as popular. It would be hard for Tebeau to be successful in Kansas City, stated the St. Louis weekly.[22]

The 40-year-old James Manning had been in baseball for almost 20 years. He had started his career with Springfield of the Northwestern League in 1883, and spent the next four years bouncing around National League clubs, before ending his career with Kansas City of the old American Association. Manning would hit only .215 in the big leagues, and stayed on in Kansas City with the Western Association and Western League teams. He purchased the Western League club and remained in the western Missouri town until 1901.

Manning was very popular in Kansas City, but in this year he gave up the ownership of the baseball club to become majority stockholder of the Washington franchise in the new major American League. Manning managed the Senators to a 61 and 73 season while losing a fair amount of money. In addition to the extremely high salaries in the American League, there was concern the National League might renew its lease on the old park in Washington, D.C., which would lead to the American League franchise losing even more money. Manning decided to sell his stock to another stockholder, Fred Postal. It was also reported Manning left because American League president Ban Johnson had too much power, which prevented club owners from doing what they considered right for their club and the league. As Manning still held an option on the lease on the only park in Kansas City, he decided to

James Manning — The Kansas City favorite would take the K.C. Western League franchise through its first year of battle with the American Association (Transcendental Graphics/theruckerarchive.com).

return there. Manning also sold high-explosive compound for a big powder firm, causing *Sporting Life* to comment, tongue in cheek: "The stuff will come in handy if Tebeau makes too much headway in Kansas City."[23]

Charles "Kid" Nichols was born in 1869 in Madison, Wisconsin. He had played in 1887 and 1888 with Kansas City in the Western League and Western Association. In 1889 Nichols went to Omaha, and then to Boston in the National League the following year. The future Hall of Famer pitched for the Beaneaters from 1890 to 1901, winning 329 games and losing only 183. He posted 30 or more victories in seven of his first nine years there — in 1890 and 1895 he would only win 27 and 26 games, respectively. After the 1901 season Nichols obtained his release from Boston to go to Kansas City as joint owner with

Kid Nichols — The popular and famous Boston pitching ace would give class and a big time name to the Western League's Kansas City team (baseballguru.com).

James Manning; Nichols ran the playing side of the game and Manning the business end. It was reported neither Manning nor Nichols could sell his shares without the consent of the other. Both Charles' and his wife's parents lived in Kansas City, adding to their anxiousness to return to the city. Philadelphia writer Ernest J. Lanigan had high praise for Charlie Nichols, both as a player and a person, upon his leaving the Boston club. Lanigan wrote of the new Kansas City manager/owner:

> He was a general favorite with the local public, as well as with the enthusiasts of every city he visited, and the appearance of a Boston team with the "Kid" will for some time to come resemble a production of *Hamlet* with Hamlet omitted. For 12 successive years he wore the uniform of the Boston National League Club and in that time he always behaved himself and gave to the management his best service. He did not dissipate and became thoroughly liked for the gentlemanly way he always conducted himself on and off the field. Here in Philadelphia we have ever considered Nichols as one of the really great pitchers in the history of the national game.[24]

The American Association soon gained a distinct advantage in Kansas City when it was reported George Tebeau had control of three baseball sites in the city, recently securing a one-year lease on old Exhibition Park for $3,000 plus repairs, taxes and insurance. President James Whitfield claimed the Western League had a one-year option on the park, but the rent demanded was so excessive Manning declined, believing he could build a new park cheaper. Tebeau had actually subleased Exhibition Park from Manning the year before. Manning had renewed his lease on the park in the spring of 1901 with the intention of putting a team in the proposed Western Association. When this deal fell through, Manning had a ballpark on his hands that was costing him about $3,500 for the year. Manning owned the American League club in Washington, and Tebeau leased the park in Kansas City for his 1901 Western League team at a high price.[25]

Whitfield and Manning looked over sites in December and found five or six that would make a good park. Whitfield thought Tebeau's actions in loading himself with the leases of three ballparks would not hinder the Western League club but would hurt Tebeau's bottom line, as the leases took $8,000 out of the American Association owner's pocket. In early January 1902 Manning secured a park at 16th and Indiana, about six blocks from Tebeau's park, on the same streetcar line. It was questioned if Manning's park would draw fans, as the streetcars had to pass within twenty feet of Tebeau's park, which could not help but make a difference.[26] Work began at Manning's Western League park in March, calling for seating for 5,500 in the grandstand. When completed in April, it was said to be a big improvement over the old Exposition Park. As a money-producing investment, Manning and Charlie Nichols signed a five-year contract with the Missouri and Kansas university football teams to lease the new park on Thanksgiving and other days at such a favorable rent that the owner's percentage of the receipts would more than pay for the cost of the new park.[27]

Shortly thereafter it appeared the Western League–American Association war would be fought on additional fronts. In December 1901 word was being spread that Milwaukee would be awarded a franchise in the new Western League, with Fred C. Gross, formerly involved with the Milwaukee American League club, likely to be awarded this franchise. However, after the first of the year in 1902, Jim Manning told reporters Milwaukee was no longer being considered for the Western League. Manning also said Denver and Colorado Springs would be out. He thought the Western League would consist of Omaha, St. Joseph, Kansas City, Sioux City, Rockford, Peoria, Dubuque, and either Des Moines or Louisville.

Fred Gross told the Milwaukee press in early January that he was out of baseball, and two teams in Milwaukee would prove to be an expensive proposition to the clubs' backers, especially the team that did not hold its own in a pennant race. However, on January 17 W.T. Van Brunt, James Manning and Thomas Burns came to Milwaukee to talk to Gross about the franchise. Upon leaving on the afternoon train, the three announced Milwaukee would definitely be in the Western League. When asked who would supply the money to finance the new club, "the trio of Westerners were as dumb as oysters," claiming they had promised not to name the backers. It was reported Gross was not interested in backing the club, although he was willing to lease the grounds to the Western League and "dispose at a sacrifice the uniforms the Brewers wore last summer." Thomas Burns had told Gross that "a brace of capitalists unknown to Milwaukee" wanted to supply money to a franchise in the Cream City.[28]

Most important, Fred Gross was owner of Milwaukee Park on 16th and Lloyd, where the Brewers had played since 1895. In December Western League President Whitfield said he had closed a deal for the ballpark on Lloyd Street and a decision would be made soon on which of the several applicants would receive the Milwaukee franchise. But soon it was reported no lease on the Lloyd Street grounds had been secured, and that Harry Quin and Charles Havenor of the American Association were negotiating for the park. This would shut out the Western League franchise from the only available grounds in Milwaukee and also save the American Association club the expenses of erecting new stands at the grounds Quin owned at Eighth and Chambers. Gross said he would not lease the park to anyone until he received a substantial payment. On January 10 James Whitfield signed a two-year lease on the park on 16th and Lloyd. Quin announced he would build his own park at Eighth and Chambers, where a few years earlier Athletic Park stood, but now was being used by Troop A First Cavalry. Troop A was told to vacate the property by March 1, and new stands and bleachers were built for the new Athletic Park. Upon completion, Quin leased the ballpark to the Milwaukee Brewers Baseball Club for 10 years, the baseball club paying six percent interest on a mortgage of $16,000 in lieu of rent for the first year.

In December George Tebeau sold his interests in the Denver franchise and the lease on the park at Sixth Avenue and Broadway to the Western League, which meant there would be no fight in Denver. At the time it was reported D.C. Packard was left entirely out of the deal, and that A.B. Beall of Minneapolis had negotiated the deal while working for the Western League. Beall said he did not know who would be in charge of the franchise, although some reports placed him at the head. At the time Tebeau said he was happy with the sale of the Denver club and would concentrate his efforts in Kansas City.

James Whitfield, however, told the press the Denver franchise was vested in the Western League and could not be sold until the league ratified the sale. He noted that no decision had been made by the Western League on ownership.[20] It was thought that J.R. Crabb, owner of an amateur baseball team and the leasee of Union Park in Denver, stood a good chance of obtaining the franchise, as he held the lease on the only available grounds in Denver outside of Beall's Broadway Park.[30]

President Whitfield announced a few days before Christmas that A.B. Beall had decided to stick with the Western League and leave Minneapolis. According to Minneapolis sources, Beall had traded the local franchise for Tebeau's Denver interests and would manage the Denver team in 1902. Word in Minneapolis was that if Walter Wilmot could raise $4,000, he could purchase the franchise. It was also reported that George Lennon, who owned the St. Paul American Association club, wanted to purchase the Minneapolis franchise and put the title in the name of two residents of the city. If this was in fact the case, the *Minneapolis Journal* warned Hickey to stop the transaction, as syndicated baseball would not be popular in the Minneapolis/St. Paul area.[31]

Walter Wilmot — The Minneapolis Miller manager had played for years in the National League and ran an early player recommendation bureau (Transcendental Graphics/theruckerarchive.com).

Wilmot purchased the Minneapolis club and two ballparks — Nicollet Park at 31st Street and Nicollet Avenue and Minnehaha Driving Park on Minnehaha Avenue at 34th Street for Sunday games — for a cash consideration. This move pleased the Minneapolis fans because Wilmot had always been popular in the city and was thought to be the man capable of producing a winner. Before the season began, the Minneapolis Base Ball Association would incorporate with a capital of $10,000 by Wilmot, S.E. Hoops and Edward A. Johnston.

The 38-year-old Wilmot had managed or played in Minneapolis from 1896 to 1900. Prior to that, he had played in the National League with Washington (1888 and 1889) and Chicago

(1890 to 1895). He also played a number of games with the New York Giants in 1897 and 1898. In the 1890s Wilmot ran a recommendation bureau for aspiring young players. He would attempt to match players with clubs by providing averages and writing letters of recommendation. In 1901 Wilmot started the season in Louisville but took over the Grand Rapids team, both in the Western Association. His Grand Rapids club lost $3,000 on the season, and then lost the pennant when two games were thrown out of the standings after the campaign concluded. With much turmoil going on in the Western Association, Wilmot decided not to return to Grand Rapids. It was reported after the 1901 season that Wilmot intended to return to his home in Minneapolis and conduct his retail cigar business. As it turned out, he had no business to return to and instead continued his very good position selling his Paul Jones whiskey to local dealers for a Louisville firm.[32]

Western League President Whitfield also told the press that George Lennon in St. Paul would come back to the Western when the American Association collapsed. However, Lennon had made it clear he would not return to the Western League. "I have a franchise in the American Association and shall stand by it. St. Paul is too big to associate with Des Moines and Colorado Springs and won't consent to support minor league ball when it can get the same on a par with the major leagues. The American Association is entirely independent, and, aside from respecting contracts, is at liberty to get the best players that money can secure. It will cost more, but I believe St. Paul wants the best it can get and will pay for it."[33]

Meanwhile, William Rourke in Omaha had abandoned the American Association. Furthermore, he was threatening to enjoin the A.A. from putting a club in Omaha, as he owned the Western League franchise there. President Hickey replied that the American Association refunded Rourke's $500 deposit, plus an additional $100 for running expenses, even though the Association was not legally bound to do so. Hickey said nothing prevented the American Association from putting a team in Omaha because Rourke forfeited all rights when he broke faith. "We will go ahead as if Mr. Rourke had never been on earth," Hickey told *Sporting Life*.[34] The Omaha correspondent to *The Sporting News* doubted Hickey really wanted to put a second club in Omaha, or that anyone would support it. "This town will give one team good support, but no reason exists to think that it will support two, or that anyone in his sane mind would risk money on such a proposition."[35] Yet Hickey still maintained the American Association would occupy the Nebraska city. In December he offered a franchise in Omaha to Buchanan Keith, who had owned the Western League team in Omaha for two years. Keith declined the offer, believing two clubs would not pay in Omaha, and he did not wish to challenge Rourke.

While the Western League was having success in Omaha, its chances of putting a club back in Des Moines were looking slimmer. The ability of many franchises to field a club in the Western League or American Association depended on ballpark access or availability in the city. The owners of the ballpark the Des Moines team had been playing in were said to be asking a substantially higher rent. As there was no other available place in the city for baseball grounds, the franchise might be forced to leave. There were rumors that William Rourke might purchase the club and transfer it to Indianapolis or Louisville.

William A. Rourke, who was causing such a stir in the Western League/American Association baseball circles, was born in Ohio in 1863. His baseball career began in Zanesville in 1885 before moving on to Duluth of the Western League and then in 1887 to his first tour in Omaha, at that time in the Western League. Making stops in numerous minor leagues from Minneapolis to Texas over the next ten years, Rourke was hit with a pitch in the eye, affecting his eyesight and cutting short his playing career. His first manager's job had been at Grand Island in the Nebraska State League in 1892. He later managed clubs in Omaha, Bloomington, Birmingham and St. Joseph. In the winter of 1899, Rourke and Buchanan Keith purchased the Omaha franchise in the new Western League, making good money in the 1900 season. The next year Rourke bought out Keith, and the stage was set for Rourke's dealings in 1902.[36]

On December 30–31, 1901, American Association members met at the Hotel Baltimore in Kansas City. All eight cities were represented, including Omaha, with Milwaukee's Harry Quin serving as a proxy for that city. A constitution was adopted, uniform ticket prices to games set at 25 cents for general admission and 50 cents for grandstand seats, an equal division of gate receipts decided on, and a 10 percent guarantee fund established. In the matter of uniforms, it was decided all teams would wear white uniforms at home, with the exception of Kansas City, which was allowed to wear blue at all times. The traveling uniforms would be left to the judgment of each team. Quin, who owned a sporting goods store in Milwaukee, not only supplied uniforms for his Brewers but later secured orders to supply the uniforms of Kansas City and Louisville.[37] In a move to strengthen Thomas Hickey — and thus his association — each member of the league placed a three-year lease of his ballpark with Hickey.

After the American Association meeting, Thomas Hickey offered William Rourke $5,000 to leave the Western League for the A.A. Rourke took the offer under consideration but asked for more time. The Omaha owner told a St. Paul reporter he thought the American Association offer was "a grandstand play to place me in an unenviable light with the Omaha baseball public."

Rourke said Hickey and his men were trying to make it appear he was standing in the way of Omaha fans seeing a good baseball team. The Omaha owner said to the newspaper man:

> To show that it is not true, and to refute all claims of Mr. Hickey that this so-called association intends to give Omaha a higher grade of the national game than she has ever enjoyed before, they thus boldly offer, in fact invite me to fall into their circuit with the very team with which I intend to represent the Western league here next summer. If my team will be capable of giving the people high class ball in the American, what should be expected of the same men in the Western league? Does that strike the ordinary fan with the idea that their body intends to give us a higher class game than we have heretofore and will hereafter enjoy?[38]

Other sources reported Rourke was asking $7,500 for his franchise. Hickey declined this price and said he would put the money into improvements at the American Association playing grounds. It was announced that local businessman Frank W. Bandle would run the Omaha American Association club with the backing of two Wisconsin men — Cornelius Corcoran, an owner of Corcoran Brothers Grocers and an alderman in Milwaukee's Third Ward, and Adren L. Buell of Berlin. Frank Bandle was popular in Omaha, having played ball there in the 1880s, and it was thought he would be able to sell stock to local people. As it stood, Bandle owned 55 percent of the stock, Buell and Corcoran 45 percent.[39] In early January 1902, Hickey announced grounds had been found at 20th and Paul streets. These grounds were on three streetcar lines and only 10 minutes from the business section of town.

The Western League met in Kansas City on January 14–15, 1902, and announced the Denver franchise had been awarded to Durand C. Packard. A lifelong baseball fan who was said to have been one of the original supporters of the Syracuse Stars in 1876,[40] Packard initially made his money in Denver by being involved in the Manhattan Gold and Silver Mining Company, and later went into real estate and insurance. He was involved in the forming of the Denver club in the Western League in 1900, soliciting funds to build a grandstand. It was said Packard's "integrity was beyond question and his word as good as gold."[41]

The Western League now had five solid franchises with owners: Kansas City, James Manning; Omaha, William A. Rourke; St. Joseph, W.T. Van Brunt; Colorado Springs, Thomas F. Burns; and Denver, D.C. Packard. The application from Milwaukee was approved on the first day of the meeting. Tommy Dowd, a former big league ballplayer from Holyoke, Massachusetts, who had played briefly with the Brewers in 1900, said he wanted the Milwaukee franchise. However, his request was declined. Instead, a committee was appointed to try to induce Milwaukee capitalists to back the club. The application of Des Moines from previous owners Frank Flynn and W.P. Chase was also sent to committee, as were applications from Pueblo, Peoria, Sioux City and Indianapolis. A.B. Beall of Minneapolis was expelled from the Western League because he had transferred his parks in Minneapolis to George Tebeau of the American Association in exchange for the latter's park in Denver. Tebeau had then transferred the parks in Minneapolis to Walter Wilmot. This was seen as infringing on Packard's rights in Denver and killing the Western League's chances in Minneapolis. Beall would later sell this Broadway Street park in Denver to D.C. Packard. At the second day of the Western meeting, it was decided that 10 percent of each game's gate receipts would be placed in a general fund to defray league expenses. A sinking fund also was established, with each club required to deposit $500 by the next meeting. The life of the Western League was set at four years.

The idea of two teams in Milwaukee did not sit well with everyone. *The Sporting News* Milwaukee correspondent, Arthur M. Marsh, was certain the fans would not support a Western League team. He wrote: "It must be remembered that Milwaukee was in the American League the last two seasons. We saw teams from Chicago, Boston and Philadelphia play, and if anybody thinks for a moment that they will patronize teams from Des Moines, Colorado Springs and St. Joseph, they will be said mistaken. The jump from the American League to the [American] Association was far enough without getting any lower."[42] The *Milwaukee Sentinel* showed which camp it would be in when it declared in March, "It is an insult to already outraged senses of patrons of baseball here to have Milwaukee included in a league which is composed of St. Joseph, Peoria, Colorado Springs and Des Moines, and the additional fact that contract jumping is fostered by the men owning clubs in those cities should earn for the Western league the stamp of disapproval. Milwaukee has been in these fly-by-night leagues before and suffered and the lesson learned in the past will never be forgotten."[43]

As a matter of fact, whether or not a club would be in Milwaukee was still in doubt. The *Milwaukee Sentinel* said the idea of putting a club in the city was not being given any credit outside of the Western League headquarters, claiming the public and press laughed at the idea. The *Sentinel* believed "it was a moral cinch that a club in Milwaukee would not draw flies."[44] But within a week, it was reported that both Tommy Dowd and Hugh Duffy were anxious to take control of the team. Dowd claimed to have sufficient backing to finance the club.

On February 20 Fred Gross, owner of Milwaukee Baseball Park, told the *Milwaukee Sentinel* he had three backers but did not identify them. It was believed W.T. Van Brunt from St. Joseph had guaranteed the Milwaukee franchise against losses, in addition to paying about $9,000 for the rental of Gross' ballpark.⁴⁵ All of what Van Brunt paid cannot be certain, as a report in April said the Western League as an organization would assume the entire expense of maintaining the parks in both Milwaukee and Kansas City.⁴⁶ In late February it was reported the Western League was trying to get local businessman Rudolph Giljohan, who had part ownership in the Milwaukee Western League club back in the 1890s, to take the Milwaukee franchise. Giljohan declined to be involved with the club.⁴⁷

Although many felt Colorado Springs had too small a population to support a Class A minor league team, *The Sporting News* saw the city's baseball success from a different angle:

> Some think Colorado Springs is too small to be a success. They forget that the town during the base ball season is about three times the size of its usual population and that the people who are there are a class who have the means to enjoy themselves and have nothing else to do. A base ball game in Colorado Springs is a society event among the people who journey there to spend the summer months. In addition to this season tickets find a ready sale and the income from this source alone is a profitable investment for the club owners.⁴⁸

To convince the eastern teams of the Western League to travel to Colorado Springs and Denver, these two cities were to charge 40 cents for general admission instead of the quarter charged in the other cities. To appease local fans, Burns and Packard received permission to sell 200 books of season tickets at 25 cents a game. There was still the additional 25 cents for a grandstand seat. Kids under 12 were only charged 15 cents and another dime for grandstand seats.⁴⁹

Meanwhile, the Omaha situation was heating up. According to reports, A.L. Buell, Joseph Turner and Cornelius Corcoran of Milwaukee had formed a company to back the American Association club in the Nebraska city. However, there were too many difficulties involved in securing a ballpark for them to make headway. The major difficulty was the refusal of the city council to permit the closing of a street in order to build a park. Some even questioned why the American Association was considering Omaha. The *Milwaukee Sentinel* wrote:

> Why the American association should be troubling itself about Omaha is something baseball men cannot understand. It is not a sporting center, and never will be. If it made good in baseball last year, there is no doubt that some other city of the same size would have turned out much larger crowds. The only excuse the association magnates have to offer for their persistency in going after Omaha is that when they outlined their circuit last fall they included that city in

their prospectus, and to leave it now would be a confession of weakness. This position is ridiculous and untenable...."[50]

It was thought that Louisville would be a better choice than Omaha. The *Milwaukee Sentinel* reported Larry Gatto, a former director of the Louisville baseball club, said he was willing to invest $5,000 to place a club in Louisville. The newspaper reported, "Louisville is one of the liveliest sporting cities in the Middle West, the support it has given harness racing and baseball, although it was almost invariably represented by inferior teams during its existence in the National league, stamping it as a factor in the sporting world.... Louisville will improve the circuit from a geographical standpoint as well as a pecuniary point of view."[51]

The American Association owners met in secret in Milwaukee at the Davidson Hotel on January 19. At this meeting it was determined to transfer the Omaha franchise to Louisville. In early February the transfer was officially announced. *The Sporting News* believed the American Association owners had never really intended to put a team in Omaha unless William Rourke would sell his franchise to them. When this did not happen, the Association turned its head toward Louisville.

At first the news was received in Louisville with lukewarm enthusiasm since the local backers still were hoping for a stop in one of the major leagues. But soon it was reported George Tebeau would run the franchise and was in Louisville looking for possible investors as well as a playing site. The day after it was announced that Tebeau would place a club in the Falls City, the names of his entire team were made public, making it appear that the move had been planned for some time.

George Tebeau would leave the Kansas City franchise and its players in the hands of attorney Dale Gear, who was said to be more popular in K.C. than Tebeau. Tebeau soon sold his interests in the Kansas City franchise to A.L. Buell, Cornelius Corcoran and Joseph Turner—the three who were to own the Omaha franchise. Buell said he and his partners would attend exclusively to the financial end of the franchise and Gear would handle the playing end. Gear was given part ownership of the club, and would also pitch for the team.

Dale Gear, the 29-year-old son of a Kansas farmer, had pitched with the Washington American League team owned by James Manning in 1901, winning four games and losing 11. Prior to that he had pitched four years in Kansas City with the Western League team, and he was well known and well liked by the K.C. fans. Gear was also an attorney, receiving his degree from Kansas University, with an office in Kansas City. While with Manning in Kansas City and later Washington, Gear had learned much about the baseball business, and he was certain to do well in Kansas City.⁵² In what today seems extremely odd, Gear was also secretary of the Players' Protective Association.

However, Doc Shively of the Kansas City press doubted George Tebeau was completely out of Kansas City. He wrote, "If they show me a bill of sale, I might believe Tebeau has sold out, but there would have to be some pretty strong oaths to the document to convince me."⁵³

The American Association was now complete. *Sporting Life* of March 8, 1902, gave the following officers in its list of baseball clubs:

> Columbus: J.F. Bryce, President; John Grim, Manager
> Indianapolis: William H. Watkins, President and Manager
> Kansas City: George D. Hardesty, President; Dale Gear, Manager
> Louisville: George Tebeau, President and Manager
> Milwaukee: Harry D. Quin, President; William Clingman, Manager
> Minneapolis: H.A. Winslow, President; Walter Wilmot, Manager
> St. Paul: George Lennon, President; M.J. Kelley, Manager
> Toledo: Charles J. Strobel, President and Manager

The American Association held its league meeting in Chicago in March, setting a schedule and adopting the playing rules of the American League of 1901. The most important of these rules was the non-usage of the new National League rule that foul balls not caught before the batter had two strikes on him would count as a strike. It was thought counting foul balls as strikes would cut down on offense.

President Thomas Hickey was very confident in his American Association. He had this to say:

> The affair has passed the stage where we even consider the Western League as a factor. They are doing nothing to warrant consideration, and are getting little from the press or public. All baseball authorities who are not prejudiced recognize the natural successor to the old Western under Ban Johnson and when reporting time comes you will find us with the strongest kind of a circuit and teams prepared to play the fastest kind of ball.⁵⁴

Hickey also announced he would move his offices from St. Joseph to the Cable Building in Chicago in February. This move was made to gain the support of the Chicago press, hopefully resulting in having his league receive much more newspaper coverage.

Since the first of the year the franchise situation in the Western League had been heating up. In mid–January, W.T. Van Brunt, Thomas Burns and James Manning visited William Watkins in Indianapolis to see if he would take over a franchise in the Western League. Watkins declined. However, the Western let it be known it was still interested in placing a team in Indianapolis to compete with the American Association club there. It had been hinted that streetcar magnate Hugh McGowan was interested in backing a team in Indianapolis, but he said that he had too many irons in the fire to think of a baseball club. Reportedly, the Western League continued "tendering all kinds of specious temptations" to get Watkins to join them.[55] Talk of a Western League club in Toledo was also heard. Reported price tags of $26,000 to buy out Indianapolis and $46,000 for Toledo stopped these deals. However, the real reason was the fact that American Association President Hickey was the only person authorized to dispose of the franchises. All the Association owners gave him the right to hold their territory and only he could authorize a transfer or sale.

On February 17 Western League president James Whitfield decided to form a stock company in Peoria and place a team there. The co-operation of a solicitor was secured, and sums ranging from $5 to $100 were received from a number of people. As the entire sum amounted to less than $1,000, the prospects of a Western League club in Peoria were "correspondingly dubious" at this time.[56] The hopes of adding Sioux City to the Western were gone, as that Iowa city had decided to join the Iowa-Illinois League. It was reported that Des Moines might also join this league.

At its March 12 meeting, which was held in Denver, the Western League formally admitted Milwaukee and Peoria. Once the ballpark situation was cleared up in Des Moines, Frank Flynn's club also officially became part of the Western. Des Moines' ballpark, Athletic Park, was two to three blocks from the business center of town, at Fourth and Grand Avenue. It seated about 1,800 spectators in the grandstand and another 1,200 in the bleachers. The team leased the YMCA park on SW Ninth Street to play its Sunday games.[57]

The Western League set up a 140-game schedule that had numerous conflicting dates with the American Association teams in Milwaukee and Kansas City (although the schedule was not immediately released). The Western also opted to operate under the National League playing rules, adopt the Spalding ball, and suspend its salary limit. The league also decided to stop the practice of allowing umpires to call a game in the city in which they lived in order to cut down on appearances of favoritism.

At this point, Peoria and Des Moines still did not have the proper financial backing. The pro–American Association *Milwaukee Sentinel* thought the two clubs were "traveling a rock road," and gave this opinion of the new Western League: "Lacking in capital and players and with a circuit which is a monument to the stupidity of the men guiding its affairs, the Western league of to-day is a grotesque object."[58] President Whitfield, Van Burnt and old-time ballplayer William Hart met in Peoria and called a meeting of those interested to get the backing needed. By mid–March, only $3,500 in stock had been secured, but by April the call was successful, with all $5,000 in stock subscribed. Later in the month, all the stock in the Des Moines club was sold, and Frank P. Clarkson was elected president.

The Western League now stood like this:

Denver: D.C. Packard, President; Parke Wilson, Manager
Colorado Springs: Thomas F. Burns, President; William Everitt, Manager
St. Joseph: W. T. Van Brunt, President; Bryon McKibben, Manager
Omaha: William A. Rourke, President and Manager
Kansas City: James H. Manning, President; Charles A. Nichols, Manager
Milwaukee: Fred C. Gross, President; Hugh Duffy, Manager
Des Moines: Frank P. Clarkson, President; Joe Quinn, Manager
Peoria: no president; William Hart, Manager

The Sporting News thought this was a fairly good league — with two exceptions — thus believing a six-club Western League would be a better idea.

> A city that paid the Detroit Club only $700 for a season's series in 1900 and was a rank failure in 1901 is not worth fighting for. It would be better for the Western League to have six paying cities in its circuit than to invite disaster by taking in two others that are likely to be unprofitable. Competition in Kansas City is necessary and Nichols' club should be self sustaining at home and a money-maker on the road, The Omaha, Denver and Colorado Springs clubs will be profitable, providing the salaries of their players are not excessive. St. Joe is counted on to do as well as in 1901 and Des Moines, with good management, should do much better. Peoria and Milwaukee are not good base ball propositions and the prospects are that the promoters of the clubs in these cities will have to stand heavy losses.[59]

Even with the Western League set, rumors persisted that Milwaukee would not be part of it. "An authentic source" reported the Robisons were contemplating transferring their St. Louis National League team to Milwaukee and playing at the Lloyd Street Park, where the Western League team was scheduled to play. It was reported Milwaukee capital was behind the move, but no names were given.[60] Of course, this never occurred.

Although the Western League had numerous owners and backers, William T. Van Brunt of St. Joseph was the biggest. Born in 1858 in Perth Amboy, New Jersey, he was brought to St. Joseph from Scranton, Pennsylvania, around 1890 to help his brother with the development of the railway company, and became the president and general manager of the streetcar system. The company was sold for several million dollars to a syndicate headed by E.H. Harriman in 1902. Van Brunt continued as president of the company in St. Joseph, which included the streetcar system and electric services, even after E.H. Harriman sold to Seligman & Co. and E.W. Clark for $3,500,000. Van Brunt was also the president of the Furnaceville Iron Company and Sinnemahoning Iron and Coal Company.⁶¹ W.T. Van Brunt was reputed to be "one of the most liberal men ever connected with baseball and is considered a thorough sportsman and an enthusiastic baseball fan."⁶²

In addition to owning the St. Joseph club, the multi-millionaire Van Brunt had financial interests in the Milwaukee, Kansas City, Peoria and Des Moines franchises. How much he had in each club is not known. For example, in Milwaukee Hugh Duffy only admitted Van Brunt held a few shares of stock. The St. Joseph magnate would only say about the Milwaukee franchise that the Western League "had a fund on hand ample to meet any contingency."⁶³ It was said Van Brunt and Thomas Burns from Colorado Springs had promised William Rourke in Omaha any losses he sustained would be taken care of if he stuck with the Western League. A report in *The Sporting News* claimed Van Brunt supplied all the money to put Nichols and Manning in Kansas City.⁶⁴

Why W.T. Van Brunt took such a financial interest was commented on in *The Sporting News* prior to the opening of the season. It was thought that Van Brunt and Thomas Burns felt they had been wronged by Thomas Hickey and George Tebeau when these two pulled out of the Western League and took Kansas City, St. Paul and Minneapolis with them to the American Association. After convincing other Western League men their league got the short end of the stick, it was decided to "enter into a war of extermination" with the Association. Thus, "while the Western League promoters would not refuse to accept profits, they expect the balance to be on the other side of the ledger, and the placing of clubs in Kansas City and Milwaukee by the Western League in opposition to those of the American Association has been done apparently with the idea of revenge."⁶⁵

The *Milwaukee Sentinel* thought Van Brunt's identity with five clubs could lead to suspicions that if attendance did not meet expectation, the league standings could be manipulated. The newspaper also argued that "it can be readily appreciated that where there is not healthy rivalry and local ownership a league built upon other lines must be lacking in the qualities which make baseball attractive to the public."⁶⁶ Charles Havenor, the secretary of the Milwaukee American Association club, thought Van Brunt would be lucky to get out of the season losing only $40,000.

With Van Brunt being the "angel" of the Western League, a report surfaced suggesting the American Association had the same arrangement. In March 1902 it was reported that Charles Clark, son of the Untied States senator from Montana and one of the wealthiest men in the country, was the financial backer of the entire American Association. His backing would explain the bundles of money given in advance to players, in addition to the money being spent on ballparks by Association teams. This report was labeled as false, with Clark having no financial interest in any American Association club, only partial ownership in Milwaukee's Athletic Park, which was owned by his cousin Harry Quin. However, in late March, Quin traveled to San Francisco to visit his cousin, and was quoted upon his return: "You know Mr. Clark is interested with me in the Milwaukee club and $10,000 doesn't look any bigger to him than a postage stamp does to me. He has promised me all the money I want for my baseball business and if necessary would be willing to back the whole league."[67]

President Thomas Hickey of the American Association was certain his circuit would do more than hold its own against the Western League, especially in Milwaukee. He was quoted as saying, "We will go ahead just as though the Western League did not exist, and I don't think it will hurt us any. Milwaukeeans care nothing about the small towns in the Western league and the Milwaukee club, if it materializes, can hardly expect much patronage. The Western league was a failure last year and I see nothing better in prospect for it this season. The men at the head of it are apparently new in the business, or they would not attempt to include a city the size of Milwaukee in their circuit of comparatively small towns."[68]

Comparing populations of the cities in the two leagues from the 1900 federal census shows the advantage Hickey's American Association had over the Western League:

Milwaukee	285,315	Milwaukee	285,315
Louisville	204,731	Kansas City	163,752
Minneapolis	202,718	Denver	133,859
Indianapolis	169,164	St. Joseph	102,979
Kansas City	163,752	Omaha	102,555
St. Paul	163,065	Des Moines	62,139
Toledo	131,822	Peoria	56,111
Columbus	125,560	Colorado Springs	21,139

Even the pro–Western League *Sporting Life* foresaw the troubles in the Western League–American Association standoff. In its March 22, 1902, edition, the Philadelphia weekly wrote:

> The Western League has finally completed its circuit, which, by the way, falls far short of what its projectors had originally hoped it would be. Notwithstanding the handicap of an inferior circuit, however, the Western League exhibits no abatement of its set purpose to make a finish fight with the American Association. At its schedule meeting last week the Western League decided to schedule against the opposition clubs in Milwaukee and Kansas City, and craftily ordered the withholding of the schedule until the last moment in April. This was done

presumably to prevent any immediate shift of dates by the opposition, although it is not probable that the American Association would make such a move which might be construed as a confession of weakness or fear, although it would be good business judgment. The Western League also suspended its salary limit, not so much as a war measure as to enable it to compete with the American Association for players. In effect, however, it will amount to a war measure and it will make the fighting more costly for both leagues. Assuming that the two rivals will stubbornly maintain their antagonistic attitude there is nothing to expect but a losing season for both leagues. The four clubs in Milwaukee and Kansas City are doomed to sure loss, while all the other clubs must suffer from their excessive salary lists. It will simply narrow down to a question of "survival of the fittest," in which sympathy will not cut little tea. The chances of the battle, it must be truthfully said, favor the American Association by reason of a greatly superior circuit, one better calculated to stand the exhausting drain of the conflicting cities than the Western League's chain of small towns. As the great Napoleon so aptly expressed it: Providence is usually on the side of the heaviest guns.

The pro–American Association *Sporting News* gave a dismal assessment of the Western League in its February 22, 1902, edition.

The Western League is not showing energy in making good its claims or promises to the people. Its Milwaukee team is a myth, without a manager. It controls a park, but has no players. It is questionable whether a rival team should be placed in the Cream City in view of its geographical location and its inability to secure a footing in Indianapolis and Toledo, as was contemplated. The cost of travel over a circuit with Denver at one end and Milwaukee at the other must be considered. The Cream City is not capable of supporting two teams and it is doubted if the 1902 patronage will pay the operating expenses of one club next season. The Western circuit should be settled at once and work began on the Kansas City park. If Des Moines and Peoria are to be given franchises, let the awards be made and preparations made to place good teams in those cities.

However, the Milwaukee Western League club was beginning to solidify. Fred C. Gross was named head of the franchise but was protected against any deficit by the guarantee of W.T. Van Brunt of St. Joseph. On March 9 the Milwaukee Western League team signed a manager, Hugh Duffy. Because of this guarantee from Van Brunt, Duffy's team would be known in some circles as the Angels, although they were officially the Creams. Throughout the season the team would not lack for nicknames, also being called the Duffmeyers, Orphans and Remnants.[69]

Hugh Duffy was born in Cranston, Rhode Island, in 1866. His big league career — which led to a Hall-of-Fame enshrinement — began in 1888 with Chicago. In 1890 he jumped to the Players' League and then went to Boston of the old American Association. From 1892 to 1900 Duffy played in Boston with the Beaneaters. Duffy was a first-class hitting outfielder. After batting

Hugh Duffy — The legendary Boston outfielder piloted the Milwaukee Western League "Angels," and served as president of the club for two years (Library of Congress).

.282 in 1888 and .295 in 1889, he never hit below .300 until 1898, when he posted a .298 average. In 1894 he had hit .440, an average that has not been topped since. Hugh also led the National League in home runs in 1894 and 1897. Duffy was signed to manage the 1901 Milwaukee entry in the American League and reportedly bought former manager Connie Mack's shares in the club. The 1901 Brewers finished in last place with a 48–89 record, with Duffy hitting .302 while playing 79 games in the outfield. After the season there were reports Duffy would return to Boston and play center field while giving up managing as his troubles with American League umpires "was the golden spike that finished the job which marked the finale of Duffy's managerial aspirations."[70] However, he was in demand as a manager. Shortly before the first of the year, he was offered management of the Jersey City club in the Eastern League. There was also gossip connecting his name with Buffalo of the same league. The job Duffy was after, however, was the business manager of the Boston American League club, a position that was eventually given to Joseph Gavin. Duffy complained he had been promised the position along with ground privileges by Ban Johnson and Henry Killilea, which led to his passing up a number of other advantageous offers.[71] The truth might have been that Duffy had a two-year contract with the American League Milwaukee club and had to honor that with the Western League. In addition, Duffy was very popular in Milwaukee, and reportedly would own half of the Western League club.

Suddenly, the unexpected happened to the Western League. James Whitfield, the 47-year-old Irish-born president of the Western, committed suicide at his home in Kansas City on April 7. Whitfield had been having financial difficulties, and a lawsuit he filed against a newspaper for libel was weighing on his mind. These pressures, plus the heavy work schedule as president of the Western League, began to take its toll. He had been under a doctor's care for a few weeks, but had been working hard to get his circuit in order.

In late March there had been a report that W.T. Van Brunt and some other Western League owners wanted Michael Sexton to replace Whitfield as president of the Western League, feeling Whitfield had "not been as aggressive and successful as they expected."[72] Sexton was president of the Indiana-Iowa-Illinois League, but he stated he would not resign that position. Nothing came of this report at that time. After Whitfield's death, D.C. Packard in Denver was offered the presidency of the Western League. He turned it down, believing the president should be a man with no connections to a club in the league. There were reports Sexton was again being talked to, as was Charles D. White, formerly president of the Eastern League, and Sandy Griswald, the sports editor of the *Omaha World-Herald*. In the meantime Van Brunt took charge of the league.

James Whitfield — The first president and early guiding force of the Western League before financial difficulties and a lawsuit, combined with the pressure of running a league, led to his suicide (*St. Paul Globe*, April 8, 1902).

Van Brunt came to Milwaukee in late April to set up the franchise. Hugh Duffy was elected president of the baseball club and George Ladendorf became secretary and treasurer. Ladendorf had been in baseball for some time and was to handle the cash from the receipts at the ballpark. Duffy was in charge of the remainder of the money. Van Brunt guaranteed the club against losses. Fred Gross, who had been listed at times as president or secretary-treasurer of the Milwaukee club, was now out and had no connections with the club. With Duffy as president, manager and left fielder of the team, a Milwaukee critic remarked "that if President Duffy were to order Manager Duffy to fine Left Fielder Duffy there would probably be trouble."[73]

On April 17 Michael H. Sexton was appointed president of the Western League, and kept his job as president of the Three-I-League. He immediately let the players know where he stood. He said that when the American Association opened its season, any player who had deserted any of the Western League teams would be fined in accordance with the National Agreement schedule. In essence, that date was the player's "last day of grace."⁷⁴ *The Sporting News* had high praise for the new president:

> Mr. Sexton, in one year, has established an enviable record as a base ball executive and he will give his time and talent in the discharge of his dual duties with integrity and impartially. He has so far escaped the petty criticisms which time-serving and truckling officials come in for and has won the confidence of press and public that he is not subjected to the suspicions that club-owners, in their selflessness, direct at those who stand between them and the law. Mr. Sexton believes in wholesome base ball and expects those behind the clubs as well as those who play the game to conduct themselves as sportsmen.⁷⁵

Michael H. Sexton was born in Rock Island, Illinois, in 1863. He was the chief of police in Rock Island when he became president of the local baseball club in 1898. In 1901 he was active in forming the Illinois-Indiana-Iowa League, being elected its first president. In later years Sexton would preside over the Three-I League and the Mississippi League. In 1909 Sexton was chosen as the head of the National Association of Minor League Baseball clubs, and held that position until December 1931.⁷⁶

Michael Sexton — As Western League president, he guided his league through the two-year war (National Baseball Hall of Fame Library, Cooperstown, New York).

Sexton, who moved the Western League's headquarters to Rock Island, thought the circuit was in better financial shape than the American Association. He doubted if the Association's Milwaukee and Kansas City franchises could last the season. The new Western League president thought the players saw the American Association's financial prospects were not good, and he believed that was the reason so many were jumping that league.

As the American Association did not respect organized baseball's reserve clause, its owners felt free to deal with any player who had not signed a contract. But the Association was against signing players who had signed a contract in another league. The Western, Eastern, National and American leagues did not follow this lead, declaring the American Association was "marked for the slaughter,"[77] and signed a number of American Association players already under contract. (Some of these signings will be discussed in Chapter Two.) By mid–April the Association had lost at least 20 players who had been signed to a contract. As the contract jumping continued, there was a growing sentiment in the Association to retaliate for player raids. After three star players of the Kansas City American Association team jumped to the K.C. Western club, Thomas Hickey spoke on the matter to the editor of *Sporting Life*: "At present it is the policy of the American Association to avoid dealing with contract jumpers. If the Western League and some of the other base ball organizations continue their piratical course it may be necessary to adopt retaliatory measures. This, however, will be the last resort."[78]

Ballpark locations as well as player signings were a tool in this upcoming war. Another tacit was brought out in the baseball war in February. The manufacturers who furnished baseball supplies to the leagues were asked to help in the fight to put the American Association out of business. For example, it was reported that a strong influence was being brought upon the Connecticut and Pacific-Northwestern leagues to discontinue the Victor ball and accept the Reach or Spalding ball. These two companies would then furnish a war fund to be used in the extermination of the American Association. As it turned out, the American Association adopted the Reach ball over the Victor ball. The American Association actually had little worries regarding equipment, as Harry Quin was reported to be doing a land office business in furnishing supplies from his sporting goods store in Milwaukee to the various Association clubs.

To put an end to some of the press rumors and leaking of information, in March the American Association adopted a resolution providing for penalties ranging from a fine of $250 to franchise forfeiture for violation of secrecy from Association meetings or discussions.

Obviously Kansas City and Milwaukee would be the major battlegrounds in the Western League and American Association conflict in 1902. The Western League schedule would have 21 conflicting dates in Kansas City with their American Association rivals, and 23 conflicting dates were scheduled in the Cream City. Milwaukee Brewer president Harry Quin added to this by issuing a challenge to Hugh Duffy to play five games to determine which Milwaukee team was better. Duffy slyly said he would be willing to accept but was afraid the Western League would not let him because Quin's Brewers were in "an Outlaw League."[79]

Two

♦ ♦ ♦ ♦

Filling Rosters and Jumping Contracts

After the 1901 season there were reports of numerous players jumping from the National League to the American League as the war between the major leagues continued. The player signings not only affected the two major leagues, but as players from the various minor leagues were signed — some reserved, some already under contract — all leagues were financially impacted as salaries rose drastically.

The newly formed National Association of Minor Leagues declared any player who jumped his contract to play for a National League or American League club would have to pay a fine before he was able to return to the minors. If the player jumped a Class A club, which the Western League was, he would have to pay $1,000 in cash to return. It was believed that by the end of October 1901 eight Western League players had already signed with National League clubs.

The California League was not a member of the National Association of Minor Leagues and also had raided the Western League heavily in 1901. Thomas Hickey, before leaving the Western League, said he would have revenge on that organization. In November George Tebeau went to California to sign players. Tebeau, who still owned the Kansas City club, was looking for players to strengthen this team as well as the Denver team, which he still had an interest in at the time. Other players signed were to be placed in other cities of the new league. However, Tebeau had only limited success in signing players. In January 1902 D.C. Packard, owner of the Western League Denver club, also went to California with his wife, who was in poor health, with the intent to sign some players.

Some teams had players signed from the previous year, or in the case of the Western League, on their respective reserve lists. By mid–December it was claimed that all the Western league teams except Kansas City and Denver had the players from their 1901 teams signed. As it turned out, this was far from the truth.

Of course, the outlaw American Association had no players under reserve. By early December it was reported that American Association clubs were signing players, many under reserve to the Class B Western Association teams. John Grim, the new manager in Columbus, was said to have 21 players — "all top notchers" — under regular and personal contracts.[1] Shortly after the first of the year, Tebeau in Kansas City was said to have 16 men under contract. Charles Strobel in Toledo claimed to have received enough applications from amateur and professional players to fill a half-dozen teams. At the American Association meeting of December 30–31, 1901, president Thomas Hickey gave the names of players signed by each team. Kansas City had 13, Indianapolis six, Columbus nine, Toledo eight, Milwaukee seven, and St. Paul more than 20. Minneapolis had signed none, the only person under contract being manager and owner Walter Wilmot. Which players and the exact numbers were difficult to determine. Unless players had signed personal contracts with the club in question, it was good practice not to announce names each club was interested in. Once it was known a club was interested, other managers from rival leagues immediately offered the player more money.

Salaries for players were higher than ever in both the American Association and the Western League. Charles Comiskey, owner of the American League Chicago White Stockings, warned the American Association magnates in simple terms: "If you go above a monthly $2,000 limit for a team, you will lose money." As some teams were said to be as high as $3,000, losses were easily foreseen. Comiskey told American Association owners that it was once possible to make some money by selling players to the major leagues after the minor league season, but since the A.A. was not part of the National Agreement and did not have an agreement with the American League, this source of revenue was not open to them.[2]

The American Association did not recognize the reserve clause in any league's contracts, but was decidedly against signing any player who had signed a contract in another league.

By December 1901 the minor leagues (with the exception of the "outlaw" American Association and the California League) were back in the National Agreement with the National League, which, of course, was having its own war with the new American League. For this reason, American League president Ban Johnson, who was a friend of Western League president James Whitfield, said he could do nothing officially to help the Western League in a baseball war.[3]

Teams already had been signing players in December. Of the numerous early signings before the first of the year, Omaha reported that Captain Ace Stewart had signed "Coal Miner" Brown, a pitcher who had worked for Terre Haute the previous year. Brown is known by another nickname, "Three Finger." Mordecai Brown would go on to win 239 major league games in a Hall-of-Fame career. Brown was coming off a 25-win and 8-loss year with Terre Haute, and would win 27 with Omaha in 1902.

Naturally, players jumping contracts and leagues not respecting reserves were big issues. In January 1902 Secretary J.H. Farrell of the National Board of Arbitration issued rules and fines for players under contract and reserve who jumped leagues. A schedule of fines for the clubs and players was published, and the threat of blacklisting players was emphasized. As can be imagined in a baseball war, any fines threatened before players could return to National Association leagues would not be enforced. An editorial in the *Evening Wisconsin* shortly after the season began provided one example.

After winning 27 games for Omaha, "Miner" Brown would win 239 games in the big leagues as "Three Finger" Brown (Library of Congress).

The farcical feature of the fining system of the National Association of Minor Leagues was brought to light yesterday. Harry Truby, who played in the Western Association last year, decided that he would leave his surroundings in the league and take up new quarters at Louisville with George Tebeau's team. He signed with Tebeau and practiced with the Colonels, but George concluded that Truby was not fast enough for the Colonels, and as he refused to work overtime and get in something like half-way condition, why the Louisville manager decided to "can" him. Accordingly Truby was released yesterday and he was immediately signed by Manager Billy Hart of the Peoria club of the Western League, the rival of the American Association.

Now the question arises, did Truby pay the $1000 fine that the National Association of Minor Leagues threatened to impose on all players who started the season with the American Association? Not on your tintype! Truby did not pay one cent of the fine, and what is more, he does not intend to, nor does the Western League expect him to pay any fine. The Western League was glad to have him join one of their clubs and forget about the $1000 fine. This only proves how farcical the threat of the National Association of Minor Leagues becomes.[4]

George Tebeau was of the opinion that Western League players could sign with American Association clubs without fear, as the Western contracts had a clause stating the clubs agreed to pay players $10 for the privilege of renewing their contracts. Tebeau claimed not one player was paid the $10.[5]

After the first of January 1902, teams picked up the pace of signing players. In the Western League Kansas City manager Charles Nichols went east to sign players for his club. Returning manager Byron McKibben of the St. Joseph club reportedly signed a number of players, but in January lost Tim Flood, his second baseman, to Brooklyn of the National League. Flood had accepted advance money from McKibben but returned it when he signed with the Superbas. Flood had reportedly also signed a contract with Sacramento of the California League. By mid-month, Colorado Springs reportedly had 16 players signed, Omaha 14 players, Des Moines and St. Joseph 12 each.

William Watkins in Indianapolis soon reported that he had a number of good players under contract, including Bill Fox as his captain and second baseman. Fox had played with Cincinnati of the National League in 1901, hitting a lowly .176.

Charles Strobel in Toledo said he had 27 men under contract. Although some had never taken part in a professional game, Strobel said their amateur work stamped them as fast young ballplayers. It was reported an unusual feature of the Toledo team would be an Elk outfield, as every man in the outer garden was a member of that order, as was Strobel.[6] One nice find for Strobel was Homer Mock, who had pitched in the Connecticut League in 1901. The 20-year-old, who was a glass worker when not pitching, did not have much experience but had been sought after by many major league clubs. Charles Strobel told a rather humorous story to a reporter regarding the signing of Mock on a visit to the player's hometown of Lancaster, Ohio:

> After his [Strobel's] arrival at the hotel he sent word to Mock to call on him. After supper the big fellow strolled into the office and made himself known. He was immediately made acquainted with the object of Strobel's visit, and was asked what he expected for his work the coming season. The pitcher answered that he was sorry, but that he did not feel that he was at liberty to sign a contract, as he had promised to give the Connecticut league people first call on his services. "I'll give you $175 a month," said Strobel. Mock couldn't sign the contract quick enough.
>
> Before the ink was dry he turned to Strobel and said: "I guess you might have got me for $50 or $75 a month if you had waited a little longer." Before the Toledo manager left the town Mock intimated that a little Advance money might come in handy. Strobel was agreeable to the proposition and inquired how much was necessary. "Do you think $5 would be too much?" asked Mock.

Two. Filling Rosters and Jumping Contracts   37

The magnate almost fell off his chair, as he had expected a touch for at least $50 and was prepared to stand for a hundred. The next day he mailed Mock a check for the amount, and a few days later received a letter thanking him for his generosity.[7]

The signing by Strobel of two players who had played with Dayton in the Western Association the previous year caused a stir. The Toledo owner signed Jack Burns and George Grossart to contracts. William B. Armour, owner of the Cleveland American League club, was said to be very upset over the signings because he wanted the players. Armour had owned the Dayton team the previous year, but the two players were not under reserve to Cleveland. Armour wrote to Strobel, threatening that he would go after some of his players in retaliation. Armour soon offered Mud Hen pitcher Al Pardee $300 a month, and started talks with pitcher Addie Joss. Pardee refused the offer. Joss will be discussed later in this chapter.[8]

The story was pretty much the same all over the American Association and Western League. In the Western, newly named manager Billy Everitt in Colorado Springs had most of his team signed. Columbus reportedly had a number of mostly new good players under contract. The Columbus management treated their previous year's players in a most liberal fashion. After having signed all of their players for 1902, and being in a position to trade them or sell their contracts, the club gave unconditional releases to all the men it did not want so that these players could garner contracts elsewhere.[9]

In Milwaukee the American Association Brewers had a new manager. At first it was reported that Frank Motz, who had played a couple of seasons in Cincinnati in the mid–1890s, was being favorably considered as the manager of the team. However, owner Harry Quin announced in mid–December that he had signed Billy Clingman to manage his team for 1902. William Frederick Clingman was born in Cincinnati on November 21, 1869. He bounced around the minor leagues from 1890 to 1894, playing a few games on two major league clubs. In 1894 he had played third base with the Milwaukee Brewers of the Western League. In 1895 Clingman played with Pittsburgh, and the next four years in Louisville of the National League. In 1900 he played with the National League Chicago Colts; 1901 found him with the Washington Nationals of the American League. In the early part of his career, Clingman was mostly a third baseman, but in 1899 he switched to shortstop.

Manager Clingman reported that he had a strong team with 18 men under contract, including young Nick Altrock, who had been under reserve to Toronto in the Eastern League. The 25-year-old pitcher had won three games with the Louisville National League club in 1898, and had been 16 and 13 with Toronto before posting a 6 and 8 record with Los Angeles of the California League.

Walter Wilmot in Minneapolis had only six men under contract but would not name them. By February 1, it was reported that the American Association teams had 112 men under contract.

As the winter continued, the secretary of the Players' Protective Association, Dale Gear, was appealing to players to disregard the reserves in their minor league contracts. Of course, the clubs in the National Association of Minor Leagues defended the reserve clause and threatened players who thought of switching leagues. By February players were disregarding the reserve and jumping their contracts. When the Kansas City Western League club signed three players under contract to the American Association club, Dale Gear (remember, also manager of the Association Kansas City club), blasted this practice: "A player who jumps his contract is not honest, and I hardly see how the manager who persuades him to jump can be considered in a better light, certainly not by base ball authorities. There is even honor in war, as barbarous and inhuman acts are condemned by the civilized nations, and honest dealings in a base ball war is the only method by which any faction can hope for toleration, and patronage of the base ball public." President James Whitfield of the Western League was quick to respond and defend his league. He said the Western was simply fighting fire with fire: "The Tebeau-Hickey people set the pace by raiding the California and Interstate Leagues, and even went so far as to try to buy Rourke of Omaha, and his entire team. Yet they talk about honor. They further conspired with A.B. Beall to injure the strength of the Western League by trading the Denver ballpark for Beall's Minneapolis buildings.... The Western League is simply fighting the attempt of Tebeau and Hickey to wreck it, and is prepared to pay more money for players than the Tebeau-Hickey combination." Whitfield ended with this telling statement: "There is little sentiment in base ball and the public will patronize the club that puts up the fastest ball."[10]

On February 11, 1902, the Players' Association issued a bulletin telling its members that "it is the duty of every member of our union and every base ball player as well, to use his best influence to defeat the unjust rule that the association of minor leagues proposes to place upon players who in their leagues dare to better themselves financially by ignoring the reserve clause in contracts. The Players' Protective Association has always favored respecting of contracts, but has consistently ignored the reserve clause."[11]

Dale Gear's position in the Players' Association and ownership of the baseball team was an obvious conflict of interest. *The Sporting News* called for him to step down from the Players' Association, feeling that he was more concerned with the success of the American Association than the welfare of the players.[12] The St. Louis weekly pointed out the American Association player contracts bound a player to the team for five months, and that he could be released upon a payment of $20 for violating any terms of the contract. However, a player had no way to terminate the contract. Also in the standard American Association contract was a clause tying the player for another year at the same salary he received in 1902. A player also had to consent to a trade without his consent. *The Sporting News* thought that "Mr. Gear and his associates have tried to retain all the slavery features of the old contract by compelling their players to waive all their rights, civil and personal," exactly what the Players' Association was complaining the National Agreement did to its members.[13] President Hickey said that the paper was incorrect and that there was no reserve clause in the American Association contracts. Hickey said that his league's contracts were modeled after those in the American League, against which he had not heard any complaints from players.[14]

Contract signings that disregarded the reserve clause picked up in February, and so did the tension between the various leagues — both major and minor. Thomas Hickey's American Association teams were signing a good number of Eastern League players under reserve. In Louisville alone, George Tebeau's team consisted of at least nine former Eastern League players, including his manager, Billy Clymer, and pitcher Patrick Flaherty, who had won 15 games with Toronto and Syracuse in 1901. Indianapolis signed Ralph Miller, who had won 13 games for Hartford of the Eastern League in 1901. The Indiana club also signed Arthur Coulter, allegedly under contract to Syracuse. However, it was claimed that Coulter had been selected and signed by Cincinnati of the National League the previous year. When it turned out that the outfielder could not make the grade in the major league, he was turned over to the Hoosiers. Coulter was then placed on the National Association's disqualified list. George Lennon in St. Paul signed Joe Bean, who had led Eastern League shortstops while playing with Rochester.[15] It was soon reported George Stallings of Buffalo had been giving Bean alluring offers to jump the American Association. At first Bean said he would remain in St. Paul to be close to his ill father, but he eventually signed and played with the New York Giants. He was cut in July and finished 1902 with Providence of the Eastern League.[16]

Thomas Hickey explained that his Association was not hampered by any salary limit. The fact that Springfield had not paid its players two years previously, followed by the Hartford club defaulting on its payment in 1901, had stirred Eastern League players to bolt. In early March the Toronto club accused Hickey of engaging two players to act as agents in order to get other players they knew in the Eastern League to jump to the American Association. The entire Eastern League was prepared to undertake "a gigantic reprisal" on

Hickey's league. A pool of $10,000—$1,250 per club—was supposedly set up. Buffalo manager George T. Stallings was to "play the J. Pierpont Morgan role in the pool ... he will set out upon his mission, bound by no restriction, but instructed to sign any and all players whose departure from the American association will tend to weaken that organization." Each of the Eastern League magnates turned over to Stallings a list of American Association players each team could use, but any players signed would be divided among the Eastern League teams, the weakest teams being given preference.[17] Harry Quin in Milwaukee thought it best that the Syracuse and Hartford clubs pay their players under contract the previous season "before money was diverted to inciting dishonorable methods."[18] This entire story was denied by George Stallings.

However, the Eastern League clubs did actively go after American Association players. George Lennon's St. Paul team was an inviting target. Pitcher Charles Chech said he received a telegram from Stallings offering him $400 a month—a $100 increase—to jump the Saints. Chech said he was pleased with the treatment he had received from Lennon and would stay in St. Paul. Stallings offered Saints second baseman Miller Huggins $325 a month; the future Hall of Fame Yankee manager also decided to stay in St. Paul, where he would hit .328 in 1902. Pitcher Dick Cogan also received tempting offers from Stallings, in addition to offers from Newark, Montreal, Toronto and Milwaukee's Western League club. Cogan declined them all and, as he said in a letter, "will be a good Saint once more."[19] Infielder Davy Brain was a different story. He had played third base for St. Paul in 1901 and signed a contract with Lennon after the season, calling for a $50 per month raise, to $250. Stallings was after Brain to join his Buffalo team, mailing him a number of letters and even sending Milwaukee manager Hugh Duffy to Chicago to try to sign the infielder. Brain signed with Buffalo for $300 a month, saying the contract he signed with the Saints was a Western League contract, and there was not a Western League club in St. Paul any longer. Brain was quoted as saying: "I gave [Saints manager] Kelley the opportunity of having me

Davy Brain—One of the early defectors from the American Association (Library of Congress).

in that association if they would pay me something near what I could get elsewhere, and I told him that I would go with him for less than anyone else." The third baseman was informed he would not be given one penny more than his contract called for, and he was gone to Buffalo.[20]

The Western League said it would continue the raids on the American Association players, with special effort to strip George Tebeau's teams. Tebeau was said to have interests in Kansas City, Minneapolis and Louisville, and this would put a large burden on him to carry on a baseball war. One of the reasons the Kansas City club was picked was because it was felt the contracts signed with Tebeau were not binding. Tebeau and Dale Gear claimed the contracts players signed before the close of the season were of a personal nature. However, *The Sporting News* was of the opinion these players signed with the expectation of playing in the Western League, and this played an important part in the fixing of salaries. Now that Tebeau and company had expanded into "a higher grade of the game" in the American Association, the weekly paper thought these players were underpaid. In addition, the contracts called for the players to play in the Western League, and since Tebeau switched to an independent league, the contracts were not binding.[21]

In late February 1902 it was being reported that six of Tebeau's players had jumped ship to the Kansas City Western League team. St. Joseph was successful in scooping up outfielder Billy Hartman and first baseman Norman Brashear from Kansas City. Tebeau also lost pitcher Al Whitridge, third baseman Gus Dundon and catcher Parke Wilson to D.C. Packard in Denver. Whitridge had signed with the Kansas City Association club two months prior to his jumping to Denver. Tebeau had transferred Dundon with him to Kansas City when he sold his interests in the Denver franchise in December, saying this was perfectly legitimate since Dundon had signed a contract to play with him and had accepted advance money. Dundon now wanted to be back in Denver. Parke Wilson had been playing winter ball in the California League and was signed for "a very large salary"[22] by Packard when the Denver magnate took his trip west for his wife's health. Packard immediately named Wilson the manager of his Western League team, which now had 12 players signed.

Parke Ansel Wilson was born in Illinois in 1867. His minor league career started in Colorado Springs of the Colorado State League 22 years later. The next year found Wilson in Denver on the Western Association team. Two years after that he was catching for the New York Giants, playing with them for seven seasons and hitting .265 in 370 games. After his major league career was over, Wilson played with Kansas City in the Western League and Montreal in the Eastern League before going to California to play with San Francisco, where he became "one of the most popular men in the business."[23]

St. Paul was also hit by raids from the Western League, in addition to those from the Eastern League. Outfielder Frank Warner had played for Des Moines the previous year, and the Western League people were bringing everything to force him to return. Warner would start the 1902 season in Des Moines. There was word catcher Bill Wilson would play with San Francisco in the California League in 1902. Wilson eventually signed with Peoria of the Western League, but it being said he was afraid he could not make good in the fast company of the American Association. He promised to return the advance money he received from St. Paul.

To add to St. Paul's troubles, the National League took some players owner George Lennon thought he would be able to count on. First, Lennon lost his star second baseman, Herman Schaefer, to James Hart's Chicago National League club. Lennon had signed pitcher Archie Stimmel after his demands for a $500 increase in salary and a $500 bonus were not met by the Cincinnati Reds. Saints manager Michael Kelley said the signing of Stimmel was not illegal, as the pitcher's agreement with Cincinnati was a conditional one, and the American Association recognized nothing but straight contracts. Stimmel would sign and play with Cincinnati to start 1902. However, he was released in May and signed with St. Paul in June. Lennon also lost pitcher Roy Evans to the New York National League team. The circumstances behind Evans' departure were given this way in *The Sporting News*:

> Evans was a great letter writer and always closed his jollying effusions with a request for more money. Most of the money was wanted to pay the expenses of Mrs. Evans, who was in a hospital in St. Louis. The last letter from Mr. Evans to Mr. Lennon was received 10 days ago, in which the writer, after giving Mr. Lennon a good jolly about the ability of his team, asked him to engage quarters for his wife and himself at the Colonnades (recommended by Kelley) and send Mrs. Evans $30, so she could come to St. Paul immediately, saying "This makes a little over $200 which I have had and I will whittle it down as fast as possible." Well, it seems he decided to cut it off at one whittling and jumped to pastures green. Mr. Lennon telegraphed him, asking what he meant by such conduct, and the clever pitcher requested him "to look it up in the dream book."[24]

That Evans would take advance money and jump should have come as no surprise to George Lennon. The pitcher had done the same prior to the 1901 season, jumping Providence of the Eastern League for San Francisco of the independent California League. He jumped San Francisco in August, going to Ogden, Utah, of the Inter-Mountain League. The Ogden folks wanted Evans back, and he was given a nice job in the railroad office. The job came, as reported by the *Anaconda Standard* "with the understanding that he would remain and play with the team again the following year. Evans did not remain long, however, until it was rumored that he was not very well posted on the coin of the

Two. Filling Rosters and Jumping Contracts

realm and that it was hard work for him to distinguish his money from other peoples." On Christmas Eve Roy Evans, with his wife and child, left town, skipping out on the $85 hotel bill. The ball player also owed more than $100 in other debts to local benefactors. Evans had received $100 advance money from the New York Giants and was done with Ogden.[25]

The St. Paul club was hit so hard by contract jumpers that manager Michael Kelley had only 12 players show up for spring training in Richmond, Indiana. He was forced to take in a number of youngsters to fill roster spots.

Two players St. Paul was able to hold on to were catcher Jeremiah Hurley, who had played with Schenectady in 1901, and Harry Lumley, who had played in Rome, New York. Lumley led the New York State League in hitting, and became property of Syracuse when the Rome team was transferred there. It was claimed Lumley signed a contract with Syracuse for $150 a month and accepted $50 in advance money. He soon signed another contract with St. Paul and accepted $50 in advance money from the Saints. The outfielder then had second thoughts, about the possibility of being blacklisted and wished to return to Syracuse. The Syracuse management said it would return the advance money to St. Paul, but then Lumley asked Syracuse to sell his release to St. Paul so he could stay there. Syracuse management was not willing to do this. Both Hurley and Lumley were banned by the National Association for contract jumping.

The Milwaukee American Association team also had problems with other leagues. In February Charles Jones, who had signed with the Brewers and accepted $100 in advance money, signed a contract to play with Denver of the Western League. Jones, who had played the 1901 season in Denver, returned the advance money to Milwaukee management. In March catcher Al Shaw had defected to Buffalo of the Eastern League, taking his $100 in advance money with him. In mid–March the *Milwaukee Sentinel* reported manager Byron McKibben of the St. Joseph Western League club tried to induce Kid Speer (signed by Milwaukee) and Ed Lewee (signed by Kansas City), who were working out in Milwaukee, to jump from the American Association to the Western League, offering them $50 a month more on their contracts. Both refused.

One of the tricks used in this player signing battle was to antedate contracts with players who were already under contract with another team. It was reported Connie Mack worked this dodge in signing Clyde Robinson of Kansas City, who had signed with George Tebeau on August 18, 1901, but later signed with Philadelphia under a date of August 5, 1901. In late March 1902 Robinson went back to the Kansas City Association team after getting in shape with the

Athletics and receiving advance money. His contract with the Blues had been $700 less on the season than he was to receive in Philadelphia, so it was believed Kansas City upped the ante. It was also thought Robinson knew he would be used as a utility player by Mack, and would play more in the minor league. Two weeks later, Robinson deserted the K.C. American Association team for the Kansas City Western League club. Manager Dale Gear called "the midget third baseman" an ingrate and guilty of a low down, dirty trick. However Gear's rantings were not taken too seriously when it was remembered Robinson had come to Kansas City from Philadelphia under a cloud.[26]

By mid–April it was reported that at least 20 players had jumped their American Association contracts to go to the Western, National or Eastern league. The St. Paul club was hit hard, losing four starting players. Louisville also reported losing four players, and Kansas City five, but not all of these were projected starters. American Association President Hickey declared that players who had jumped their Association contracts would never be allowed back.

The *Milwaukee Sentinel* was

Clyde "Rabbit" Robinson — A double contract jumper drew K.C. manager Dale Gear's ire (Historic Photograph Collection/Milwaukee Public Library).

one paper very opposed to this contract jumping, and saw terrible ramifications if it continued. In a sporting editorial the paper wrote:

> Sportsmen like honest methods and patronize honest games, but the moment an iota of taint appears in any branch of athletics its future is clouded. Baseball has been an honestly played game. The players have formed no collusions to work a "brace game" on the public and the profession has always been esteemed an honorable one. But if the magnates, the men who supply the financial backing and are looked upon as being responsible for the integrity of the game, begin a campaign by bribing players to jump contracts and disown honorable obligations, why will not the patrons of the diamond be warranted in believing that the games are "fixed" at the instigation of the club owners for the purpose of catering to their pecuniary interests and deliberatively thrown to give gamblers a sure thing?[27]

Columbus was also having its problems with players jumping. Catcher Jack Zalusky and first baseman Jim Hart had signed contracts with the Senators and received advance money. Columbus had purchased Zalusky and some other players from Walter Wilmot for whom they had played at Grand Rapids in 1901. However, Zalusky could not reach an agreement with Columbus and signed with the Chicago National League club. When the Chicago Colts decided they had enough catching, they agreed to let the catcher go to James Manning's Western League Kansas City team. Wilmot decided he wanted Zalusky back, but under the rules of the American Association Zalusky belonged to Columbus. Club president Thomas Bryce told league officials Zalusky would play in Columbus or nowhere in the American Association. Zalusky, the son of a Minnesota police officer, was willing to return to the American Association, but only to Minneapolis. If forced to play with Columbus the catcher said he would go to Kansas City. American Association president Thomas Hickey stepped in, asking Bryce to give up his claim on the player in order to keep him from jumping to the Western League. After some consideration Bryce allowed the player to go to Minneapolis. Zalusky resigned his position at the local flour mill and began training at the university in March to join the Millers. Wilmot was delighted to have Zalusky, believing he had no equal when it came to throwing and fielding.

The Wheeling club of the Western Association claimed to have signed outfielder Jim Hart for the balance of the 1901 season and all of 1902. The situation was settled in March when Hart purchased his release from Wheeling and stayed with Columbus. However, in April it was reported in the Columbus papers that Ed Barrow of Toronto was attempting to get Hart and pitcher Harvey Bailey to jump their Columbus contracts for his Eastern League team. Bailey also stayed with Columbus, winning 23 games for the Senators in 1902.

There was a growing sentiment in the Association to retaliate for player raids. In April three star players of the Kansas City American Association team — outfielder Fred Ketcham, catcher Tom Messitt and third baseman Clyde Robinson — jumped over to the K.C. Western club. Each had signed a personal contract and received advance money with the Association team. Thomas Hickey spoke on the matter to the editor of *Sporting Life*: "At present it is the policy of the American Association to avoid dealing with contract jumpers. If the Western League and some of the other base ball organizations continue their piratical course it may be necessary to adopt retaliatory measures. This, however, will be the last resort."[28] Within days manager Dale Gear of the Kansas City Association club said he had conferred with owner A.L. Buell, and his club would not seek to get the three players back. Gear believed he would secure players as good or better, but the three owed him the advance money and board. Charlie Nichols of the Western League Blue Stockings said all this talk was simply for effect. He said Gear knew the Western League club would pay back the advance money and board and that the jumping was no surprise. The Western League club guaranteed the three players their money for the entire year would be paid no matter what happened to the league. Buell refused to offer the same guarantee when the players went to him, and they proceeded to sign with the Western League club.[29]

Another jumper from the Kansas City A.A. club to the Western was pitcher Jake Weimer, who had been the ace pitcher on Tebeau's 1901 Western League team. On April 11 Dale Gear filed an injunction to restrain Weimer from playing with the Western League team. Gear claimed Weimer was "a pitcher of unusual ability" who signed with the Kansas City club in the old Western League on August 14, 1901, for the 1902 season. Weimer's contract had been transferred

Jake Weimer — Even though he was involved in a stubborn contract court case between the two warring Kansas City clubs, he would pitch the entire season with the Western League Blue Stockings, finishing with a .625 winning percentage (Library of Congress).

to the American Association Kansas City club, which Weimer ratified. The original American Association contract was for $850, but the Western League increased the amount to $1,500. In court Weimer's attorney claimed the pitcher had signed the contract believing he was to play in the old Western League, not the new American Association. The judge ruled the contract was with George Tebeau, not the Western League, and granted a temporary injunction.[30]

Western League Kansas City owner James Manning suggested he was not concerned with the case:

> They can't touch Weimer in any possible way. I consulted attorneys before these men were signed, and also since, and all opinions are to the effect that they are wasting time and money. No court in the country will hold that a man must work for one man when he can get more for his labors from another. Then, too, what if they should get an injunction here, they would have to enjoin us in every other city in the league to prevent our playing him. The whole thing is a gigantic bluff to scare other players out of jumping who are on the verge of doing so now. We are not at all frightened about their action and will meet the issue squarely.[31]

The proceedings for a permanent order were postponed until mid–May. Both leagues agreed to allow Weimer to pitch in the state of Missouri until a final judgment was given. The suit was postponed a few more times and soon dissolved. Weimer would start the opening game for the Western League Kansas City team in Colorado Springs and play the entire season with Manning's Blue Stockings.

The contract jumping dispute involving the most famous player was that of Addie Joss. Joss, called "the Chinese god of the Western Association,"[32] had pitched for Charles Strobel in Toledo in 1900 and 1901, winning 19 and 25 games, respectively, in those years. After the 1901 season the 21-year-old went back to his home in Wisconsin and attended Beloit College, where he was a very good football player. Reports stated that Joss had signed with Brooklyn of the National League as early as August 18 and accepted $400 in advance money, although Joss said he had not received any advance money. Toledo owner Charles Strobel said the pitcher was still his property, as he had signed him and a number of other players for the 1902 season on August 12. Strobel correctly cited that until September 30, 1901, the Western League had been under the protection of the National League, a protection he and other owners paid for. Brooklyn owner Charles Ebbets wanted to meet with Joss to discuss the matter, but the player told Strobel he would stay in Toledo and reportedly signed with the Mud Hens in February 1902, accepting $150 in advance money.

In March it was reported that Joss had signed a contract with Cleveland of the American League. The Toledo press took the young pitcher to task. On April 19, 1902, the Toledo correspondent to *Sporting Life* wrote:

> Strobel surely received the most ungrateful treatment on record, even in these days of contract jumping. There was a time last year that whenever Joss appeared in a box the fans threatened to mob Strobel. Joss at the time looked like a very cheap amateur and was generally hit to the woods. But Strobel saw that he had the talent and kept him on the pay roll while all the local papers were calling for his scalp. The last four or five weeks of the season he made good and developed into a tower of strength. When he left Toledo at the close of the season he took Strobel by the hand and said "if all the team desert, you will find I will stay with you." He voluntarily signed the contract for this season, but when Armour of Cleveland showed him the $500 bill he forgot his pledge and sneaked off to New Orleans like a whipped cur.[33]

At first Strobel said he would take no legal steps to force Joss to pitch in Toledo, as he had plenty of pitching. But the Toledo magnate soon changed his mind. On April 2 a Toledo grand jury handed down an indictment charging Adrian Joss with obtaining money under false pretenses. The charge was that Joss had returned only $100 of the $150 advance money he received from Strobel. This was a felony charge, and Joss could land in the state penitentiary. The warrant was placed in the hands of the Franklyn County sheriff, who waited at the train station to arrest Joss when the Cleveland team arrived in Columbus, Ohio, before the regular American League season began. However, Joss had gone on to St. Louis for the A.L. opener. President Kilfoyl of the Cleveland Blue Birds said that Joss would surrender to authorities when the team came home, and the club would post his bail and fight his case for him.[34]

On April 28 Addie Joss, in the company of American League vice president (and principal Cleveland owner) Charles W. Somers, turned himself in at Toledo. Bond was set at $500 and signed by two local coal dealers. The trial was set for May 1. Charles Strobel was on the offensive, saying that in the event Joss was not convicted, he would go to the United States Supreme Court to endeavor to enjoin him from playing with Cleveland. Strobel said he was also in the process of starting proceedings to collect damages from the Cleveland club in a civil suit, claiming his business had been interfered with. The case lingered in the court until July, when Cleveland released pitcher Jack Lundbom to Toledo with the understanding that Strobel would withdraw his suit against Joss. The big 25-year-old Lundbom was said to have the qualities to make an excellent pitcher but lacked experience. He would win but one game with the Mud Hens and lose six, before being returned to Cleveland in August.[35] Joss would do much better in Cleveland, winning 17 games in 1902. Addie Joss would go on to pitch nine years in Cleveland, winning 160 games while losing only 97. He also threw a perfect game in 1908 and a no-hitter in 1910. He became sick during the 1910 season, and pitched his final game on July 11. On April 14, 1911, Adrian Joss died of tubercular meningitis in Toledo, two days after his 31st birthday. He would be inducted into the Baseball Hall of Fame in 1978.

The attempts by Western League managers to induce American Association players to jump leagues continued after the 1902 playing season began. In early May it was reported that St. Joseph manager Byron McKibben went to Toledo and registered in a hotel under an assumed name while attempting to get Kansas City pitcher Barney Wolfe, second baseman John O'Brien and shortstop Ed Lewee to sign with his club for more money. All three refused.[36] Wolfe, who in 1902 would win 19 games for the Blues while losing the same number, had been an inviting target for Western League clubs. In April Blue Stocking manager Charles

Addie Joss — The future Hall of Famer was involved in a major contract dispute between the American Association, National League and American League in 1902 (Library of Congress).

Nichols and Billy Everitt of Colorado Springs asked Wolfe for a conference to convince him to jump to "the Rubber Legs." The *Kansas City Journal* reported: "'Old Smiles' went, but when they began giving him the bull con they were told a few things. 'When the time comes,' said Wolfe, 'that my word is not good, then I hope that I won't be able to play baseball or anything else.'"[37]

President Hickey of the American Association publicly stated that he was against contract jumping. He was in favor of a reserve clause in the major leagues, but not in the minors. His reasoning was that the big leaguers had already reached the limit of salaries, while the men in the minors were just beginning. In Milwaukee Hickey told a reporter that any player who jumped a Western League contract would not be allowed to play in the American Association. Hickey said it was a business decision: "Should a man jump any organization to play for us he is likely to jump us for another team. Such dishonesty will not be tolerated in the Association."[38]

However, Western League men were telling *Sporting Life* a different story. Claims were being made against Minneapolis' Walter Wilmot that he had sent letters to some St. Joseph players offering them more money and the promise of steady employment, which would be impossible if they stayed in the Western League, because it was about to disband. St. Joseph owner W.T. Van Brunt immediately reported all that the Western clubs were in good financial standing and did not owe their players any salary. Van Brunt also claimed letters had been received from the Milwaukee American Association team offering Western League players bribes to jump their contracts.[39] When a misunderstanding over a player's contract came up later in July, and the Brewers were again accused of attempting to sign Milwaukee Western League players, Milwaukee Brewer president Harry Quin sounded off.

> The statements that we were after Western League players are false. We have no agents doing such business, and anyone who made such a claim is acting on his own responsibility and not ours. No one had any authority to approach any of Duffy's players, for what good would it do? Even if the whole team wanted to jump to our organization we would not take them. We went on record some time ago as being opposed to contract jumpers, and we have had no occasion to change our views. When we do we will come out and announce the fact and then go to the enemy's camp and brandish the greenbacks in the faces of the players. Then if they want the coin we will do business, but until we decide upon that policy it will be well for the Western League people to stop harping about it. If we lose a few thousand dollars, or make a few thousand, all well and good. The public does not give a rap whether we make money or not. We feel confident that the Association is a much faster organization than the Western League.[40]

George Tebeau came under fire in April for his signing of third baseman Bob Schaub for his Louisville team while he was reportedly under contract to Toronto in the Eastern League. Charles Havenor, secretary of the Milwaukee Brewers, said his club would not play Louisville if Tebeau was playing contract jumpers. Tebeau said Schaub was not jumping a contract, since he had signed the third baseman the previous fall.[41] American Association President Hickey said he wrote to the Eastern League to find what Schaub's status was, but having never received an answer, permitted him to play. The situation resolved itself when Toronto released Schaub in April.

Tebeau apparently was still trying to get Western Leaguers to jump well into May, as he was accused of tampering with Billy Hartman, Norm Brashear and Frank Roth of St. Joseph. The first two players St. Joseph had taken from Tebeau. Van Brunt, the chief backer of a number of Western League clubs, also accused the Milwaukee American Association people of sending letters offering four of his players more money to jump their contracts. In addition to these American Association offers to Western League players, it was reported that a number of Denver's pitchers had received letters from managers in the Utah League inducing them to jump the team. None would, however.

The Sporting News correspondent from Wilkes-Barre, Pennsylvania, H.G. Merrill, was very much against contract jumpers. He believed jumpers should be forced out of the game and made to seek other employment. But he also blamed management for the situation. In a biting editorial on the practice of contract jumping he wrote:

> The flopping of players during the past three or four months, largely influenced and countenanced by team owners and managers, has had but one effect. It has created, within the minds of the array of ball players, the disposition to disregard contracts — to disregard any bond created between manager and player. The fact is, unless the thing is speedily stopped, ball payers will come to the belief that, from caprice of any form, they may break any contract they may make with utter impunity. Both elements — manager and player — have contributed, and are yet doing so, to the very thing that will ultimately put the nation's sport into great jeopardy. The managers during the past winter have been maneuvering and have corralled men from various sources, using methods that others have adopted, and when the time came for men to report, have found their calculations all wrong. Then a fearful howl ensued and reprisals were in order. The fact is, the various managers have had their own personal goals to effect, and all went above them in the subtle manner peculiar to the man certainly looking for the best and at everything. In every move of diplomacy, just as in every horse trade, some one gets the best end of the matter. And it is the same spirit that actuates the sharper against the sharper, or the sharper against the unsophisticated in a horse-trade, that has actuated the men who have been making the majority of the player movements during the past few months. Many of them have reaped that which they have sown, but the sport is forced to sustain the effects of the ill-advised and unwarranted action. I did not admire the reservation privileges and powers of the past, and care little whether present reservations are in any way respected. But when it comes to a contract of any sort involving an agreement of any kind between player and manager, I say it ought to be respected and every manager ought to keep his hands off the player.[42]

The American Association showed it was against contract jumpers with a decision in a case involving pitcher Wily Dunham. The previous fall Dunham had agreed to go to the St. Louis National League club for a set salary and a $100 advance. The club accepted his offer but never sent the advance money. After waiting a reasonable amount of time, Dunham signed with Columbus, telling the Association owners that St. Louis had no claim on him. The St. Louis club thought differently and appealed to Thomas Hickey, who sent the matter before the board of directors of the American Association. The board awarded the player to St. Louis. Even though Columbus Owner Bryce wanted the player, he gracefully acquiesced to the decision. However, there were those in Columbus who believed that the board of directors, composed of Tebeau of Louisville, Watkins of Indianapolis and Lennon of St. Paul, wanted to weaken the Columbus team.[43]

The Philadelphia weekly *Sporting Life* took note of the American Association's stance on player contracts:

> As a matter of justice to the American Association, attention should be called to the fact that this is practically the only important base ball organization in the country whose skirts are absolutely clean in the matter of contract-breaking. To the best of our knowledge there is not within its ranks one player on whom any club of any league has any contractual hold. Of reserve-jumpers there are many in the American Association, but that is another and less serious thing. Reservation is a matter solely between clubs and leagues. As players are not party therein, and not bound thereby except by force, they violate no obligation of their own in ignoring or escaping from reservation whenever leagues themselves open the door. That the American Association should have closed its doors to contract breakers during a state of war, and resolutely refused to be driven into a war of reprisal in face of attempts upon its players, is a remarkable fact that deserves more recognition and commendation than has as yet been accorded it. In this matter the American Association has risen superior to all base ball organizations, not excepting the National and American League.[44]

But the American Association was not that pure. Before most could read this article, Toledo and Kansas City signed two players reportedly under contract in the Connecticut League. Later reports out of Denver were that Walter Wilmot of Minneapolis had been in the Colorado city attempting to tempt players to jump their contracts. It was said Wilmot was acting on his own, as a sort of agent. However, this story was not generally believed, as Wilmot had "bundles of bones which he displayed liberally to all the players he approached." The presumption was that he was an agent for the American Association. None of the Denver players signed. As Hickey had issued the order that all jumpers would be barred from his league, the players looked at the offers as a possible means of kicking them out of baseball.[45]

The jumping continued into the season, and on occasion clubs took immediate action. In June Danny Shay left the St. Paul American Association club to play for the San Francisco team. He was arrested just prior to taking a train to the West Coast on a charge of having overdrawn his account with the Saints. He was arraigned in court and fined $25, promising to repay $138.25.[46]

Later in June Ed Cline, an umpire in the Southern League, was accused of attempting to convince a number of Indianapolis players to jump to that league. He succeeded in getting third baseman Charles Babb to jump to Memphis while the Hoosiers were in Louisville. Another player to be tempted by the Southern League was pitcher Sam McMackin of Columbus. It was reported McMackin was "out on a drunk" with Ed Cline and attempting to get a number of players to jump their contracts. Senator manager John Grim suspended McMackin without pay and fined him his entire remaining salary. Columbus owner Thomas Bryce, feeling sorry for McMackin's family, later remitted the fines, gave McMackin's wife the salary due him, and released the lefty. Sam caught on with the Milwaukee Brewers shortly thereafter.[47] One Columbus player, second baseman John Evans, however, did jump to Memphis of the Southern League. In July the National Association declared that Babb and Evans were ineligible to play in the Southern League and were to return to their American Association clubs. This order, however, was overruled by the Southern League president, causing a major "squabble" in that league.[48]

In Louisville captain Billy Clymer stated that he received an offer from an Eastern club to jump his contract for $400. He replied that he would not be at liberty to accept offers until September 23. Indianapolis first baseman George Kilm had also been tempted by the San Francisco Pacific League club to jump.

As late as mid–July shortstop Bobby Lynch left the St. Paul club for Colorado Springs of the Western League while complaining about the treatment he had received from teammates. Lynch said he was not a contract jumper because he had been playing with the Saints without a signed contract. Interestingly, Lynch was playing for St. Paul even though he was supposed to have reported to Connie Mack's Philadelphia Athletics, but Lynch claimed he never signed with the A's either. Saints manager Mike Kelley put a good spin on the jump by Lynch, saying the shortstop left "just in time to save an unpleasant scene." Kelley said he had been "not at all satisfied" with Lynch's play and was about to release him.[49] A month later the young shortstop was looking to return to the American Association, still claiming he was not a contract jumper.

The National League was also attempting to sign American Association players already under contract. In Louisville it was reported that the New York Giants had tried to get pitcher Pat Flaherty and outfielder John Flournoy to jump. Flaherty would say nothing, but Flournoy admitted the New York club sent him a railroad ticket and instructions to report immediately. Both players had been on the Eastern League reserves when George Tebeau signed them. New York had purchased Flournoy's release from Providence and claimed he belonged to them. Flournoy said Providence had no claim on his services because that club had failed to pay him in full the previous year. Both players would remain with Louisville.

The Eastern League was not done raiding American Association clubs after the season began. In July the Buffalo club managed to get the premier shortstop in the Association, Billy Nattress, to jump from Columbus. Nattress was said to have received a large increase in salary and a bonus of several hundred dollars.

In the face of all this jumping and attempts at inducing players to leave the American Association, the A.A. directors met in Chicago in July and decided to continue their policy not to play contract jumpers or to indulge in any retaliatory measures against other leagues.

It should be noted that not all dealings between the American Association and organized baseball were in a bad light. In June it was reported that Connie Mack of the Philadelphia Athletics offered to trade a good player or pay cash for the release of Milwaukee Brewer manager Billy Clingman. Harry Quin declined, considering Clingman too valuable a manager and player to let go. Quin said this about the offer: "Connie Mack made the offer for Clingman in good faith and did not try to get him away from us by any underhand methods. He was open and fair about it and offered a good price for his release."[50] Later, American Association President Hickey was informed by the National Association of Minor League Clubs that shortstop Tom Owens of Toledo and outfielder Fred Odwell, recently signed by the Louisville club, were under contract to Springfield of the New England League and Montreal of the Eastern League, respectively. Hickey immediately ordered the two players back to their respective clubs. However, after Odwell signed a sworn affidavit that he had not signed a contract with Montreal, and the Eastern League club would not send Hickey the alleged contract, Hickey reinstated Odwell to the American Association.[51]

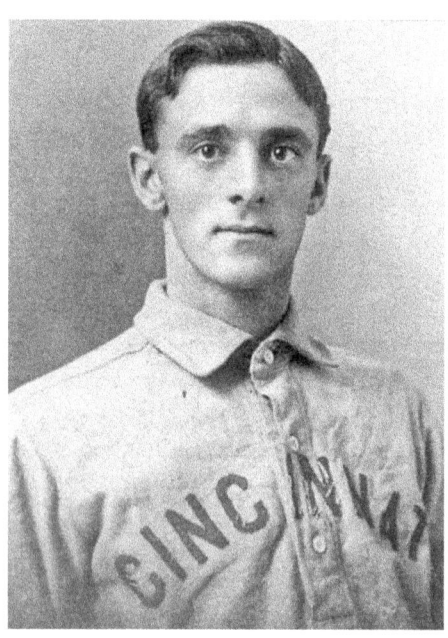

Fred Odwell — Ordered back to his original club by the A.A. president, he was allowed to remain in Louisville when no proof was provided that he jumped a contract. He would break his manager's jaw with a thrown ball meant for an umpire (Baseball-Birthdays.com).

It was not only the American Association clubs that were being hurt by contract and reserve jumpers. In Colorado Springs infielders Buck Francks and William Devereaux jumped to the

California League and were therefore thus being banned by the National Association. Pitcher Joseph Kostal also jumped his Denver contract to play with Spokane of the Northwestern League. E.F. Mohler, Bob McHale and Henry Schmidt would all be banned for not recognizing their reserve to Denver and leaving for the California League. Schmidt was said to have accepted $75 in advance money from Denver. The case of McHale showed a different side to all this jumping by players. His aging mother lived in Sacramento and he preferred to be near her. At 32 years of age, McHale, now in the outfield, knew he had only two or three more years left in the game, and he felt if he remained near his home in California, he would be better able to find work after his baseball career ended.[52]

The California League was actively attempting to sign Western League and American Association players well into the 1902 season. In June it was reported that M.E. Fisher, a captain of detectives and owner of the Sacramento club, was in Kansas City trying to sign Jake Weimer and Rabbit Robinson of the Western League Blue Stockings, in addition to Billy Wolf and Kid Nance of the Association Blues. None of the players jumped. However, in August third baseman Bill Phyle jumped his Minneapolis contract to play for San Francisco.[53]

During the March 30, 1902, Western League meeting, President Whitfield announced the players Western League clubs had signed to date. Omaha, Colorado Springs, Kansas City, St. Joseph and Denver had complete or nearly complete rosters filled. Due to their late entry into the league, Milwaukee, Des Moines and Peoria had fewer players signed.

Soon Hugh Duffy in Milwaukee said that he had 12 men under contract and several promised from the American League. Duffy was reluctant to give out names, and it was thought that he was waiting for the American and National leagues to cut some of their surplus players, thus picking up some talent. One reason Duffy was not giving out names of players he was interested in can be seen in the signing of George McBride by the American Association Brewers. Duffy was interested in the local lad, but when he tipped his hand, the Brewers "secured McBride's signature to a contract before Duffy dreamed that any other club wanted him."[54]

The two other latecomers to the Western League now had managers. Billy Hart was named as the Peoria manager. Hart had been born in Louisville in 1865 and played his first games with the Chattanooga Lookouts and Memphis Browns of the Southern League in 1885. He was in the big leagues in 1886 with the Philadelphia club of the American Association. He pitched again for the Athletics in 1887 before playing five years in the National League and then finishing his big league career in 1901 with Cleveland of the American League. Hart's major league pitching record was 66 wins and 120 losses. In

Billy Hart — The veteran major leaguer served as manager of the Peoria team (Library of Congress).

between many of these big league stops, Hart played for a number of minor league teams, mostly in the Western League and Western Association. As Peoria's manager in 1902, Hart's first signing was the noted catcher Harry "Farmer" Vaughn of Cincinnati.

Joe Quinn took over the manager's job in Des Moines, signing to play second base and manage for $300 a month.[55] Quinn was another veteran ballplayer, having spent 17 years in the big leagues, dating to 1884 with the St. Louis Maroons of the Union Association. Quinn was born Christmas Day 1864 in Sydney, Australia. He had the dubious honor of being the manager in the 1899 season for the Cleveland Spiders, whose 20 and 134 record is the worst in major league history. Quinn's record as a player/manager was 12 and 104. Playing second base, Quinn committed 31 errors but hit a respectable .286 that year. Quinn's only other managerial experience was with the St. Louis Browns of 1895, finishing with 11 wins against 28 losses. For his major league career, which ended in 1901 with the Washington Senators, Quinn hit .262, amassing 1,800 hits. Quinn had an off-season occupation different from most ballplayers; he ran an undertaking business in St. Louis.[56]

It was thought that the American Association had put together a very strong league, far above average for a minor league. In early exhibition games with major league clubs, the St. Paul Saints defeated the St. Louis National League club "in a most decisive manner,"[57] Indianapolis whipped the Cincinnati Reds in two of three games, Columbus also trimmed the Reds, Kansas City lost to the American League champion White Stockings by close margins. The Brewers also defeated the Reds in games in Cincinnati. At the same time, the Western League clubs were having little success with major league clubs, losing a majority of the games played.

Regardless of what spring training showed, the teams of both the Western League and American Association were ready to begin the 1902 season.

Three

♦ ♦ ♦ ♦

The 1902 Playing Seasons

The majority of American Association clubs decided to have their teams report for spring training at home, or as close as possible. This was an economic decision due to the heavy expenses of starting up the league. Also, any surplus in the treasuries might be needed to help the Association through the upcoming year of war with the Western League and other circuits in organized baseball. For example, Toledo, Kansas City and Columbus trained at their home ballparks when weather permitted. St. Paul and Milwaukee trained in locations near Indianapolis.

The American Association began its 1902 season on April 23. Indianapolis was host to the Milwaukee Brewers, the Hoosiers winning 5 to 4 behind the five-hit pitching of Win Kellum. Attendance in Indy was estimated between 3,500 and 4,000, despite a cold and windy day. In Toledo the visiting St. Paul Saints lost to the Mud Hens 8 to 7 in eleven innings before a paid crowd of 1,500. (The Associated Press gave an attendance of 3,500.) How many of those in the stands were city officials would be interesting to know. In January the Toledo city council contemplated making club owner Charles Strobel pay a $100 license fee to play baseball in the city. Strobel said if the fee was passed, he would not issue a free pass to any city officials. Strobel complained he had issued $1,000 worth of free passes yearly to city officials.[1] (Unfortunately, I could not find if this fee passed the council or not.) Strobel was also having troubles with the owner of the grounds where his Armory Park was located. The owner wanted to raise the rent $450 for the season. Strobel thought of relocating, and even secured an option on another piece of property that was not as accessible as Armory Park. Before the season began, Strobel accepted a $200 raise in rent and decided to increase the seating capacity at the park by 500 to 600 people.

The opener in Columbus drew 3,300 to see Senators pitcher Wiley Dunham give up only three hits in shutting out Minneapolis 5 to 0. The Millers pitcher, Joe Corbett, also allowed only three hits, but eight errors by his teammates helped pin the loss on him. The fourth game that Opening Day was in Louisville, where the hometown boys were whipped by Kansas City 16 to 6 before an estimated crowd of 5,000.

The Louisville Colonels played the 1902 season in a new park. When George Tebeau first announced he was placing a team in Louisville, it was said he would purchase the old National League grounds on 28th and Broadway and build a newer and bigger grandstand. The "cigar box stand" was one of the main reasons the Western Association club had folded in Louisville the previous year.[2] The National League was reluctant to give anyone a lease on the grounds, fearing it would end up somehow in the hands of the American League. It was soon announced a local real estate person was looking to purchase the old ballpark and divide it into lots. Tebeau was looking seriously at two other locations to put his ballpark. One was at Seventh and Kentucky, in the heart of the city. One problem with this location was the owner of the property objected to Sunday ball on the grounds.[3] The other location was a square between Fifth and Sixth, L and M Streets, located 19 minutes from the business center. These grounds were about a mile closer to the city than Churchill Downs, and reached by the same streetcar line. Tebeau had one other location in mind, at Preston and Camp streets. He asked the public to respond by postcard what their preference was. "Every person, male or female, white or black, [was] eligible to vote," and about 3,000 votes were cast. The fans favored the Fifth and M Street location. However, the Street Railway Company would not give Tebeau any assistance with new cars. The company said this section of town was reached by the Fourth Street cars, which already were overburdened with travel to Jacob Park, and thus would be unable to provide adequate baseball service on the line.[4]

At the end of February Tebeau leased the grounds from W.H. Dulaney bounded by Seventh and Eighth streets, Kentucky Street and Garvin Place. It was said this was really the tract Tebeau had been after all the time, with the talk of the other locations a way to disguise his real intention. It was reported he signed a ten-year lease on the grounds at $2,800 a year. This location was only a few blocks from the most fashionable portion of Louisville. The park was only a seven-minute direct streetcar ride from the business center and a ten-minute walk from Fourth and Broadway.[5]

Before George Tebeau could begin erecting a ballpark, an injunction was filed by nearby property owners claming their property would be ruined by ball games, which they declared to be a nuisance in a residential section of town. It was also claimed "that bad boys and men would congregate and make the neighborhood unfit for decent and self-respecting people." A Methodist congregation, whose church was within a block of the proposed park, also lodged a protest against the building of the park. A temporary halt was put on all plans and Tebeau immediately filed a demurrer. The objection was substantiated by Judge Shackelford Miller. The judge held that baseball in itself was not a nuisance and that the property owners' only recourse was a suit for damages or a criminal prosecution if they considered they had suffered any harm.[6] Tebeau had asked the neighbors whether they had any objections to having a ballpark in this location when he secured an option on the property. At that time there were none. There had even been a petition circulating that the park be located in the neighborhood, as the signers thought the park would increase the value of their property. For these reasons it was surmised by some that Western League people had sent an emissary to Kentucky to fight their rival behind his back.[7] Tebeau would spend at least $15,000 putting up his ballpark, which he named Eclipse Park, after the heroes of the old American Association days.[8]

Once the season began, Louisville, which had always been a good Sunday ball town, was drawing crowds so large on Sundays that it was thought the ballpark's seating capacity was entirely too small. The bleachers on weekdays were also close to capacity, as Tebeau was off to a good financial start in Louisville. Tebeau showed his good business sense when instead of attempting to compete with the Saturday Kentucky Derby, he switched the baseball game to be part of a Sunday double-header, and drew between six and seven thousand fans.

Columbus, in particular, continued to draw excellent crowds on this opening homestand, having a crowd of 10,000 on the first Sunday game and more than 8,000 the first Sunday in May. Weekday attendance ranged from 1,200 to more than 2,000. Before the season had begun, a new left field bleacher section was completed at Neil Park (thus named since it was owned by Charles and Thomas Neil of Columbus, from whom Thomas Bryce would purchase the park in November 1904 for $41,000[9]), adding 1,000 needed seats to accommodate these larger crowds. Another improvement for the players at the ballpark was the erection of a large clubhouse, fitted with hot and cold water and several fine bathtubs.

In Indianapolis William Watkins was running up against political opposition regarding Sunday ball. The American Association schedule called for Sunday game in Indianapolis, even though there was a state law prohibiting this, but not enforced uniformly. Indianapolis mayor Charles Bookwalter said there would be no Sunday ball in his city. Watkins at first threatened to leave the city if he could not play Sunday ball, but then decided to circulate a petition to change the mayor's mind. Watkins planned on playing the first scheduled Sunday game against Kansas City on April 27 in his Indianapolis park, but "out of respect for a handful of cranky ministers and a mayor who doesn't believe in baseball, yet permits the saloons to stay open on the Lord's Day,"[10] he decided to postpone the game until later in the season. The Hoosier owner, knowing his club could not be self-sustaining without Sunday ball, secured the old Western Association park in Marion, a city about 70 miles northeast of Indianapolis. The owner of the park, C.W. Haldermann, would only lease his park if some weekday games would also be played there, which Watkins agreed to. At least one American Association owner, Charles Strobel in Toledo, was against the Marion move, believing Marion could not attract paying crowds.[11] The Hoosiers played their first Sunday game in Marion on Sunday, May 4, defeating the St. Paul Saints 4 to 1 before 3,500 people. However, for the rest of the season, the Hoosiers would either transfer the scheduled Sunday home games to the other team's city or simply postpone the game.

The Canadian-born William Henry Watkins had been associated with baseball in Indianapolis since 1884, when he played the infield with the American Association club, and hit a weak .205 in 34 games. Late in the season he took over the managerial reins of the club, which won only 29 games against 78 losses. Watkins' playing career was nearly over — he was hit by a pitch, which threatened his life for a time[12] — but his managerial career was just beginning. In 1885 he started a four-year stay in Detroit, then in the National League, and placed second with an 87 and 36 record in 1886. Watkins' Detroit team won the pennant the next year with a 79 and 45 record. Later in 1888 Watkins left Detroit to take over the American Association club in Kansas City, where he had considerably less success. After having jobs in Sioux City and St. Louis, Watkins returned to Indianapolis with the Western League club in 1896 and finished in second place with a 78 and 54 record. He piloted the Pittsburgh National League club in 1898 and 1899 to average seasons. On November 25, 1899, Watkins purchased the Indianapolis American League (formerly the Western League) club from John T. Brush and a few minor stockholders for between $10,000 and $15,000.

William Watkins — The veteran baseball man owned and managed the Indianapolis American Association club (Transcendental Graphics/theruckerarchive.com).

Three. The 1902 Playing Seasons 61

Watkins was highly thought of as a baseball man, as can be seen from this pre-season report in *The Sporting News*:

> Watkins has put together one of the best teams seen in Indianapolis for some time. Watkins demands his players have the ability "to play the inside of the game." Anybody that knows Watkins knows that he never would stand for a team of stupid players. Intelligence is one thing that the Indianapolis manager has insisted on above all else. Stupid players upset Watkins quicker than anything else and for this reason we are getting assured that the local team will play the game right "up to the handle," the way that Indianapolis teams have done in the past. The team has already turned a number of clever tricks in its preliminary work, showing that Watkins has his eye open for the finer points of the game.[13]

The second batch of American Association Opening Days in 1902 took place on May 10. Kansas City opened before 2,500 with a 5 to 4 win over the Columbus Senators. In St. Paul an imposing parade led by the Minnesota State Band, followed by the mayor and 230 members of the Order of Base Ball Rooters, made its way to Lexington Park. Despite cold and disagreeable weather conditions, 3,184 persons turned out for the game to see Charles Chech shut out Indianapolis on four hits in a 4 to 0 victory. The Minneapolis Millers opened at home the same day and defeated the Louisville Colonels 9 to 4. The weather in Minneapolis was also terrible and only 1,000 braved the cold. With no parade or concerts before the contest, it was one of the tamest Opening Days the city ever experienced. Milwaukee's opener against Toledo was rained out.

Milwaukee had gone into the 1902 season not only with worries about the Western League rival in a ballpark less than two miles away, but with threats of boycotts against the club owner, Harry D. Quin. Quin was owner of the Quin Blank Book and a sporting goods supply company in downtown Milwaukee. Quin ran into trouble when he received bids for the building of his baseball park from an iron works company that was on the carpenter's union unfair list. The problem was solved when Quin agreed to use only union carpenters at the work site. However, there was word around the city that Quin's Brewers were to be boycotted. About two weeks before the season started, the president of the Carpenter's District Council

Charles Chech — This St. Paul Saint pitcher tossed a four-hit shutout on Opening Day 1902 (*The Sporting News*, December 14, 1901).

attempted to end this misunderstanding by sending out a letter saying the report of a boycott was false.[14]

In fact, a boycott had been called for, not by the carpenter's union but as a result of some alleged unfair labor practices resulting in a strike of bookbinders at Quin's bookstore. The bookbinders' representatives put Quin's ball club on the unfair list and sent out communications to other American Association cities' unions to boycott the Brewers when they played in their cities.[15] In Louisville, St. Paul and Toledo, the unions adopted resolutions to not patronize Quin's ball team. In every city in the circuit, stickers were placed outside the ballpark warning organized labor unions not to patronize the Milwaukee club. In Louisville and St. Paul the boycott was said to be a bust, but it "without doubt hurt the other gates of the Hickey league." Members of the union attending a baseball game in Toledo were fined one dollar, and a strict watch was kept at the gate to identify attendees. Attendance was down in the Ohio city enough was thought was given to transferring the Brewer–Mud Hen games scheduled there to Milwaukee, where attendance was not hurt much by the boycott. Thomas Bryce of Columbus later said the boycott cost $5,000 across the Association.[16]

Charles Strobel also found himself in trouble with the Central Labor Union in Toledo when he said some bad things about labor unions. The Toledo club owner was an accredited member of the musicians' union and was expelled from that organization on the technical grounds he had missed three successive meetings.[17]

The Brewers' home opener at the new Athletic Park took place May 11 on a cold day, with a northeast wind "chilling the spectators to the marrow and benumbing the fingers of the players."[18] The attendance was 7,000, including 6,272 paid. The Brewers — clad in cream-colored blouses and pants with blue trimming along with blue stockings and caps — beat the Toledo Mud Hens in 12 innings on a walk to player-manager Billy Clingman, a stolen base, and a hit by catcher Kid Speer.

On Memorial Day Columbus was solidly in first place in the American Association race with a 23 and 13 record. A bit behind was Indianapolis with 19 wins and 11 losses, followed closely by Louisville's 20 and 12 record. St. Paul was in fourth place with 18 wins against 14 losses. The other four teams were all under .500. The Senators were playing very good ball and had "not played a single rotten game this season, nor has it ever gone to pieces."[19] The team was leading the league in fielding, sacrifice hitting and base running, and ranked third in hitting. The pitching was doing a very good job, and at this early stage of the season the talk was of the success of local pitcher Ivor Wagner. He had only a half-year of experience in professional ball and to this point showed excellent promise. Wagner would tail off and post a 14 and 19 record for 1902. One of the problems with having a successful minor league club was the major leagues were continually searching for talent. Recently, the New York Giants had offered to purchase Terry "Cotton Top" Tucker, but Senator Owner Bryce said the third baseman was not for sale for any price.

Columbus had been involved in one of the better-played games in this early season when the Ohio team took on the St. Paul Saints in that city on May 22 before 1,491 fans. In the one hour-and-twenty-one minute game both Harvey Bailey of the Senators and Charlie Chech of the Saints gave up only four hits, and neither team made an error. After Phil Geier recorded the first hit of the game off Bailey, the ballpark rabbit "tore madly across the diamond," pleasing the fans. Columbus scratched out a run in the seventh inning and ended up winning the game 1 to 0. Because of this outcome, the *St. Paul Globe* wrote "The rabbit will be shot if he shows today."[20]

* * *

The Western League 1902 season opened the same day as the American Association, on April 23. In Omaha the Indians beat the Milwaukee Creams 11 to 4 in front of 2,500 spectators, following the usual downtown parade that Mayor Moore headed in an automobile. In Des Moines the home team lost to Billy Hart's Peoria team 6 to 2, even though Distillers pitcher Chester Cox walked eight batters. A small crowd of between 1,500 and 2,000 attended the game. Although the weather was chilly in Denver, a crowd of 5,000 saw the home nine lose to the St. Joseph Saints 6 to 5 in eleven innings. Denver continued to have great crowds on this initial homestand, with the Sunday game against Kansas City drawing 6,800 people, the largest crowd ever to see a ball game in that city.

The Denver owner, D.C. Packard, had gone out of his way to provide a pleasant atmosphere for both players and fans. The latest equipment was ordered for the players, and he even had a bathroom erected on the grounds for the benefit of the players after the game was over. The press was also thankful, as Packard made special arrangements for reporters. His press box had seating for six persons, with seats provided for the representatives of the four Denver newspapers, the Associated Press and the *Colorado Springs Gazette*.[21]

The game in Colorado Springs drew between 3,500 and 4,500 to see the Millionaires beat the Kansas City Blues 5 to 2. The game was played in the new park in the Ivywild suburb. Colorado Springs owner Thomas Burns had begun his plans for the new ballpark early in the year. He paid $16,000 for the land and put $5,000 into the park, which would seat 3,500. The new grounds would on occasion be called Boulevard Park, as it was north of the new street railway line on the boulevard road beginning directly west of Jenkins Pond (at today's Cheyenne Boulevard at Tejon Street), but would also be known simply as Base Ball Park. The park was only a five-minute ride from the center of town on a streetcar, and it was said on a pleasant day more people would probably go down into Ivywild to take a look around than ever had visited the place in one day before.[22] Western League president Michael Sexton had high praise for the ballpark: "Do you know that the diamond is the finest in the country? Well, sir, it is. I tell you that sodded infield is a wonder. It is the nicest park that I have laid eyes on for some time."[23] To celebrate this new baseball park and the opening of the season, the Colorado Springs Millionaire fans were treated to the "remarkable sight" of three gold-mining executives taking the field from their box seats:

> For the space of probably a minute and a half three men, representing probably $50,000,000 gave an imitation of a baseball team at work while a leading member of the bar and former judge of the district court, presided as umpire. Mr. [William Scott] Stratton entered the pitcher's box. Mr. [James F.] Burns [brother of owner Thomas Burns] doffed his coat and got behind home plate and Mr. [E.W.] Giddings stepped to the plate with bat in hand. Judge [Ira] Harris stood to one side in order to allow Mr. Stratton a full swing of the arm. As the multimillionaires took their positions another fond cheer went up. Mr. Stratton, after carefully measuring the distance, threw the ball. It went straight for the center of the plate though a trifle high. Mr. Burns was ready to receive it but Mr. Giddings interposed the bat and the ball sailed off toward second base. Another cheer went up and then the real millionaires vacated the diamond.[24]

The other four teams in the Western League opened at home on Friday, May 2. Kansas City beat Denver 9 to 6 behind Jake Wiemer's pitching. The attendance was reported to be 2,500. In Peoria the Distillers scored four runs in the eighth inning to win 5 to 3 over Des Moines in front of 3,100 fans. The St. Joseph Saints opened with the largest crowd to ever attend an opening in the city and beat the Colorado Springs Millionaires 5 to 3. The Sunday game was another record breaker. In Milwaukee the Creams could collect only three hits off Arthur Alloway, as Omaha won 2 to 0.

This Opening Day in Milwaukee is a fine example of attendance variations in the press. The *Milwaukee Sentinel* reported an Opening Day crowd of 700. The *Milwaukee Journal* and *Evening Wisconsin* gave the crowd at 1,500, causing the *Journal*'s sportswriter to comment: "One of the local scribes says that there were but 700 people at the game yesterday. Wonder where the other 700 were when he did his counting? Or perhaps that is as high as he can count?"[25] However, Omaha manager William Rourke said he did not receive enough money in Milwaukee to pay his railroad fare out of the city.[26]

Three. The 1902 Playing Seasons

On Memorial Day Omaha was leading the Western League with a 25 and 7 record, followed closely by Kansas City's 26 and 8 record. The only other team in the Western over .500 at this point was Denver, with 19 wins and 13 losses. Both Milwaukee and Des Moines had only won nine games; Milwaukee had lost 21 and Des Moines 22. The Omaha Indians, whose home uniforms were white with a big red O on the left breast adorned with a red cap and belt and blue stockings, were playing magnificent baseball, both in the field and at bat. Johnny Gonding was having a superb season behind the plate, and the club's three outfielders — Frank Genins, Tom Fleming and Bob Carter — were doing extraordinary work. Frank Owen had been winning games at a fantastic rate and was said to be the best fielding pitcher seen in many a year.

Frank Owen — The Omaha hurler, said to be the best at fielding his position, would finish the 1902 season with the fourth best winning percentage in the Western League (Library of Congress).

Not talked of much but an important part of baseball was where the teams stayed on the road. We have the story behind where the visiting teams stayed while in Omaha in 1902. All Western League clubs stopped at the Millard Hotel at 13th and Douglas streets in downtown Omaha. Manager Byron McKibben had stayed at the Millard during a spring exhibition on the suggestion of Omaha manager William Rourke and was very pleased. McKibben wrote a letter to James Manning of the Kansas City Blue Stockings, and word passed through the league. The rates at the Millard were as low as $2 per day on the "American Plan" and $1 and up on the "European Plan."[27] The Millard Hotel burned down in February 1933, killing seven firemen and injuring 22 others. No guests perished in the fire.[28]

One incident stands out in this first month of Western League play. The game in St. Joseph on May 13 was interrupted and then postponed by a strong storm. Saints shortstop Artie Ball, while leaning against a wire fence, was struck by lightning before the game was stopped. Ball was unconscious for three hours, and his left arm was temporarily paralyzed. He recovered at home for some time and was able to join the team later.[29] Artie was released to Peoria in early June.

Again in St. Joseph on May 22, the one thousand fans in attendance saw two well-pitched games. In the first game Frank Barber of Milwaukee held the Saints to three hits. Unfortunately, his fielders committed four errors in one inning, in addition to his walking two batters in the same inning, resulting in a 5 to 2 loss for the Creams. In the second game Milwaukee's John McPherson pitched a good game, giving up only six hits and two runs. But the Saints' Frank Parvin was "absolutely invincible," pitching no-hit ball for eight innings. In the ninth Charlie Hanford hit a little pop-up into right field that fell for a single. Parvin finished with a one-hit, 2 to 0 victory.[30] The very next day in Des Moines Tom Barry pitched another gem, a two-hit shutout of the Denver team, giving the Midgets a 2 to 0 win in a game played on exceedingly wet grounds. The highlight of the game was Des Moines player-manager Joe Quinn's grandstand catch of a "flaming liner" and resulting double play.[31]

* * *

Of course, without direct competition it is hard to tell which league had the better quality of play. A month into the 1902 season, the *Milwaukee Sentinel* gave the overall nod to the American Association. In its May 18 edition, the paper's sports editor, A.W. Friese, wrote: "Out of all the teams that have played here so far the work of the Omahas alone has been above reproach and by comparison the others have looked mediocre. The standard of play in the Burns–Van Brunt league is considerably below that set by the American Association, and Milwaukee people have not been slow to appreciate that fact, as the attendance indicates."

Overall the American Association was not drawing as well as expected, and the Western League not as well as the Association. For example, on Thursday, May 8, there were a total of 5,100 people at the four American Association games and 2,400 in Western League parks. The Milwaukee Western League Creams that day drew the dubious honor of the lowest attendance of any club in a major league or upper-class minor league with an attendance of 154.[32] Attendance figures in Louisville and Columbus had been very good. The Columbus-Toledo series over the Memorial Day weekend drew 20,000 for the four games, including the 11,000 who attended the Memorial Day doubleheader. By mid–June Columbus owner Thomas Bryce said his team had played to 76,000 people in its 32 games. Toledo was also doing fairly well in drawing crowds. However, crowds were disappointing in the other American Association cities.

The head-to-head battle for attendance in Milwaukee and Kansas City was showing the American Association the big winner. In late May Kansas City Association treasurer A.L. Buell told the press his club had outdrawn Manning's Western League club in every game played.[33] Newspaper attendance estimates support Buell. Opening Day on May 10 in the American Association Park drew 2,500, while only 250 attended the Western League opener. The next day, a Sunday, Gear's Association team drew 4,000, while Manning's Western team attracted 1,800. The weekday crowds showed similar or even bigger gaps in attendance, with the American Association team drawing 600, 1,000, 820 and 850 compared to the Western's 250, 200, 150 and 200. The following weekend Gear's team drew 750 on Saturday and 5,000 on Sunday, compared to 750 and 550, respectively, for Nichols' team. Things were not much different when the American Association club returned on Memorial Day to again go head to head with the Western League club. Facing the Milwaukee Brewers in a double-header, the Blues drew between 5,000 and 6,000 spectators, while the Western League club drew 3,400 against St. Joseph.

In Milwaukee the discrepancy between the two teams' attendance was even bigger. In head-to-head dates, the Association Brewers usually outdrew the Western League Creams by a three-to-one margin or more. The first head-to-head game was on May 11, but the 5,000 at Athletic Park who came to see the Brewer–Mud Hen game cannot be compared to the 300 at the Creams' Milwaukee Park, as this was the Brewers' Opening Day. The following day, 900 attended the American Association game, while only 150 were on hand to see the Creams. The pattern continued during the homestands. For example, on May 15, 16, and 17, the Brewers had crowds of 600, 500 and 3,000, while the Creams only had crowds of 100, 100 and 250. The Sunday, May 18, games drew 5,000 at the American Association ballpark and only 550 at the Western League grounds.

President Thomas Hickey assessed the American Association and said he was very satisfied with the attendance, He thought the Western League would have a difficult time making it past the Fourth of July. Hickey blamed the Western League's problems on syndication. With W.T. Van Brunt practically owning five of the eight clubs in the Western, the league was in effect a cooperative instead of a competitive concern. *The Sporting News* took a more non-objective view of the situation but came to similar results. The weekly believed five of the clubs in Hickey's circuit were in good condition. Columbus was the "bulwark" of the Association, and Louisville was getting satisfactory support. St. Paul, Kansas City and Milwaukee were considered to be doing well. Even though Watkins in Indianapolis had transferred his Sunday games to Marion, indications seemed to point to Indianapolis being out of the league by July. Minneapolis was "a good or bad ball town according to the team it has." The paper did not think Toledo would support the "makeshift team" Strobel had put together. *The Sporting News* editor concluded his assessment with the observation: "The American Association's chief danger lies in the top-heavy salary list of its clubs, and its victory over the Western League will be barren if there are breaks in the circuit before the half of its scheduled games are played."[34]

In the Western League Omaha was doing well in attendance. William Rourke, who had made a number of improvements to the playing area before the season began, increased the park's seating capacity in May. The Sunday, June 1, game drew an estimated 10,000 spectators. Denver was also beginning to attract large crowds. The Memorial Day afternoon game (part of morning-afternoon double-header) drew about 10,150 people — 9,941 paid — more than the stands could hold, and the crowd spilled onto the field. The double-header featured five home runs by Denver players, all inside-the-park hits, as the fences in Denver's park were too far away for anyone to hit a ball over.

As of June 1, a semi-official statement was made that the sinking fund of the Western League showed a balance of $21,000. It was reported that all the Western League clubs except Milwaukee and Kansas City were making a profit, with Denver and Omaha thousands ahead. Although it was claimed Des Moines was in "satisfactory shape," it appeared the club was having some financial problems. The club released three players — "Still Bill" Hill, Bill Dammann and Mike Hickey — to reduce salaries. Manager Joe Quinn denied this, saying Hill and Dammann were not pitching up to the standard of the Western League, and Hickey was released because of his broken arm.[35]

* * *

After Memorial Day the Louisville Colonels were a hot club and soon overtook Columbus for the American Association lead. Columbus owner T.J. Bryce ascertained his team's slump was to due to "dissipation," and he identified the offenders. Soon Dan Lally "got on another toot," showed up on the field in an intoxicated condition, was fined and suspended. He was soon traded to Minneapolis. In about 10 days the club had fined one pitcher, two outfielders and a second baseman. Finally, two players were released and one suspended for dissipation. It was reported the fans were patting Columbus management on the back for attempting to rid the team of the problem drinkers.[36] Another part of the reason Louisville was able to climb into first place was that Columbus was being hit hard by players defecting. By mid–July seven of the team's best men had jumped their contracts. These actions were not taken well in the city. It was reported the Western League agent recruiting players was escorted to the train depot by policemen for his own protection.[37]

However, Louisville's play on the field had much to do with its leading the league. The Colonels had two of the three leading pitchers in the league by June 21. Perry Coons owned eight wins and only two losses, while Pat Flaherty had a 12 and 5 record.

After losing three of four to Louisville, the Columbus Senators hosted Indianapolis and had one of the best-pitched games of the season tossed at them by Win Kellum. The Indians pitcher allowed only a single by Roney Viox with two outs in the eighth inning, and no Columbus base runner reached third base in the game, as Indianapolis won 3 to 0. Another fine pitching performance was put on by Hank Olmsted of the Milwaukee Brewers on June 13, when he allowed only three hits in the twelve innings he pitched against the Minneapolis Millers. Olmsted left with the game for a pinch-hitter in the twelfth inning with the game tied 4 to 4, and the Brewers scored a run two innings later to give the win to another Brewer pitcher. To add one more game to this list of impressive first-half season pitching performances was that of St. Paul's Dick Cogan on June 30 against Columbus. The Saints pitcher allowed only two hits, both to Senator right fielder Claude McFarland. He did display some wildness, walking two and hitting two batters with pitched balls, but the effort was enough to win the game 2 to 0.

After the games of July 4, the 1902 American Association pennant race looked like this:

Louisville	44	20	.688	Kansas City	31	34	.477
Indianapolis	39	24	.619	Milwaukee	26	37	.413
St. Paul	36	28	.563	Minneapolis	24	38	.387
Columbus	34	31	.523	Toledo	21	43	.328

Louisville was leading the Association with excellent hitting. Of the regular players, first baseman John Ganzel was leading the league by hitting .350 as of July 1. Ganzel had played the previous year with the New York Giants but was released, having averaged only .215 in 138 games with the National League club in 1901. Ganzel was signed by Louisville in the winter of 1902 and was making more money in the American Association than he had in the National League. His teammate, shortstop Lee Tannehill, was hitting .339, while outfielder John Flournoy was at .305. Three other regulars were hitting over .290. Even pitchers Perry Coons and Pat Flaherty were hitting heavy: Coons .379 with 54 at-bats, and Flaherty .313 in his 64 at-bats.

* * *

Even though Kansas City was not drawing that well, the team was playing good ball, and by June 6 temporarily overtook Omaha for the lead in the Western League pennant race. The Blue Stockings were helped considerably when Bryon McKibben's St. Joseph team swept a four-game series from Omaha. The Saints returned home, and helped Omaha regain first place, by winning three from Kansas City, including handing manager/pitcher Charlie Nichols his first loss of the season after he had won his first nine games on the mound. The Saints also showed themselves to be a lucky team. In the June 11 game, Blues pitcher Norwood Gibson gave up only two hits and struck out fourteen, but the Saints won the game 4 to 3 on a missed throw by Tom Messitt. The St. Joseph Saints might have been lucky, but Norwood Gibson ran into a bad streak of pitching luck. A week after losing this wonderfully pitched game, he matched up against Peoria, from where the lad resided. For twelve innings he shut the Distillers out, allowing only one scratch hit. Then in the thirteenth inning he lost the game on another scratch hit, a steal, and a solid hit. His Kansas City teammates had managed nine hits but could not score off Willie McGill.

On June 5 the Denver Grizzlies and Colorado Springs Millionaires started the all–Colorado series in Ivywild park. Both clubs had run afoul of other Western League owners in their choice of team mascots. President Thomas Burns of Colorado Springs had a mountain lion that he wished to carry about, and D. C. Packard in Denver wanted to take a grizzly bear along with the team. "When the two plans were laid before the other magnates they shook their heads and asked that nothing of the kind be done. The grizzly will, therefore, remain the pet of a West Side butcher shop, and Mr. Burns' mountain lion will retire to a menagerie."[38]

The Western League was putting on an exciting pennant race. Denver continued to play good ball and jumped into the lead. After the games of June 20, Denver was in first place with a 33 and 17 record (.660), Kansas City with one more win and one more loss (.654) was in second place, and Omaha in third place with a 32 and 18 record (.640). At this point in the season no other team was playing above .500 baseball. Colorado Springs was having a hard time signing good players. One of the reasons was there was an impression among baseball men in the East that the cost of living in Colorado Springs was exorbitant.[39]

Denver was playing this fine ball with a truckload of injuries and sick players. First baseman Ira Davis had been playing with a cracked bone in his shoulder. Shortstop C.E. Radcliff was sick in bed in St. Joseph with bilious fever, "evidently from over drinking Missouri River water."[40] Manager-catcher Parke Wilson was out of the lineup for a few weeks with a knee injury. Jack McConnell took his spot, but numerous injuries to his hand put him out for two months. Outfielder Walter Preston was sick with a slight rheumatism but was able to play on occasion. Outfielder Joe Wall had been out for some time,

Three. The 1902 Playing Seasons

being recently released from the hospital with leg problems. As a result of all this, Wilson was forced to use two pitchers in the outfield. As a matter of fact, when outfielder Preston was ejected from a game, Wilson was forced to have three pitchers covering the outfield positions. The Grizzlies lost pitcher Charles McCloskey to Little Rock of the Southern League in a contract dispute. Pitching superbly for Denver was "Pop" Elwood Eyler. On June 1 he pitched a one-hit 8 to 0 shutout against Peoria, after having shut out Milwaukee in his previous start on six hits. To top this off, on June 10 the Grizzlies executed the first triple play seen in Denver. Playing against Colorado Springs, a short fly was hit over Radcliff's head. It appeared the little shortstop had no chance to catch the ball, and the runners on first and second took off. When Radcliff made a fine catch, both runners were easy outs.

Soon the Denver Grizzlies' injuries and lack of pitching caught up to them. The team went on a two-week losing streak. The only game Denver won was in St. Joseph, by Charles McCloskey, and this game was disallowed by league president Michael Sexton. Denver owner D.C. Packard said he had been negotiating with Little Rock to purchase the pitcher's release for $500 but had not closed the deal when he pitched for his Grizzlies. Packard said the mistake was his and accepted the throwing out of the game.

As Independence Day 1902 came to a close, Denver had fallen to third place in the Western League:

Omaha	41	20	.672	St. Joseph	28	34	.455
Kansas City	40	25	.615	Colorado Springs	25	34	.474
Denver	34	26	.567	Peoria	19	34	.358
Milwaukee	30	26	.536	Des Moines	20	38	.349

* * *

As June continued, most clubs in both the Western League and American Association were reporting better crowds, some, such as Louisville, extraordinary crowds. However, the two Milwaukee teams could make no such claim. Although the team was beginning to play better ball, the Brewers could only draw a crowd of 200 in the June 10 game and 400 two days later. Meanwhile, a few miles south, the Creams drew 450 against Peoria but only 100 for the June 12 game. Crowds in Milwaukee on this homestand for both teams were steadily at 400 or so for the Association Brewers and under 300 for Duffy's Western League Creams. The Sunday games of June 15, however, attracted large crowds for both teams' double-headers. The Brewers drew 3,500 for the twin-bill with the Millers, while the Creams put 2,200 in the seats for the contests against Kansas City.

By late June the *Milwaukee Sentinel* was reporting Hugh Duffy's Western

League Milwaukee club was already about $5,000 in the red for the season. The club's operating expenses were about $3,000 a month more than the receipts, partly due to bad weather, which kept the attendance down at Milwaukee Park. It was alleged that three drafts for $2,000 each had been received from the Van Brunt-Burns syndicate by Duffy since the start of the season. The American Association Brewers had also been affected by the weather but were enjoying better patronage than the Creams. However, club treasurer Charles Havenor told a newspaper reporter he would be satisfied if the club did not cost $5,000 in excess of gate receipts for the year.[41]

Not only were the two Milwaukee teams vying for patronage at their ballparks, but in June the two clubs were involved in a player misunderstanding. It had been announced Ed Kenna, a pitcher who had been released by the Philadelphia Athletics in May, had signed with the American Association Brewers. But when Kenna arrived in Milwaukee, he was with the Western League Creams. Reportedly, Brewer manager Billy Clingman sent transportation for Kenna to his representative in Philadelphia, former Brewer Pete Husting, and Brewers president Harry Quin sent an order for advance money to Al Reach. However, in the meantime, Kenna received transportation and $75 in advance money from Creams manager Hugh Duffy and came directly to Milwaukee. Kenna said he was sorry for the misunderstanding and would like to play for the Brewers but could not after accepting the advance money.[42] Ed Kenna was the son of the late Senator John C. Kenna from West Virginia, he had been the quarterback of the West Virginia football team, and he had played baseball for Wheeling in the Western Association to help pay his way through college. He began writing poetry in his spare moments and later published a book of his poems titled *Lyrics of the Hills*. This earned him the nickname "the Pitching Poet."[43]

Ed Kenna — Known as the "Pitching Poet," after a contract misunderstanding, this son of an ex-United States senator finished 1902 with the second highest winning percentage among Western League pitchers (wikimedia.org).

Perhaps as a cost-cutting measure, on June 18 President Hickey ordered all teams in the American Association to carry only 14 men. Most of the clubs were already carrying this amount, but a few were as high as 16. The cut players would be offered first to other A.A. clubs before being released.

As July 4 past, all the predictions made earlier that one team or another, or entire leagues, would fold by Independence Day were remembered. As Kansas City newspaperman Ed Kundegraber said "From all surface indications the estimates are as far wrong as heaven is from the city of Chicago."[44] All sixteen clubs in both the Western League and American Association were still intact. At the Western League meeting on July 2, president Michael Sexton said the baseball war had become one-sided and that the only question undecided was how long the American Association could hang on.

It appeared most clubs in both the American Association and Western League were making money, at least according to public comments made by league officials. In the American Association it was reported all clubs would make money, with the possible exceptions of Kansas City and Milwaukee.[45] However, *The Sporting News* reported the only club making money in the A. A. was Louisville.[46] On July 4 the four American Association cities played before 36,778 paid admissions, prior to hosting 11,000 for three games the next day. This would make it appear the Association was in good shape.

At the July 1 meeting of the Western League in St. Joseph W.T. Van Brunt claimed all eight clubs were making good money and the league had more than $15,000 in its sinking fund.[47] Even the pro–Western League *Sporting Life* had doubts about this when it reported on July 12: "The [Western] League's press agents have sent out word that everything is lovely within its borders, and that every team stands to make a little money. This must not be taken too seriously. In several of the Western League cities Mr. Van Brunt may come out a little ahead, but in several, also Mr. Van Brunt will be called on to make good losses of greater or less size."[48] Cy Sanborn in the *Chicago Tribune* on July 1 gave these thoughts on the matter:

> It is a mystery to many how the minor leagues which are at war in the West can live with the small attendances reported at their games and paying the high salaries most of the clubs are paying. So bitter is the rivalry between the American Association and the Western League that both organizations have gone way beyond their depths in the matter of salaries. Only recently the Minneapolis club borrowed Pitcher Jack Katoll from Comiskey at a figure per month which would have staggered any of the old Western League magnates of five years ago, and the attendance is only slightly better now than then. There may be a gold mine behind every one of the sixteen clubs in those two leagues, and if so they will last the season out, but it would surprise no one who has watched the situation at all closely to hear a few explosions right after the Fourth, which will not be caused by gunpowder in any form, but by hot air.[49]

Neither of the Milwaukee clubs was as strong as league officials stated. There were a number of rumors that one of the Milwaukee teams would be moving out of town. Including one that suggested the Western League was to transfer the Milwaukee franchise to Grand Rapids, Michigan. Owner-manager

Hugh Duffy told a *Sporting News* correspondent: "You can bet your father Dudley will not play in Grand Rapids or any other city. Milwaukee is good enough for me and I expect to stay here with the Milwaukee Western League team so long as the public is willing to see good base ball. When the fans tire of it or when the team can't play, it's time enough to bolt; not before." Other printed reports said there was an effort being made in the Western to drop Milwaukee, and then the American Association would in turn take its club out of Kansas City. Yet another rumor floating around town was the Milwaukee American Association team would be transferred to Evansville, Indiana. Both Harry Quin and Hugh Duffy said no stock should be taken in any of these reports and rumors.[50]

* * *

The second half of the American Association season started on a bad note for Toledo second baseman Jack Burns. On the night of July 4, Burns attended a performance at the local theater with a friend and was boarding a streetcar when he was shot in the left breast, just below the heart. The bullet glanced off, leaving nothing but a scar. Burns missed only a few games, and would hit .229 in the 127 games he played with the Mud Hens in 1902.[51]

The Columbus Senators continued to falter, and John Grim resigned as manager, it being said "while a perfect gentleman and good ball player, but he was of too easy a disposition to make a successful manager."[52] His place was temporarily taken by Bobby Quinn and then George Fox. John Grim signed with the Indianapolis Hoosiers to play first base.

Indianapolis continued to win, while Louisville, hampered by injuries, finished July by losing six of seven games. On July 31 the Hoosiers and Colonels were tied for the American Association lead with identical 58 and 31 records.

As the pennant race heated up going into August, so did the back-room negotiations. A report circulated that two American Association cities would be dropped to make room for Nashville and Memphis. Although denied, it was reported George Tebeau had written manager Charles Frank of Memphis to set forth the advantages the Southern League might receive by withdrawing from the National Association of Professional Base Ball Leagues and allying itself with the American Association. Memphis had been having trouble in the Southern League at the time while playing a number of players who had jumped contracts from other teams.[53] Nothing came of this report, but Memphis and the Southern League would fight a battle of their own.

Louisville played good ball in August and opened a three-game lead over Indianapolis by August 28. The Colonels had posted a 77 and 37 record, compared to the Hoosier's 74 and 39. The only other team to have a win percentage over .500 in the American Association at this late point was St. Paul, at 63 and 52. Second-place Indianapolis won three games from the Toledo Mud Hens before facing Louisville. On September 1, approximately 4,500 fans — the largest crowd that ever attended a morning game in Indianapolis — saw Tom Williams beat the Colonels 9 to 4 to close the gap between the two clubs. In the afternoon a record-breaking crowd of nearly 16,831 jammed into the stands and onto the field to see the Hoosiers stroke 21 hits in a 17 to 3 route of Tebeau's team. The Kentuckians came back the next day with an 11 to 3 win, before Indianapolis closed its home schedule with a 7 to 4 victory. Attendance in Indianapolis for these four games against Louisville was 28,454. On September 4 the Hoosiers were in first place, a half-game ahead of the Colonels. A week later the Hoosiers increased their lead to a game and a half over the Colonels.

Injuries plagued the Louisville Colonels during the last weeks of the season. Star shortstop Lee Tannehill was out with an injury. Outfielder John Flournoy became a disturbing element on the team and was suspended. In addition, the Louisville management and players were convinced umpire Charles Tindell was favoring Indianapolis to win the American Association pennant and mistreating the Colonels. On September 20 Minneapolis and Indianapolis played a game in the pouring rain until the Hoosiers tied the score and then plated two runs to go ahead. Tindell called the game after the Millers batted on account of rain, giving Indianapolis the win. The next day Louisville was scheduled to play a double-header in Minneapolis. The Colonels won the first game 6 to 2. In the second game Tindell, again umpiring, called the game on account of darkness after three and a half innings, at about 4:30 P.M. The first anyone knew of the decision was when the umpire walked off the field. The crowd was furious, and the Louisville players and Tindell argued to the point the umpire had to seek shelter in the park's box office under the protection of two police officers.[54]

The pennant went down to the last day of the season, Indianapolis and Louisville both scheduled to play three games in the Twin Cities. The *St. Paul Globe* claimed both of these triple-headers were tainted. In its coverage of the games, the paper wrote that Louisville's George Tebeau "induced the Minneapolis management to forfeit games to Looieville [sic] yesterday on a twelve-minute schedule. The daring move compelled the Saints to leave their noonday beans untouched in order to reach the ballpark in time to lose the necessary three in a row to the Indians before the sun reached its sink." According to the *Globe's* version of events, the Millers were instructed "to move into the tardy-scholar class." While the Louisville players were on the field, the Minneapolis players remained in the clubhouse. The regular umpire, Charles Tindell, did not appear for the game, so Cy Torrence, a Minneapolis Miller pitcher, was named acting umpire. Torrence "bravely paraded out in front of the Miller stands and declared in a voice choked with sobs and tobacco juice that his team mates being delayed at luncheon, had forfeit a game to Looieville [sic]."

After a twelve-minute wait, Torrence came out and announced the second game was also forfeited to Louisville. Finally, a game was played, which Louisville won 4 to 0. However, "several of the deluded ones in the stands [attendance was given as 300] insisted that they had paid the gate for a double bill." Another game was played, but it was initially billed as an exhibition game in the press box. When Louisville went on to win the game 4 to 3, the contest was reported as a regular season game.

Meanwhile, across the river the Saints managed to lose the three games in their triple-header, before an announced crowd of 140 fanatics. The summary of the last inning of the second game let readers know what the *Globe* thought of this contest. The score was tied 2 to 2 in the ninth inning when we pick up the action: "...after [Indianapolis leadoff batter George] Hogriever had been walked [Saints pitcher Charlie] Chech heaved [Bill] Fox's bunt about a mile. G. Hogriever compelled several thrills by his mad dash for the plate. [St. Paul right fielder Harry] Lumley, not taking any chances on Hogriever slipping and breaking a leg, waited for the high sign before finding the ball. G. Hogriever's run won the game." In the third game the Hoosiers scored three runs in the sixth inning and four runs in the seventh inning to take a commanding 11 to 6 lead when "a cloud moved over the sun and before it got by [umpire] F. Figgmeier called the game on account of darkness."[55]

The *Globe* was quick to blast American Association officials in an article on September 23:

> It must be admitted that the finish of the season was a disgrace. It may have meant much to the association to land the pennant in Louisville, but the public supports the ball game because it believes that of all the professional sports the ball game stands out the one clean sport. The games at Minneapolis and St. Paul were deliberately thrown to the teams fighting for championship honors. St. Paul enthusiasts, realizing that the game was being played, did not raise a loud objection at the part taken by the St. Paul team, for with Clymer on the Louisville team, the fans here were willing to see Watkins win out.
>
> Watkins was excused, but this does not excuse the finish of the association. By making a farce of the windup the club owners themselves did more in a few days to injure the new association than was done all season by the members of the organization of minor leagues and other enemies of the American. This is one thing that the American Association will have to live down.

Three. The 1902 Playing Seasons

The 1902 American Association ended this way:

Indianapolis	96	45	.681	Columbus	66	74	.471
Louisville	92	45	.671	Milwaukee	65	75	.464
St. Paul	72	66	.521	Minneapolis	54	86	.385
Kansas City	69	67	.507	Toledo	42	98	.300

The Hoosiers won the pennant without a .300 hitter. They won with excellent fielding, and led the league in team fielding percentage and base running. Statistician E.S. Barnard of the *Columbus Dispatch* charted a number of interesting records of the 1902 American Association season. His evaluation of why the teams finished where they did is of special interest. Barnard felt Indianapolis and Louisville finished as the top teams of the league in part because they were fortunate in keeping the majority of their original team intact. Neither club used a pitcher who was not under contract to them at the beginning of the season. The injury of Lee Tannehill late in the season is probably what shifted the balance in favor of Indianapolis to win the pennant. The fairly good pitching staff of St. Paul could not overcome some "wretched fielding" (the team's 397 errors ranked second worst in the Association), and the Saints were never a factor in the pennant race. Kansas City was "shot full of holes" by the Western League before the season started and never had a chance. Dale Gear had made a game fight to land the team in the first division. Columbus was hit hard during the season by contract jumpers and dropped from leading the Association for the first two months to a dismal fifth place. The Brewers in Milwaukee were hampered by injuries that kept the team continually at a disadvantage. Walter Wilmot never got his Minneapolis pitching into satisfactory shape but did manage to overcome a horrendous

Lee Tannehill — The Louisville shortstop's injury contributed to the Colonels not capturing the A.A. title in 1902 (Library of Congress).

start, having lost 17 of the first 21 games of the season. Barnard commented that last-place Toledo was "a rank failure from start to finish." The Mud Hens had a good corps of pitchers, but the other players, with an exception or two, were not in the same class as the other Association clubs, and the club was poorly managed.[56]

* * *

The Western League pennant race opened up a bit after the Fourth of July, with Omaha taking a commanding eight game lead by July 17 while winning eleven of thirteen games. During this two-week stretch the Western League exhibited some fine pitching. The July 10 games give a fine example of this. Saints pitcher Harry Maupin and Milwaukee Creams pitcher Frank Barber were locked in a classic pitcher's battle in St. Joseph. Both pitched ten innings of scoreless ball. Finally Milwaukee scored one run in the eleventh, and Barber held down St. Joseph in the bottom half of that inning for the win. Both pitchers gave up eight hits. In Kansas City Jake Weimer shut out Peoria in a 2-hit, 5 to 0 victory. Denver's Elwood Eyler gave up only four hits while Tom Barry of the hometown Des Moines Midgets give up five, but the home team (in addition to the Midgets, the team was referred to as the Hawkeyes and Undertakers, the last because manager Joe Quinn ran an undertaking business in St. Louis[57]) scored three runs to the Grizzlies' two to tag the loss on Eyler. While not a pitching matchup for the ages, in Colorado Springs first-place Omaha beat the Millionaires 4 to 2 in a game played in only 58 minutes. Perhaps the best one-day pitching performance in the season was given on July 6 in Omaha. Mordecai Brown pitched the first game of an afternoon double-header against the visiting Denver Grizzlies, giving up five hits en route to a 2 to 1 win. In the second game Brown again took the mound and gave up only four hits, winning this game 6 to 1. In the two games the future Hall of Famer surrendered only two runs and nine hits, struck out 12, and walked only two batters. Brown received a well deserved rest the next day, as Frank "Yip" Owen (from Ypsilanti, Michigan) pitched a two-hitter against Denver, winning 1 to 0.

If it seems as if great pitching was all that happened in the Western League, two games on July 22 show that was not always the case. In Des Moines the home team collected 21 hits, scoring 17 runs, to beat Kansas City 17 to 6. The Blue Stockings hit safely 14 times. Eight doubles were hit in this game, and Josh Clarke and Charley O'Leary of Des Moines had four hits each. The game, amazingly, was played in one hour and forty minutes. The same day in Denver the Peoria Distillers had 24 hits to beat the Grizzlies 11 to 5. In this game there were four triples. Even the Peoria pitcher, Eugene

Cox, had four hits this day. And in a third game on July 22, the Colorado Springs Millionaires scored 12 runs on 15 hits to whip the visiting Milwaukee Creams 12 to 6. Two home runs were tagged in this contest.

In late July Denver won nine straight games, including a four-game sweep of first-place Omaha, to get in the thick of the pennant race. The team's 53 and 34 record as of July 31 put the Grizzlies only four games behind first-place Omaha. Denver was hitting very well, with four regulars — second baseman Tom Delahanty, third sacker Gus Dundon, outfielders Emil Frisk and Charlie Jones — batting higher than .300. Kansas City had fallen to third place with a 48 and 40 record.

On the other side of the Western League map Peoria was having a very tough time. The Distillers had won only eight games on the road all season. The team's 22 and 58 record put Peoria solidly in last place. Although the Peoria news media said the players were one of the highest-salaried teams in the Western League and there was no excuse for this losing, the *Milwaukee Sentinel* said of the team: "Peoria is a weak outfit, the team being composed largely of has-beens and it is not extra creditable to beat them to death."[58] Add to this the fact that the Peoria ball grounds, at the Lake View race track grounds about ten minutes from the heart of the city, had been inundated by rain for ten days in late July. When the water became so deep small boys were swimming around home plate, the club transferred the three scheduled home games against the Creams to Milwaukee.[59]

As August continued, the Western League race heated up. By mid–August it was a tight three team race. Omaha still led Denver (which had lost seven of nine) by four wins, but Kansas City had clawed its way back into the race and was only one win behind Denver. Hugh Duffy's Milwaukee Creams then went on a tear to share first place with the Omaha Indians. In the last few weeks of August, the Creams took three of four from Des Moines and two of three from first-place Omaha. The Denver Grizzlies came into the Cream City and lost four games handily. After winning the first two games from the Millionaires of Colorado Springs, the Creams' seven-game winning streak was ended. However, a new streak was immediately begun as Duffy's men swept four from hopeless Peoria, finishing with a four-hit shutout by Ed Kenna. Milwaukee then traveled to Peoria, where the Creams swept the five-game series. Peoria had failed to win a game from Milwaukee the entire season. In the meantime, Denver managed to stay in the race by winning two of three from Omaha.

During this late–August pennant race, Western League patrons were given some exceptional pitching performances. In St. Joseph on August 24, the Saints' Frank Parvin gave up only two hits to the Kansas City Blue Stockings, winning

2 to 0. The same day in Omaha Mordecai Brown allowed three hits in his 5 to 0 victory over the Colorado Springs Millionaires. Brown was also very effective in the second game of this double-header, giving up only five hits and one run. However, Frank Foreman was better, allowing no runs on the five hits he allowed. The next day Milwaukee's Merle Adkins shut out Peoria in a 10 to 0 win. The gem of this August 25 pitching was in St. Joseph. Kansas City's Jake Weimer started the game but was ejected by umpire Gus Moran in the first inning for "conduct unbecoming a ball player," after walking two batters. Norwood Gibson replaced him and allowed no hits and struck out seven in a 3 to 0 combined no-hit victory over the Saints.[60]

St. Joseph	AB	R	H	PO	A	E	Kansas City	AB	R	H	PO	A	E
Maher, ss	4	0	0	1	3	0	Katcham, cf	5	1	3	3	0	1
Brashear, 1b	3	0	0	8	0	1	Waldron, rf	5	1	1	3	0	0
Hartman, cf	3	0	0	7	2	0	Miller, lf	4	0	2	0	0	0
Belden, lf	2	0	0	4	0	0	Robinson, 2b	5	0	2	4	2	0
Rohe, 2b	3	0	0	3	2	0	Jacobs, 3b	5	0	1	0	3	0
Roth, c	4	0	0	3	1	1	Kemmer, c	5	0	1	6	1	0
Hall, 2b	4	0	0	1	0	0	Shannon, ss	4	0	0	2	1	0
Parvin, rf	3	0	0	3	0	0	Risley, 1b	3	0	0	12	0	0
Maupin, p	3	0	0	0	3	0	Weimer, p	0	0	0	0	1	0
							Gibson, p	4	1	2	0	2	0
	29	0	0	30	11	2		40	3	12	30	10	1

KC   0 0 0 0 0 0 0 0 3—3
St. Joe 0 0 0 0 0 0 0 0 0—0

2-Base Hits — Miller, Gibson; 3-base hit — Miller; Sacrifice Hits — Brashear, Rohe, Maupin, Miller; Stolen Bases — Hartman, Robinson; Left on Base — St. Joe 7, KC-7; Walks — Maupin 8; Gibson 4, Weimer 2; Strike outs — Gibson 7; Time of game 2:00, Umpire Moran; Att — 900

On August 26, fans in Colorado Springs were again treated to a double-header of great pitching. In the first game the Millionaires' Harris McNeely gave up only two hits, but his teammates could not score with the five hits they collected off Omaha's Arthur Alloway, with the home team losing 1 to 0. In the second game Colorado Springs reversed the score, the only run coming in the seventh inning on a single by Billy Everitt, a sacrifice fly by Tom Fleming, a passed ball and an RBI double by Art Granville. Both pitchers, Frank Owen for Omaha and Harry Newmeyer for Colorado Springs, allowed only four hits. Shutouts were also recorded this day by Ed Kenna of Milwaukee and Fred Glade of St. Joseph, both pitchers allowing only four hits.

On August 28 Milwaukee and Omaha had identical 66 and 44 records, closely followed by Kansas City at 64 and 48, then Denver with its 63 and 50 record. In the next two weeks it was the third-and fourth-place teams that climbed to the top. Denver won 14 of 15 games and on September 11 stood on top of the Western League with a 77 and 51 record. Kansas City was now in second place with 74 wins against 52 losses. Omaha and Milwaukee had 72 and 71 wins, respectively, to be positioned in third and fourth place.

As if last-place Peoria was not having enough problems with its losing ways, its grounds were flooded and a number of games had to be transferred in late July. Later in August it was announced the team's remaining home games had to be moved, owing to the Central Railway Company leasing the ballpark to a circus for September performances. Games with Kansas City and St. Joseph were transferred to those Missouri cities.

To add some non-baseball excitement in Peoria, Milwaukee catcher-infielder Harry Vaughn had a run-in with W.W. Mitchell, proprietor of the Mitchell Hotel, in the bar of that establishment. Vaughn had started the season with the Distillers but had been released and signed with Hugh Duffy's team in July. The incident occurred after Vaughn took Mitchell's stepdaughter on a streetcar ride. When the couple returned, an argument ensued and Mitchell received "a flesh wound in the forehead and a hole in the fleshy part of his hand, which he claims was made by a bullet." Vaughn admitted to striking the girl's step-father over the head, with an umbrella. He denied having a revolver, and none was found on Vaughn's person at the police station. Mitchell decided he did not want to prosecute Vaughn, stating the "only revenge he wishes is to ruin the contour of Vaughn's physiognomy." The police captain investigating the case thought it was merely the outcome of a drunken brawl. Nevertheless, the ball player appeared in court the next morning and posted a bond of $500. Two days later, Harry "evidently had enough of Peoria and wished to take no chances of being dragged back here in the fall to answer to charges of assault with a deadly weapon," pleaded guilty to assault, and paid a $40 fine.[61]

In an incredible act, on September 17 the Colorado Springs club decided to forfeit the game to Kansas City to honor the late W.S. Stratton, part-owner of the Colorado Springs baseball park, as his remains were lying in state in the Mining Exchange building. The Millionaires also forfeited the next two games to the Blues. Another oddity to modern-day baseball fans was a tripleheader in Omaha on September 18. Not only were three games played in one day, but the Indians beat the Peoria Distillers in all three games in times of one hour twenty minutes, one hour even, and 56 minutes.

The stage was now set for the final weekend of the season. Entering these series, the top four spots in the Western League took this shape:

Denver	81	54	.600
Omaha	82	55	.5985
Milwaukee	79	53	.5984
Kansas City	80	54	.597

On Saturday, September 20, Milwaukee beat Omaha 3 to 2, pinning the loss on Mordecai Brown. In Colorado, Kansas City beat Denver 7 to 6 to tighten the race even more, while putting the Milwaukee Creams in first place.

On Sunday, September 21, the Kansas City-Denver game was rained out. This was the first postponement of the year in Denver, and it was estimated the clubs lost $4,000 or more in ticket sales, as a record crowd of more than 12,000 was expected at Broadway Park.

The Sunday Milwaukee-Omaha game at Omaha's Vinton Street baseball yard was played before a crowd of 7,000 to 8,000 fans. Neither team scored in the first three innings; pitchers Frank "Yip" Owen for the Omahogs and John McPherson for the Creams gave up only a hit each. In the fourth inning the Western League pennant took a turn against Milwaukee. The exact sequence of what happened differs in newspaper accounts, but the basic facts come through. The leadoff batter for Omaha in this fourth inning was Robert Carter. Some reports say that before the inning started Milwaukee manager Hugh Duffy went to umpire August Moran and insisted the fans in the playing area be removed. How many fans is open to question. The *Milwaukee Sentinel* reported "the crowd had surged on the field"; the *Milwaukee Daily News* reported the "crowd overflowed the foul lines." The *Omaha Daily News* commented "a dozen spectators were propped up against the left field fence."[62] Umpire Moran ordered a policeman to clear the field, but some fans were slow to leave. The umpire called for Creams pitcher McPherson to pitch, but he refused until all spectators were off the field. The umpire replied he would not wait and called a ball on the Omaha leadoff hitter. Apparently McPherson still refused to pitch, and Moran gave Carter his base on balls.

The walk to Carter brought Hugh Duffy in from his center-field position, and a few other players joined in to argue with Umpire Moran. The next Omaha batter, Joe Wright, was waiting at the plate. The *Omaha World-Herald* of September 22 gave this wonderful account of what happened next: "Then in stentorian tones, he [Umpire Moran] ordered Colonel McPherson to hurl the sphere in the direction of Mr. Wright, who stood at the plate with his sapling uplifted threateningly, but the colonel refused, and as he maintained his position, and insisted on a forensic debate of the question, Ump. Moran dispatched Mr. Wright to first on four balls that were never delivered." Omaha then went on to score seven runs on a hit batsman, along with a number of hits, errors and misplays. During this meltdown Milwaukee shortstop Frank

Gatins was ejected after threatening to punch the umpire. As Duffy returned to the bench after the inning the *Omaha World-Herald* reported he called the umpire a "robber" and "assassin," and first baseman John Thornton called Moran a "swopplespingler." The Creams never got back in the game, losing 9 to 4.[63]

Manager Hugh Duffy immediately stated he would protest the game to Western League President Sexton, based on the grounds there was no rule that authorized the umpire to call balls if the Creams failed to play. According to Duffy, the umpire would have had to wait until the field was cleared, or forfeit the game to Omaha.

On Monday, September 22, Milwaukee's hopes of a Western League pennant ended "one of the prettiest races in baseball history."[64] Kansas City beat Denver 5 to 2 for its 82nd win against 54 loses.

Back in Omaha, Duffy's team ended the season with another ugly incident in front of the Ladies' Day crowd. The game was a scoreless tie through six innings. In the seventh inning Brewer second baseman Frank Miller was ejected from the game for arguing a call with Umpire Moran. The next inning Jack Evers, who entered the game as Miller's replacement, got into a fight with Moran. It appears Evers struck the umpire either with the sleeve of his sweater or his fist, and Augie Moran countered "with a good soak on the rowdy's jaw."[65] Four policemen were needed to keep Evers from Moran, who was very willing to let the player get close to him again. Evers was arrested after he struck several officers. The inning ended with Omaha scoring three runs and eventually winning 4 to 0, dropping the Creams to third place.

The Creams could not have taken first place even if the Omaha protest would have been upheld. As it turned out, all protests that had been lodged by teams were dropped at the Western League meeting a week after the season concluded. The final standings show how close a race the Western League pennant of 1902 had been.

Kansas City	82	54	.603	St. Joseph	71	68	.511
Omaha	84	56	.600	Colorado Springs	63	75	.457
Milwaukee	80	54	.597	Des Moines	54	83	.394
Denver	81	57	.587	Peoria	35	103	.254

* * *

After the championship seasons ended for both the Western League and American Association, the two Kansas City teams played a post-season series for the championship of Kansas City. The teams alternated parks and played under the league playing rules of the home team. The first game, on September

Kansas City Blue Stockings team photo — The winners of "one of the prettiest races in baseball history" — *top row left to right:* Kemmer, Cable, Weimer, Jacobs, Miller; *second row:* Gibson, Messitt, Nichols, Shannon, Risley; *bottom row:* Waldron, Robinson, Ketcham (*Spalding Baseball Guide*).

26, drew 4,000 fans. The third game, on Sunday, drew the largest crowd ever in Kansas City for a baseball game to that date, approximately 10,000. The American Association Blues beat their Western League rival Blue Stockings in four of six games played, netting each winning player about $200.

Another post-season series took place between the American Association champion Indianapolis Hoosiers and the second-place Western League Omaha Indians at the grounds of the latter. The Western League team won three of five. But it was reported that it was not a fair series, as the grounds at Omaha were "so peculiarly built" that a team that had never played there was at a distinct disadvantage. For example, the pitcher's box was on a hill, and the pitcher threw the ball down at the batter's head. The Indianapolis pitchers could not master this pitching box.[66]

One post-season city tournament that did not come off was in Milwaukee. American Association club owners Harry Quin and Charles Havenor had been challenging Hugh Duffy to pit his Creams against their Brewers since July. Duffy declined the offer, saying the players' contracts ended on September 22 and he had no control over them after that. Havenor offered to pay the salaries of both teams for the series, but most of the Western League players were not in favor of the games, declaring they wanted to get home as soon as possible.

Three. The 1902 Playing Seasons 85

* * *

At the Western League meeting in September, league treasurer W.T. Van Brunt said the 1902 season was better than expected financially. His report showed a balance of more than $10,000 in the league's sinking fund. Denver had the highest attendance in the league with 137,000. Omaha was close behind with 132,000. The attendance in the rest of the league was reported as: St. Joseph (90,000), Colorado Springs (72,000), Milwaukee (69,000), Des Moines (62,000), Peoria (58,000), and Kansas City (53,000). How accurate these figures were is open to debate. After the season local newspapers gave Milwaukee's attendance as not more than 40,000. The Omaha correspondent to *The Sporting News* gave the Indians home attendance as about 150,000, or 18,000 more than Van Brunt's report.[67]

Western League president Michael Sexton had this to say about his league's season: "The condition of the league could not be better than it is at the present time. The salary lists of the clubs have been very high, much higher than would have been necessary had there been no signs of war in the air. As a consequence a few, a very few, of the clubs have lost money; but most of them, a big majority of the eight clubs have made money."[68] The financial success (or failure) of all the clubs is not known for certain. Sexton would report Denver, Omaha, St. Joseph and Colorado Springs made big money, while Milwaukee and Des Moines showed small profits. According to the Western League president, Kansas City and Peoria lost only a little money. Milwaukee was reported to have finished $1,100 to the good. However, other reports said the Cream City club lost about $5,000.[69] At the October minor league meetings, it was stated by National Association of Minor Leagues secretary Thomas Murnane that W.T. Van Brunt and Thomas Burns lost $70,000 backing the Western League.[70]

Secretary J.J. Barton of St. Joseph had this to say about his club's 1902 season: "We have had a good season and have made money. We have not made a fortune, I admit, nor have we made as much as several of the other Western League cities, but we have not gone in the hole. The season has been a better one than we had either last year or the year before. We have given the fans a better class of ball and I believe that the fans have all been satisfied with the way they have been treated. The attendance at the games has been good and it was seldom that we had to pay guarantees to the visiting teams."[71] Toward the end of the season the Saints drew exceptionally well, even having weekday crowds of more than 1,500, helped by the large amount of people in town for the state fair.

President Sexton said there would be no changes in franchises for the next season, but there might be some changes in ownership in Milwaukee and Kansas City. He hoped these two cities would be backed by home capital—"stock companies composed of the best men, financially, in the towns." Sexton reported there would be no change in managers, however. The popular Charley Nichols and Hugh Duffy would remain at the head of the teams. Regarding any chance of peace between the Western League and American Association, Sexton declared there would be none until the A.A. got rid of Thomas Hickey, George Tebeau and George Lennon.[72] As the Des Moines correspondent to *The Sporting News* wrote, "The war is to go on merrily."[73]

When the season ended, President Hickey of the American Association declared the initial season "a decided success."[74] He said all the franchises made money, with the exception of Milwaukee, which lost only a little. Hickey claimed even Milwaukee would have been able to make a profit had its owner, Harry Quin, not had to face a union boycott in some cities. Milwaukee's home attendance was given as not more than 55,000. However, after the season, a court hearing, which will be discussed in detail in Chapter 6, asserted the club lost $4,876.25.[75] Columbus reportedly finished with "a handsome balance" in the treasury, even after spending almost $3,000 on ballpark improvements.[76] The team had lost no games to rain despite an exceedingly rainy season, and its total attendance of 152,855 was very gratifying. George Tebeau in Louisville had said on September 1 he already had cleared $10,000 on the season with 22 road games to go. Tebeau gave his estimated home attendance at 150,000, which could easily have been more had not many grandstand seekers been turned away because of a lack of room. Kansas City drew a total paid attendance of 87,967, compared to the Western League's 53,000 in that city. Indianapolis was said to have made about $6,000 on the season.[77] In Toledo the team was "quite liberally patronized at home," especially on Sundays, with an estimated 70,000 season attendance.[78] President Hickey at this time said there would be no changing of cities for 1903. He did comment there would be a new park in Kansas City the next year, with grounds already having been leased.

The war in Milwaukee had drained both clubs, as attendance was slim in both ballparks. For example, in late July with both clubs in town, the Western League Creams drew crowds of 150, 250 and 300 against last-place Peoria, while the Brewers only drew crowds of 200, 300 and 250 against last-place Toledo. In early August, with the Brewers hopelessly out of the pennant race and the Creams fighting their way back into it, attendance started to turn in favor of the Western League team. On Saturday, August 2, the Brewers drew 1,000 to the Creams' 800, but 800 of those in attendance at the Brewer game were newsboys with free passes.[79] The next day the Western League Creams outdrew the American Association team 5,000 to 3,000. A week later, with the Brewers out of town, the Creams were drawing weekday crowds of 350 to 600 and weekend crowds of 1,500 to 6,000, which was considerably better than earlier in the season.

The actual attendance in Milwaukee was hard to determine, but other club managers were not fooled by inflated attendance reports. After the season the *St. Paul Globe* wrote: "In the good old summer time now past there were days in Milwaukee when the free paper — the passes — helped considerable in permitting the visiting teams to discover that the stands were occupied, and it might be observed that with eight towns drawing the Milwaukee crowds of last season the American Association would have finished rather suddenly."[80]

If two teams competing in the same Wisconsin city did not hurt enough, Milwaukee encountered the wettest summer in a long time: many games were rained out, and others played in the rain. The low attendance had sparked a rumor toward the end of the season that Milwaukee's American Association club would transfer all its home games to other cities, but Brewer president Harry Quin immediately denied the story.[81]

The Sporting News of October 18, 1902, summed up the 1902 situation between the Western League and American Association the best in a comprehensive and honest look at the facts:

> The American Association, in the light of the success the magnates met with the first season, is not only the logical league for the territory which it occupied, but it is entitled to be classed as the third strongest league and circuit in the country. Primarily it would be a wise move for all leagues and magnates to recognize the American Association's right to its territory, basing such an action upon the fact that its managers and leaders made a thorough success of the venture, contrary to the claims put forth by those who, at its inception, denounced it as an "outlaw association," sure to meet with failure. It can not be said that the Association was carried through the season at a heavy loss and that the majority of magnates lost money. Weak spots developed as is always the case in every base ball circuit; but on the whole the organization was a surprise to its most sanguine adherents. Its first year did not see the usual maneuvering made necessary to hold weak leagues together, not a change being made in circuit or manager or magnate. Since this organization is in the field to stay, for the good of the game, the minor leagues of the country should speedily take action — with the right spirit permeating all overtures — such as will recognize the American Association's right to the territory, and in turn the Association would willingly recognize and respect the minor league reservation. By this time the minor league managers and owners doubtless realize what a costly move it is to support two clubs in the American Association circuit, and that too, in cities where the Association is not only established, but where local capital is invested in the Association teams, furnishing superior advantages and prestige.
>
> The American Association has little to fear from the continuation of the present strained relations, or fight, if it may be so termed, for it is now firmly

entrenched in its territory, while the same can not be said of its opponent, the Western League. Unless the minor leagues declare a truce and make overtures for a settlement of the present difficulties the American Association managers will continue to disregard the reservation rights of minor leagues and take from them a far greater number of players than was the case during last winter and spring. The matter of securing strong minor league talent for the association teams of 1903 will not be difficult of accomplishment this winter, simply because the players have a knowledge of the actual strength of the American Association and the good salaries paid by its managers, while last year the whole matter of carrying the league though the season was regarded by the players as a doubtful problem ... the American Association leaders fully realize that their prospects for securing any number of good men from other circuits are of the best, and expect to do the very thing unless the minor leaguers come to a thorough realization of the situation as it confronts them. The association teams will lose many good men, since the American and National League managers are rushing after this season's stars; and these players must be replaced.

The managers of the American Association are level-headed business men. Consequently they realize that salaries for 1903 will be forced abnormally high because of the rivalry in the matter of securing players. Salaries with them, they admit, were too high last season. Jealousies and grievances should not be the cause of continuing the present high bidding for players' services, which will be sure to affect the club owners of minor leagues for 1903 worse than was the case this season. The American Association would be a big money maker, providing a settlement of the present differences could be accomplished, because it would enable the magnates to reduce salary lists from $700 to $1,100 per month. The association leaders, to making for a settlement of the differences, would meet the minor leaguers half way, and in a thoroughly conciliatory manner.... To sum up, they do not court a continuance of the present strained relations, but if the fight is to continue it will be more serious for the Western and Eastern leagues than was the case during 1902. It must be said in conclusion, that the position of the American Association managers in showing a disposition to arrange for a mutual understanding between their organization and the minor leagues that shall restore the respect of the reservation clause, is in no sense to be regarded as a sign of weakness on their part, but a desire to improve existing conditions of a financial character with themselves and others. They feel there is no just reason why the minor league club owners, from one end of the country to the other, should be forced to continue to lose money, since it is a comparatively easy matter to establish the minor league game on a profitable basis.[82]

We will see what steps were taken to achieve a partial peace between the leagues in 1903.

Four

Rowdyism and Umpiring in the Western League and American Association

Players arguing and fighting with the umpire were major problems in both the major and minor leagues at the turn of the century. Umpires were a special target, not only for players but also fans. Ban Johnson, president of the American League, tried very hard to quell this trend and protect his umpires. The larger minor leagues also made an attempt to improve the conduct at baseball games. Long before the season 1902 started, George Tebeau in Louisville said rowdyism would be suppressed and bad behavior not tolerated in the American Association, even if the offender was the star of the team.[1] Likewise, the Western League tried to make the ballpark less of a combat zone. Just before the season began, Western League president Michael Sexton sent out instructions for his umpires.

> Umpiring, in my judgment, is the most important, as well as the most arduous position on the diamond to fulfill, and good or bad umpiring will do more to please or disgust the patrons of the game than any other element.
>
> Also remember that you are absolute master of the field during the progress of a game, and have the power to order any manager, captain or player to do, or omit to do, any act that you may deem necessary to give force and effect to the rules of the game.
>
> Under no circumstances must you allow any captain or player to dispute a decision involving an error of judgment, and the captain only shall be allowed to dispute a decision involving a legal construction of the rules. Strictly enforce the rule requiring players to retain their seats on the bench until called to bat, or to the coaching lines.
>
> In very close decisions give the base runner the benefit of the doubt.
>
> Render all decisions promptly, and from firm impressions, and never try to even up any error of judgment.
>
> Under no circumstances must you tolerate vile, profane or abusive language,

no matter to whom addressed, and for each and every infraction of this rule the penalties provided for must be enforced, but no player shall be removed from the game without first having been fined.

In all aggravated cases of abusive language or rowdyism, the umpire must notify me immediately, stating all of the facts and the attitude of the officials of the home club in the matter of affording proper protection to the umpire.

Umpires are advised to retain control of their temper under all circumstances. Don't get on too familiar terms with the players and don't spend your evenings in loafing around the hotel where the players are boarding.[2]

Unfortunately, these instructions were not followed by managers, players or umpires. By all accounts the American Association was a little more successful than the Western League in curbing bad behavior, but neither scored good grades.

The rowdy behavior of fans and players started right away in the Western League. On Opening Day of the Denver season, umpire Dan Stearns' judgment was called into question by players and spectators. It was noted that "Stearns was impartial in his rottenness, giving it to either team without a particle of bias." In the ninth inning the umpire got into a dispute with Denver players and four were ejected from the game, including manager Parke Wilson. During this dispute the men in the bleachers grew impatient and started after the umpire with the "expressed intention of knocking his head into the ground." Policemen intervened and stopped the crowd before the umpire could be reached.[3]

Louisville manager Billy Clymer had the honor of being the first player to be escorted off the St. Paul grounds by a policeman in the 1902 American Association season. Clymer was put out of the May 14 game in the second inning. Later in the contest he mixed words with umpire Charles Tindell from the bench and was ordered put off the grounds. Police escorted him from the park.

Of course, some players and teams were worse in bad behavior than others.

Billy Clymer — The Louisville manager, who had many run-ins with umpires, had the honor of being the first player escorted off the St. Paul grounds by a policeman in 1902 (Library of Congress).

Four. Rowdyism and Umpiring   91

One early offender was John O'Brien of Kansas City. In an era when most games lasted an hour and a half or less the majority of the time, it took three hours and fifteen minutes to complete a 13-inning affair on May 27 in Milwaukee. It was said this was entirely due to O'Brien's continuous arguing with the umpire. The *Milwaukee Sentinel* thought O'Brien showed "a reckless disregard of the spectators, and his language, tactics and attitude toward the umpire are deserving of punishment."[4] The paper thought these early-season exhibitions of rowdyism needed to be punished quickly to stop the mounting problem. O'Brien was not disciplined by the American Association, but a month later Dale Gear released his captain–second baseman. Other venues were unhappy with O'Brien's conduct on the field, as it was reported his "bulldozing tactics with umpires and tendency to quibble over little points always brought hisses from the stand…. Any umpire with nerve enough to put him out of the game was always cheered." Unfortunately, his release was mainly due to his poor play in the field and lack of hitting, not his unruly behavior.[5] O'Brien wanted to go to St. Paul, but American Association president Thomas Hickey assigned the second baseman to Toledo. He instead jumped over to Peoria in the Western League.

The St. Paul Saints had the worst reputation in the American Association for rowdyism. *Sporting Life* of June 28, 1902, reported a game involving the Saints was an affair of continuous kicking as they wanted every decision to go their way. Any umpire in these games had his hands full.

A good example of this can be seen in the *Milwaukee Sentinel*'s account of the June 17 game in Milwaukee against St. Paul. The Brewers had scored five runs in the sixth inning to take an 8 to 3 lead. After the Saints scored a run in their half of the inning, Saints manager Mike Kelley and his players began to argue a call of Charles Tindell until the umpire finally had enough. The paper wrote of the game:

> From the time the first ball was pitched the Saints began to yelp, and in every inning they pursued dilatory tactics and used tantalizing epithets to the umpire until his patience was worn out, and then he had [Archie] Stimmel ejected from the field when he declined to cease his chatter and take his place on the bench. The spectators demanded more ball playing and less oratorical effort, but, scenting defeat from [Nick] Altrock's clever pitching, the St. Pauls went bent on mischief and tried every trick known on the diamond to rattle the left hander and his associates. In the second inning, when Huggins was on first and Shannon bunted to the pitcher, Kelley chirped, "Throw it to first," and Altrock complied, thinking Clingman was directing the play, and as a result Huggins reached the middle sack in safety and subsequently scored on Lumley's single. Every time a St. Paul player went to bat the entire aggregation, headed by Kelley, began to hoot and howl, and discipline on the field went to the dogs until Tindell drew out his watch and admonished them to play ball or forfeit the game and when they failed to comply he carried out his orders from President Hickey and gave the game to Milwaukee.[6]

Things only got worse two days later. With Tindell again umpiring, in the first inning a call against St. Paul that resulted in a run not scoring brought Kelley and his players out to argue. The players and manager were "yelling the lowest type of vulgarity," plainly heard by the spectators. The umpire was being pushed around by the St. Paul players until the Milwaukee players intervened and escorted him to the plate. However, Kelley charged the umpire and, grabbing his protector with both hands, attempted to throw him to the ground. Milwaukee pitcher Art Herman "interposed his six feet of bone and muscle" and pushed Kelley from Tindell, who ejected Kelley from the game.[7]

The fans in St. Paul also had comments from the stands for the umpires. This description provides a sample of what the umpire heard during a game in the Minnesota city. "Old man [Harvey] Bailey's cross fire greatly agitated the fanatics in the stands and much voice was used up in calling C. Tindill's [sic] attention to the matter. C. Tindill had on his store clothes, and all dressed up refused to harken to the reports from the observing ones. All this won for C. Tindill many strange and delightful titles. During the afternoon he was listed as 'the big consolidated,' 'the fat guy,' and the overworked 'lobster' title was also called into service. As C. Tindill draws a monthly stipend for all this, he continued work and refused to feel hurt."[8]

If anything, the Western League had more problems with rowdy behavior than the American Association. An incident in Denver in June showed how ugly not only managers and players could be, but also spectators. In the eighth inning umpire Gus Moran called a ball hit by Des Moines first baseman Dan Stearns a fair ball, even though it was clearly foul. This might have been enough to get the fans' ire up, but it must be remembered this was the same Dan Stearns whose judgment as an umpire put him into hot water with Denver fans on Opening Day. In a career move unheard of today, the 40-year-old Stearns had given up umpiring earlier in the month to play first base for the Des Moines club. "Doggie" Moran did not back down from the crowd at all, openly defying the crowd's demonstrations. The umpire levied numerous fines to players and Denver manager Parke Wilson. After the game, as Moran was looking for his ride back to the hotel, he encountered trouble with and some fans. Five policemen surrounded Moran, but he declared he did not need any protection and would defend himself. However, the police escorted him to the hotel. When Moran found that all fines were being paid by Denver owner D.C. Packard, he was furious and lashed out in an interview. Packard wrote a letter to Western League president Michael Sexton, saying Moran was a troublemaker and had stirred up all the rows the umpire and the Denver players had been in. Packard further claimed to have a signed affidavit to show Moran had stated he intended to fine and discriminate against Manager Wilson and

Grizzlies star second baseman Tom Delahanty.[9] Although there was no discipline against the umpire, it showed how team owners had little respect for the umpiring crew of the Western League.

A step to quell player rowdyism was taken at the Western League July 1 meeting when it was decided all fines given to players by umpires would have to be paid. Up to that point the league had been very lenient in collecting the money, due to its fear that players would jump to the American Association if fines were collected. It was also ruled clubs would not be allowed to pay the fine for the player. President Sexton would further say, "Anything that smacks of rowdyism is a thing of the past in Western League base ball," and issued a letter of advice and warning to managers and players.[10]

The warning had no effect on conduct at Western League games. From as far away as Utah, the *Salt Lake Herald* commented: "The Western League, from all accounts, now stands head and shoulders above all other minor leagues in the country for rowdy ball playing."[11] The first game of the July 4 doubleheader was forfeited to the Milwaukee Creams after the Denver Grizzlies refused to abide by a decision of the umpire in the third inning. The Creams' John Thornton was running from first to second base when he fell and unintentionally interfered with the second baseman. Denver demanded that Thornton be called out, but the umpire decided otherwise and Denver refused to continue.

Manager Parke Wilson and his Denver club were the worst offenders in the Western.[12] In a game in Omaha on July 7, Wilson was called out on strikes in the eighth inning by Umpire Swigert on a questionable call and allegedly attacked the arbiter. The police were called and Wilson was taken to a jail cell, still in uniform. Wilson was fined $100 by President Sexton for his conduct and warned any further misconduct would lead to suspension. Incredibly, the Denver correspondent to *The Sporting News* defended Wilson. Wilson's side of the story was that Swigert had ejected shortstop C.E. Radcliff for a minor offense and then called a strike on Wilson on a pitch wide of the plate. Wilson walked toward the umpire to "expostulate" when

Parke Wilson — Denver's 1902 manager would be one of the most troublesome managers for umpires in the Western League (Wikimedia.org).

Swigert threw up his hands and Wilson drew back to make a pass. The Denver manager was only bluffing and had no intention of hitting the umpire. The newspaperman admitted this was going too far on Wilson's part but thought when players of other teams had been allowed to choke umpires without any penalty being imposed, a fine of $100 for refraining from trying to land a blow was pretty heavy punishment.[13] The $100 was refunded to Wilson by the Western League owners after the season.[14]

The incident finally had an effect on Denver owner D.C. Packard, who requested that his men leave the umpire alone in the future. In a statement he told his players: "No matter if the decisions do appear wrong, and you think you are being robbed, don't go rushing out on the field and get the umpire hotter. He will only give you some worse decisions. Take your medicine like little men, and see if you can not play just so much better."[15] However, to add to the spirit of the times, Swigert was fired as a Western League umpire.

None of this appeared to stop the on-field troubles in the Western League. In Colorado Springs on July 16 St. Joseph manager Byron McKibben was tossed from the game for arguing a call. When he refused to leave the field, the game was forfeited to the Millionaires. McKibben and pitcher Barney McFadden later attempted to assault Umpire Cole with a bat. The two were arrested, taken to police court and fined $25. The case was pushed by a Colorado Springs assistant district attorney who declared he would have decent baseball in the city, or he would break up the Western League.[16] McKibben was suspended by the league but was soon reinstated with a fine.

Three days later in Denver, the Milwaukee Creams ran into a load of trouble. Umpire Davis ordered George Bone off the field in the seventh inning. Bone refused to go and a half-a-dozen policemen escorted him from the grounds. At this point Walt Preston drove a long fly to Hugh Duffy in center field, which the Creams' manager-outfielder refused to chase, and four runs were tallied. The final score was 11 to 1 in favor of the Grizzlies.

On July 31 pitcher Art Alloway and manager William Rourke of Omaha got into a fight on the bench during a game in Colorado Springs. The Indians were not doing well that day and the manager attempted to put the blame on his pitcher, who was throwing a great game. Rourke went after Alloway. The pitcher landed a few blows before players could separate the two, but not before the manager-owner received a black eye. Both men were arrested and taken to police court, where Rourke was fined $20 and Alloway $10.

* * *

Some of this terrible conduct could be attributed to the umpires. There was an unusual amount of complaints that the umpiring in the Western was below standard. After a game in Omaha in July, Milwaukee Creams Manager Duffy and Omaha Indians Manager Rourke sent a joint telegram to league President Sexton, asking for the removal of Umpire Roe. It had been cited in the press he was "without a doubt the worst ever seen here and that is saying a great deal."[17] Sexton declined the advice in this case.

The *Milwaukee Sentinel* claimed Western League umpires had been instructed to favor home teams in order to please the home crowds.[18] In its baseball coverage of August 24, 1902, editor A.W. Friese wrote:

> From every city in the Western league come complaints that home umpiring is not only permitted, but actually fostered. In Milwaukee there is ample evidence provided in nearly every game played here of the partiality of the umpire toward the Angels, [Friese's pet name for Duffy's team] and in Friday's game alone the decisions on balls and strikes were sufficient to give the home team a large margin of chances to win. The players complain bitterly of the umpiring, but say they are powerless against the syndicate which controls the destinies of the league, and therefore make the best of the situation.

Umpires in the Western League and American Association were many times former ball players, and on a number of occasions went from playing ball to umpiring in the same season. Even odder to modern day baseball fans, a number of umpires went back to playing. We have seen this in the case of Dan Stearns earlier in this chapter. Former National League star Arlie Latham umpired in the Western League in 1902, then resigned from the staff in July to play first base for Denver, where he played 33 games. Frank "Monk" Foreman was released by the Kansas City Blues of the American Association in July and was immediately signed by the American Association as an umpire. Sportswriter Ed Kundegraber thought he "should have plenty of sympathy for players who kick, as he was a warm offender himself."[19] Within two weeks Foreman resigned his umpire position to pitch again, this time in the Western League.

When Gus Moran was rumored to be leaving the Western League for an American Association job in August, he was the only umpire left on the staff who had started the season. Even though he had the respect of most players and managers, he still had problems. His difficulties in Denver in June are mentioned above, and in August the umpire would have a war of words with president Charles Barston of Peoria. On August 6 Bartson would not admit Moran to the postponed game being played on the grounds until the middle of the contest. Ben Schafstall and Jake Weimer, players from Peoria and Kansas City, umpired the 10 to 3 Kansas City win.

In August Des Moines shortstop Charley O'Leary was suspended for throwing a right hook at in-season hire Thomas Walton, which missed. Walton, who had been a prominent pitcher in the Pacific League years earlier, resigned his umpire job shortly thereafter. He said the kicking was the fiercest he had ever encountered, and he did not care to risk his life daily while making decisions.[20]

Another incident in August showed that umpires were not backed up to any degree by the league president or owners. Colorado Springs owner Thomas Burns had accused Jake Strauss of grossly favoring the Denver team in the previous series in Colorado Springs and demanded the umpire be fired. When Strauss showed up at the ballpark on August 30, Burns showed him a telegram from Western League President Sexton that said not to allow Strauss on the grounds. Upon seeing the telegraph, "Jake extracted a half fare street car ticket from his jeans," and left. Burns selected pitcher Frank Foreman to umpire, but Denver refused to supply an umpire, and the game had to be called off. The fans, about a thousand in number, were given rain checks to see the following Wednesday's game. This was all right until someone observed he could not make it to the game that day and wanted his money back. The management decided to allow the spectators this privilege and their money was returned. The *Colorado Gazette* observed: "Yesterday's farce will have a rather depressing effect on the game in this city, as several of those who imagined that they were going to lose their money were heard to remark that that finished them for the season with baseball."[21]

One of the lighter moments in the world of umpiring in 1902 happened to George Bone. Bone had played with Hugh Duffy's Milwaukee Western League team, and was appointed an umpire in that league in early August. In one of Bone's first games umpiring, Duffy took a long lead off second base when Bone, forgetting he was acting as an umpire and mentally putting himself in the game, called out to Duffy to get back to the base. The crowd had a good-natured laugh. Except for this incident, Bone's umpiring was "entirely satisfactory."[22] Another odd day in umpiring was the September 1 double-header in Kansas City between the Blues and Milwaukee Brewers. When no regular umpire was available, Milwaukee pitcher Nick Altrock, who was not to be used that day, umpired both games.

* * *

Discipline was not improving in the American Association as the 1902 season progressed. In a game between the Kansas City Blues and Milwaukee Brewers in July, an argument began after a Milwaukee player scored from third on a sacrifice fly to right field. The Blues thought the player left third base early and manger Dale Gear and his players surrounded the umpire to argue the call. When Umpire Francis walked away, Mike Grady pursued the umpire

Four. Rowdyism and Umpiring

all over the diamond. Once Grady was ordered out of the game, Bill Nance and Ed Lewee continued the disgraceful conduct.[23] President Hickey addressed the issue in late July, sending instructions to team captains to hurry up games and do less senseless kicking.

On July 31, in the first game of a double-header in Minneapolis between the hometown Millers and Louisville, Umpire Tindell called Billy Clymer out at second, causing Clymer to lose his temper. The Colonels' manager-second baseman ran at Tindell and the two men clinched but no blows were struck. Clymer was kicked out of the game, but was allowed to play the second game of the twinbill.[24] Tindell was not so lucky three weeks later. In a game in Toledo, a mob attacked him and he sustained injuries that laid him up for a bit. The umpire threatened to bring damage suits against the American Association and the Toledo club for failing to provide police protection.[25]

Problems continued in American Association parks, not only with players on the field, but from the stands. On September 1 in Indianapolis the crowd displayed some terrible conduct toward the opposing team. Dan Kerwin in right field was struck by a beer bottle while trying to catch a fly ball.

There were problems between umpires and players, as well as umpires and crowds in the Western League right to the end of the season. In Des Moines on August 30, Umpire Abbott had to have three policemen save him from a howling mob. "He evidently liked excitement, as the next day at Omaha his decisions were so rank that he had another close call."[26] The two ugly incidents by Hugh Duffy's Milwaukee club to end the season in Omaha have been detailed in Chapter 3. These incidents caused a Denver newspaper to nickname Duffy's Creams "The Rowdies."[27]

It was obvious both leagues had to address the problem during the off-season. Even Hugh Duffy, one of the main offenders during the season, agreed that effective rules to suppress kicking were needed to speed the game up. Western League president Michael Sexton was instructed to make a special effort to secure first-class umpires for the 1903 season. Before the new season began, Sexton announced he would be imposing heavy fines if necessary to cut down on "rowdyism and ungentlemanly conduct" in the Western League.[28]

Sexton gave notice that his umpires would be in charge of the games in the upcoming 1903 season. In a letter to the arbitrators he laid out what he wanted done.

> Under no circumstances will an umpire engage in an argument or dispute with any player over a decision. Deal severely with players who persist in nagging and fault-finding with your work. You are not expected to submit to insulting remarks from players just before the game is called, or just after its close, and you have the same power to punish such offenses as you have during the progress of a

game. Positively no vile or profane language will be tolerated. In punishing offenders for violations of the rules, a fine of $5 must be imposed for the first offense, to be followed by the removal of the offender from the game or grounds at the discretion of the umpire.... I will enforce the payment of all just fines imposed, and in all aggravated cases of rowdyism I will discipline the offenders in such a manner as will convince the players and public that the umpire must be respected."[29]

Sexton's new umpire crew and rules appeared to work better, for a while. The Denver *Sporting Life* correspondent said the new umpires were competent and "they conducted their part of the affair that the whole game was played by the men hired to do that work, and there was no preponderance of the umpire."[30]

However, not all problems stemmed from the players. On June 7 in Peoria Umpire Kelly called a Distiller runner out on a close play in the ninth inning, giving Kansas City a 3 to 2 victory. The umpire was immediately mobbed by about 200 men and boys carrying bricks and stones. Had the police not intervened, Kelly might have come to serious injury. Colorado Springs also encountered some fan problems, not related to the umpires. Fans had a habit of throwing their cushions onto the field, a nuisance President Burns decided to sternly suppress.[31]

The fans in Des Moines appeared to be more of a problem to the ballpark than fans in other cities. The downtown park, although a little small, was in an "ideal location" and had been "a great factor in bringing in some shekels that they [the Des Moines management] would not get if located farther from the business portion of town."[32] However, it was reported after the 1902 season the ballpark would have to undergo some repairs. To get into games without paying, "boys and cheap men" had torn off boards or cut holes in the wooden fence to see the action. On one occasion a section was broken through the floor in the bleachers and a mob entered the park before employees discovered what had happened. After the season, the scarcity of coal in the area was responsible for people taking wood to burn at home.[33]

Umpire Kelly, a new hire by Sexton, ran into trouble off the field in Des Moines on July 9. On the field he had called a Des Moines runner safe on a rundown play — which every member of the Colorado Springs team participated in — when one of the players deliberately tripped and held the runner so he could not reach second base while another player recovered the ball. All the Colorado players argued, and even after Kelly called for the game to resume, manager Billy Everitt (recently back from a three-game suspension for an incident in Milwaukee) and shortstop Buck Francks continued to kick. When Kelly had enough, he fined the two. Later in the game Kelly called a ball hit over the fence a ground-rule double. Everitt again argued with the umpire, calling him a vile name. Kelly doubled his fist to strike the Millionaires' manager but rethought the matter and ejected him from the grounds. However, Kelly did tell Everitt he would have to apologize for his language after the game. Everitt told the umpire they could finish this outside the park at that time, but Kelly refused to go and called for the game to continue. Francks kept up the commentary and was benched a few innings later.

After the game in the lobby of the Iowa Hotel, Kelly approached Everitt and demanded an apology. When Everitt refused, the umpire knocked him down. Francks entered the ensuing fight and kicked Kelly in the face, giving him a cut that required three stitches to close. When the umpire turned his attention to Francks, the player took to the street while being chased by Kelly. When he could not catch the speedy Francks, Kelly returned to the washroom of the hotel to clean up. Everitt came in and hostilities began again, with Kelly striking his head against the washstand. Bystanders finally separated the two. Kelly, sporting two black eyes, was given a grand ovation when he appeared the next day at the Des Moines park and was compelled to doff his cap repeatedly.[34] President Sexton doled out fines to Everitt for $100 and Kelly for $25 for the on-field incident, but did nothing about the hotel incident. Perhaps Francks was spared, as later in the month he left the team to travel to the West Coast where his wife was reported to be dying. While in California Francks jumped to the outlaw Oakland club.

Not all fights were with the umpires; players fought amongst themselves. On July 26 in Omaha, in the sixth inning of the second game of a doubleheader, Milwaukee Creams third baseman and team captain Jim Cockman threw a bit wide to first on a ground ball. The ball went off Jack Thornton's glove and into the bleachers. Runners advanced and eventually scored, putting the Creams behind 9 to 8. As the Creams were batting in the seventh inning (which was to be the last, as the Milwaukee club had to catch a train), Cockman began taunting the first baseman about the play. Thornton jumped up and punched his teammate. The two threw about a half-dozen punches while teammates attempted to pull them apart. It was a typical baseball fight until Cockman grabbed a bat and took a vicious swing at Thornton that missed by only a few inches. At this point the "grandstands and bleachers emptied as quickly as if they had been flipped over." The police were forced to intervene and put the two players on separate streetcars outside the park.[35] The next day Thornton was released by the Creams, and soon landed in Omaha. Troubles with teammates apparently followed Thornton. It was reported that on the last road trip of the season the Omaha players beat Jack "into insensibility" as the train was leaving Chicago before rolling him off the train onto the depot platform.[36]

Excessive arguing with the umpiring began early in the American Association in the 1903 season. In the second series of the year in Kansas City, players from both the Blues and St. Paul Saints were kicking about umpire Tony Mullane's calls and, finally, the fans joined in. Mullane had no control of the game, causing Ed Kundegruber, the *Sporting Life* correspondent from Kansas City, to write, "President Hickey must find better umpires than Mullane, or the game will become tiresome to patrons."[37] In an early May game in Columbus umpire Frank Foreman was angered to such an extent by Louisville manger Billy Clymer's actions that he called a policeman and had him escorted off the field.

In St. Paul on May 13 umpire Ellsworth Cunningham made an apparent wrong call, calling a runner safe at home, which almost caused a riot and got manager Mike Kelley and center fielder "Spike" Shannon ejected. It was claimed Kelley tore the umpire's blouse, although no one at the park, including Kelley, remembered this happening. The St. Paul manager would be suspended for five games.

An example of the frivolous arguing with umpires that took place can be seen in this account of a game in St. Paul on May 16. Minneapolis and St. Paul were tied after seven innings. In the eighth inning the Millers scored three runs to take the lead. With a runner on third and one out, the batter hit a pitch into foul territory.

> As is customary another ball was passed in from the home bench and was accepted. The bat boy chased out and got the ball that was hit in foul territory, brought it in and dropped it in the grip which contains the balls. At this juncture Capt. Yeager, with everything to lose and nothing to gain, kicked for the ball that had been hit in foul territory. There were probably half a dozen balls in the grip and three or four were offered, but it was claimed neither was the right one. The umpire was then informed that as he had in his possession the number required by the rules of the game he would get no more until another ball had passed from view. He then forfeited the game.

George Yeager, who had recently replaced the fired Walter Wilmot as the Millers' manager, certainly made "a chump play" in the eyes of the St. Paul writer.[38]

Assaults on umpires continued in the American Association in 1903. In Kansas City in May, outfielder Bob Ganley lost his temper and threw his bat toward umpire Tony Mullane, after which he was dismissed from the game. However, instead of leaving the grounds, Ganley went to the coacher's line. When ordered to sit down, he threw a baseball at the umpire and "handled the umpire a little roughly."[39] The player was then ejected from the grounds. Ganley, ordinarily not a kicker, apologized to Mullane after the game but still drew a five-game suspension from Association President Hickey.

Four. Rowdyism and Umpiring

Kansas City first baseman Mike Grady told his teammates to stop the "constant bullyragging with the umpire," and that as field captain he would take care of that end of the game. However, within days outfielder Jack Rothfuss forgot the new orders from Grady and became involved in a dispute with umpire Frank Foreman. He was immediately benched, his position taken by manager Dale Gear. Grady said the umpires received much better treatment in Kansas City than other American Association cities, although at the time arbiters declared the Kansas City critics were the worst in the land.[40]

June 12, 1903, was a particularly bad day for American Association umpires. In Columbus umpire Tony Mullane's decisions throughout the game had worked the crowd "into what may be called a baseball frenzy." After the game the crowd swarmed onto the field and surrounded Mullane, but police and players kept them away from the umpire until he was safely in the box office. However, the crowd waited until he came out, and this time the arbiter was saved only "by the vigorous efforts of the officers."[41] Mullane was finally escorted to his car.

There was a more serious incident in Indianapolis that day, leading to the Milwaukee Brewers forfeiting a game. In the top of the first inning, with the Brewers at bat, players were cheering and calling out from the bench. Umpire Cunningham claimed they were directing personal remarks at him and ordered them to cease. When it continued, he again called on them to stop and then ordered manager Joe Cantillon from the field. When the Brewer manager refused to leave, Cunningham stopped the game and called on a sergeant and patrolman to eject Cantillon. The officers talked to Cantillon and play resumed. After one batter was retired, the Milwaukee players again began yelling at the umpire. Cunningham told the police he wanted the Brewer manager put out of the park. At this point "Sergeant Boylan reached for Cantillon, who, springing from the bench, made a right hand pass at Boylan's nose. Patrolman Saugston grabbed him and Cantillon swung on him, but the blow fell short. Boylan got his revolver out of his hip pocket, after some difficulty, and [patrolman] LaPorte ran up. The three officers got Cantillion by the wrists and the back of his coat and hustled him out back of the grandstand and outside the park." The Milwaukee players packed up their gear and left the field.[41] To make matters worse, as the Brewers were leaving the field, many in the bleachers left their seats and crowded onto the field. As it was Ladies Day in Indianapolis, some of the more timid of the fairer sex feared a riot and began to leave the park. Many disappointed spectators were yelling for the Indianapolis players to fight with the Brewers and even strike the police officers. Fortunately, cooler heads prevailed and the situation calmed down.[42]

Incredibly, the Brewer manager was released once outside the ballpark. Indianapolis manager Bill Watkins came out and begged Cantillon not to have his players leave the field and disappoint the crowd of about a thousand. Cantillon's reported answer was, "Rats, just issue rain checks to your people. You can keep my share of the gate." Watkins did issue rain checks. Cantillon claimed his players said nothing out of the way and he did not say a word. He said to Watkins, "You had this thing all framed up." Watkins told the press the Milwaukee players had been boisterous throughout the entire series, which was becoming annoying to the fans, and the umpire decided to stop this sort of thing.[43]

The Brewer management was subject to a $500 fine for forfeiting the game. American Association President Hickey fined Joe Cantillon $100 for the incident. The Brewer skipper said he would not pay the fine, and gave a very different version of events. Cantillon said before the game he jokingly said to Umpire Cunningham that if he needed help (as Gus Moran, who had also umpired the day before, was sick), he [Cantillon] would help him from the bench. Cunningham became angry and told Cantillon he would not stand for any coaching from the bench. Pitcher Elmer Meredith, who was about to start the game for the Brewers, told Cunningham to just go and umpire, and was immediately ordered out of the game. Shortstop Bill Phyle protested and was also ejected. In quick succession Frank Hemphill and Larry Schlafly were also waved to the bench. Cantillon claimed he then asked the umpire: "Is this a prearranged scheme to beat us? What is the meaning of this sort of work?" At this point Cunningham ordered the Brewer manager from the grounds. When Cantillon appealed to Watkins, the Indianapolis manager went for the police. Cantillon admitted fighting with the police, but only after he had asked the officer what laws he had violated. The Brewer skipper at first claimed he did not take his team off the field, but was prevented by the policemen, who were following the orders of Watkins.[44] Cantillon later said he did take his team off the field, as the umpire's actions of ejecting four of his players had badly crippled his team.[45]

Rumors were about that Brewer owner Charles Havenor would sell the team because of the way his manager was treated, but this was immediately denied. At a special meeting of the American Association, it was decided by the owners present to uphold Hickey's $100 fine of Cantillon. The Brewer manager was barred from appearing on the bench, and Hickey actually suspended the

Opposite: Joe Cantillon — Another fiery manager whose refusal to pay a fine temporarily cost Milwaukee its franchise in the American Association (Historic Photograph Collection/Milwaukee Public Library).

ball club from the Association until the fine was paid. The American Association took temporary charge of the team to prevent managers from signing any of the Milwaukee players. The affair ended on June 18 when Havenor went to Chicago and paid Hickey the $100 fine.[46]

As these types of incidents continued, President Hickey sent this letter to his umpires in late June:

> Complaint has reached me that the players are annoying the umpires as well as the audience by coaching in a loud and boisterous manner from the bench. You will notice rule 50 states: "The umpire shall have power to order any player, captain or manager to do or omit to do any action that he may deem necessary to give force and effect to the laws of the game." You will, therefore, be governed by this rule, and if in your judgment players become obnoxious you will see to it that they are stopped immediately. Notify the manager of the club before the game starts that coaching from the bench must be stopped, and then if he does not control his players and prevent the same, he will be responsible to you.[47]

It appeared the Brewers players were not only rowdy on the field, but had some problems off the field, as well. In June, *The Sporting News* Columbus correspondent wrote of the Milwaukee players: "There were some ugly stories afloat about their dissipation while here. Some of them were seen in a downtown resort Friday morning early in a semi-comatose condition. On Friday they lost. On Saturday night there was another celebration and on Sunday another defeat."[48]

The Brewers conduct on the field showed little improvement as July moved in. In the first game of a July 4 double-header in Kansas City, three Brewers were ejected from the game. Pitcher Elmer Meredith carried on an argument too long when he hit a batter with the bases loaded. An inning later, Brewer third baseman Bob Unglaub and Kansas City runner Ed Lewee collided at third base. When the Milwaukee fielder grabbed Lewee by the arm, preventing him from advancing, Umpire Cunningham motioned Lewee home on the interference call. The Brewers were all over the umpire, in particular first baseman Jiggs Donahue, who eventually was ejected. The next inning Bob Unglaub hit a home run over the fence. While circling the bases, he stopped in front of Lewee at shortstop and punched him three times before trotting home. Police were summoned to remove Unglaub from the field. It was reported he left with no trouble while wearing a smile. This is the same Bob Unglaub we shall encounter later who lost his wife in May, and was reported to be a devout Christian who in his spare moments essayed missionary work in an attempt to convert his teammates.[49]

Given that the Brewers' manager and a portion of his team displayed such bad behavior, it seems odd and even inconceivable that Joe Cantillon umpired

Four. Rowdyism and Umpiring 105

in American Association games every now and then when the regular umpire did not show up. According to *Sporting Life,* "He does not give his team any the best of it, either."[50]

Even President Hickey was not exempt from the rowdyism of fans. In Toledo on July 12, he was hit with a stone while helping Tony Mullane exit from a crowd of excited fans.[51]

Fans caused a major problem in Indianapolis on July 31. The crowd had been unhappy with Frank Foreman's calls all afternoon, and in the ninth inning he made a close judgment against the Hoosiers to end the game unfavorably for the home nine. Hundreds of fans jumped over the fences, swarmed the field and made for the umpire. A half-dozen police were on hand and rescued him but not before someone in the crowd threw a bottle that hit Foreman in the back. The police had to escort the umpire to his hotel.[52]

One of the most serious incidents of the season occurred in St. Paul on July 26. Umpire Foreman had ordered Louisville pitcher Aloysius Egan out the game for arguing calls. Manager Billy Clymer came out to argue this ejection. Fred Odwell, who had started to his position in the outfield, picked up the ball just in back of the pitcher's box and threw it with all his force at the umpire. The ball missed Foreman but struck Clymer in the side of the face, breaking his jaw.[53] Clymer required an operation on his jaw, and was out of action for six weeks.

An extremely unusual umpiring situation occurred in Milwaukee on July 1. When umpire Ellsworth Cunningham did not arrive in Milwaukee in time for the scheduled double-header, Milwaukee pitcher Claude Elliott and Kansas City pitcher Jim Durham started the game as umpires. In the sixth inning, Milwaukee's Bill Dunleavy hit a home run. Kansas City team captain Mike Grady somehow blamed Durham for this and ordered him to the bench. The next inning Elliott had to relieve the starting pitcher, Willie McGill. The Brewers' Bob Ganley took over the umpiring for the rest of the game, as well as the second game. For what it is worth, Milwaukee won both ends of the double-header.

On July 16 Jack Haskell, considered by some the best umpire in the American Association, quit because of a $25 fine imposed on him for failing to appear for two games in Columbus. Haskell claimed he was sick in bed and could not make the trip. After negotiations with Association President Hickey, the umpire was rehired.

Terrible behavior only became worse in the American Association. On August 29 catcher George Yeager of the Minneapolis Millers was arrested in Toledo after the game and charged with assault and battery on a ten-year-old boy. Yeager had thrown a ball over the fence during the game as the crowd had been on him. After the game, a crowd of young boys followed him, yelling and hooting. Yeager threw a heavy broom that knocked the young boy down. The crowd closed in, and two policemen had all they could handle to get Yeager safely off the field as the crowd showered him with stones. Yeager was arrested and released at the station on his own recognizance to appear later.[54]

The rowdy behavior and umpire assaults continued until the end of the season. In a September game, Kansas City pitcher Arthur Alloway got into an argument with umpire Monk Foreman and pushed him around the field until manager Dale Gear intervened. Incredibly, Foreman allowed Alloway to remain in the game. Arguments continued throughout the game until it climaxed in the eighth inning when Bill Nance was called out on a close play. The Kansas City second baseman ran up to Foreman, grabbed the neckband of his blouse and shook him vigorously. Nance continued to push the umpire around the field until players from both sides stopped him. Foreman did eject this player.[55]

For his part, Foreman had not endeared himself to the Milwaukee crowd in this series. Describing the double-header in which Nance and Foreman had the above incident, the *Milwaukee Sentinel* wrote: "Umpire Foreman had clearly demonstrated incompetency [sic] in the first game and removed all shadow of doubt in the second. To his absolute lack of control and manifest incompetency is seen in the fact that the second game was probably the most disgusting to spectators that has been seen on local grounds this season." The day before the umpire had turned to the grandstand and yelled, "If you people had as much ambition for your club as you have for the umpire it would be better for you."[56] Clearly, Frank Foreman and Milwaukee did not get along.

The terrible display in these games, said to be the worst seen in Milwaukee in the memory of the oldest fan, drew a blast from the *Milwaukee Journal*. But these criticisms were not leveled at the players or umpires. The newspaper's game story dwelled on the rowdyism, and was to the point:

> However, the players are not so much to blame as the officials of the league. They are in the game fighting for every point there is to be had, and if some restriction is not placed upon them it will not be marvelous if they sometime overstep themselves in their efforts to gain a point. However, the main fault is higher; the blame of these exhibitions should be placed at the door of no other than President Thomas Jefferson Hickey. Other league presidents have found ways and means to prevent such scenes as took place at frequent intervals in both of yesterday's games.
>
> Why don't he do the same? It is enough to say that a few more such games will do more to kill baseball in the eyes of true lovers of the sport than any tail-end team would. Milwaukee fans have always shown themselves to be true

sportsmen and as such they cannot help condemning such rowdy exhibitions. It is up to President Hickey to come out from behind his "I-have-nothing-to-say" and put a stop to such displays.[57]

In January 1904 the new president of the American Association would make better umpiring and more field discipline a top priority. He said he would hire the best umpires available and give them instructions to maintain good order. Unfortunately, rowdy behavior would continue in the major and minor leagues for some time to come.

Five

League Peace but Battle Continues in Two Cities

As the fight between the American Association and Western League raged during the 1902 season, rumors of peace and franchise shifts were frequent. As early as June a story surfaced that it was the intention of the Western League magnates to try to finish the 1902 season with its present circuit, but then reorganize for 1903 with Minneapolis and St. Paul replacing Milwaukee and Peoria. In Peoria it was thought if a change were to be made, it would be best to drop St. Joseph, as attendance in the Missouri city was not good. D.C. Packard, the Denver owner, was also in favor of admitting Pueblo, Colorado. He said that city had been forging ahead in the last two years, owing to the growth of the Colorado Iron and Fuel Company's plant, and was of size sufficient to guarantee a good season. The Denver correspondent to *The Sporting News* had a definite opinion on which club should make room for Pueblo:

> Thomas Burns, of Colorado Springs, may not be in the Western League next year. He has not conducted himself like one of eight men trying to make a success of base ball, but more as though there was only one man in the league, and that man Burns. He has persistently interfered with President Sexton, has ordered umpires off his grounds without sufficient cause. Generally he has made himself obnoxious to his players, his partners in the league and to all those who have had dealings with him. Pettiness has characterized his conduct, rather than any interest felt in the success of base ball. If there is some convenient manner of getting rid of him he will be dropped and Pueblo, instead of Colorado Springs, be on the map for next year.[1]

In Denver it was believed Milwaukee would be left out, although if a foothold could be secured in the Wisconsin city, Des Moines would probably be the victim.

On the American Association side, as early as June it was rumored George

Five. League Peace but Battle Continues in Two Cities   109

Tebeau had been offered Brooklyn's place in the National League for 1903. It was not seriously believed he would accept, as one newspaper reported: "He is fully aware that claws are concealed beneath the velvet paws of the National League tabbies and that to fall into their power would mean the loss of his power and future as a magnate." Tebeau soon told the *Louisville Courier-Journal* he had no intention of leaving the American Association and going to the National League.[2]

In July it was rumored William Watkins of Indianapolis was to purchase the Toledo franchise, move his Indians there, and put the former Toledo club in some other city. In August *Sporting Life* had reported the American Association would agree to drop Kansas City, and the Western League would drop Milwaukee. The Association might then go into Grand Rapids, with the Western entering either Sioux City or Pueblo. This would make for shorter traveling distances for both leagues. One American League owner, in favor of this idea, said, "Grand Rapids is a splendid baseball town when properly handled and would fit in the circuit much better than Kansas City."[3] In October this talk was revived, this time with Grand Rapids and Detroit replacing Kansas City and St. Paul. The talk of Pueblo being part of the Western League arose periodically, even as late as April 1903, when it was reported Thomas Burns had given an option on his Colorado Springs club to J.A. Kebler, president of the Colorado Fuel and Iron Company in Denver, and that if any transfer was made, it would be to Pueblo. However, the problems in Colorado Springs were quickly ironed out.

As the 1902 season ended, some believed George Tebeau would put an American Association team in Denver the next year. Yet another rumor suggested that Minneapolis and St. Paul would be dropped from the American Association, and Memphis and Nashville added. It was being said that George Tebeau was trying to induce the two Tennessee franchises to jump to the American Association.[4] From Indianapolis William Watkins said it was true that Nashville and Memphis had applied for places in the American Association but that it would not be in the power of the A.A. to throw out present cities. One possibility was a 12-club league, which could add these two cities plus a couple of the Western League teams.[5] The directors of the American Association even went so far as to meet in Chicago in late September to discuss a proposal to form an alliance with the Southern League. Tebeau and American Association President Hickey were appointed to look into a deal but nothing ever came of the talks.

In Milwaukee there was a rumor that the two local clubs would consolidate. Negotiations reportedly had been ongoing for some time, but the problems between owners Harry Quin and Charles Havenor [see Chapter 6] stalled these talks. Which league this newly consolidated club would be in was not stated, but the team would play at the American Association Park at eighth and Chambers. *The Sporting News* reported that Evansville, the best city in the Three-I League, had applied for admission to the American Association, and if the Milwaukee situation was not resolved, the Indiana city's chances of getting in would improve.⁶

Toledo was also in the news regarding ownership issues. Charles Strobel was said to be contemplating the sale of his club to a local stock company for $10,000. Strobel said he had been approached by local businessman Charley Stevens to purchase the franchise for a reasonable price. Stevens owned a cigar store but had years of experience in the theatrical business, and was said to be one of the best amusement promoters in the business. Also in this proposed new ownership plan was New York Giants star catcher Roger Bresnahan.⁷ Strobel answered that the club was on the market if someone came up with $10,000. Stevens said that was satisfactory and asked for a 30-day option. Strobel would not give him an option, saying he wanted the total amount upon sale, and this $10,000 would not include players under contract. The bottom line for Strobel: "I guess that you will find me at the old stand next year, doing business just the same."⁸ After months of the rumor that Bresnahan and the group would take over the club, Strobel said of the young catcher from Toledo, who would go on to a Hall-of-Fame catching career: "It keeps Bresnahan busy telling the people how the game ought to be played. He is now married and I guess that will hold him for a while."⁹

Roger Bresnahan — The future Hall of Fame catcher showed great interest in purchasing the Toledo baseball club (Library of Congress).

The Western League owners met at the close of the season in St. Joseph, deciding boldly to continue the baseball war. Present at the meeting were Western League president Michael Sexton, vice-president Thomas Burns of Colorado Springs, W.T. Van Brunt of St. Joseph, D.C. Packard and Richard R. Burke of Denver, James Manning of Kansas City, William A. Rourke of Omaha, Charles T. Barston of Peoria, and James McKinnon of Des Moines. Huffy Duffy of Milwaukee wired that he was in the East on business, placing his proxy with Thomas Burns.

At the convention of the National

Five. League Peace but Battle Continues in Two Cities   111

Association of Minor Leagues in New York on October 23–25, 1902, it was arranged for representatives of the Western League and American Association to meet to forge a peace agreement. William Watkins of Indianapolis and Thomas Bryce of Columbus represented the American Association, while W.T. Van Brunt and Michael Sexton were the representatives for the Western League. The meeting was looked upon with high hopes. According to the November 1, 1902, issue of *Sporting Life,* there was "not one chance in ten that the peace negotiations will fail; if they do the world shall know the reason for the lamentable miscarriage. Peace in the minor world is assuredly in sight." After two days of conferences, propositions and counter-propositions, a plan for compromise was reached on October 28.

However, the one in ten chance made good. The bone of contention between the leagues was the Milwaukee/Kansas City territory, with neither league yielding enough to suit the other. The Western League put forth three proposals to stop the impasse, but all were rejected by the American Association. First the Western offered to vacate Milwaukee if allowed to remain in Kansas City, while the A.A. would vacate Kansas City and pay Van Brunt $5,000 for his Milwaukee ballpark improvements. Next the Western League offered to vacate Milwaukee provided the American Association took over the grounds' lease and also leave Kansas City upon receipt of $25,000 for improvements. After these proposals were rejected, the Western offered to leave Milwaukee unconditionally if the Association would similarly leave Kansas City. The American Association rejected this proposal because it felt Milwaukee was its territory before the Western League entered it as a war measure. The American Association also claimed Kansas City as its territory. The Association men reasoned that George Tebeau, who had owned the franchise in 1901, had transferred the territorial rights to the American Association. The American Association delegates felt the baseball war had been brought on by Van Brunt, and any money settlement would only be paying off Van Brunt's losses at their expense, losses estimated at $70,000.

The American Association delegates had only one proposal for the Western League, that being for the American Association to give Van Brunt a half interest in the Kansas City Association club, provided the Western League withdrew from both Kansas City and Milwaukee. It was argued this would relieve Van Brunt of two losing propositions and give him interest in a winning one, one in which he would recoup his losses in a few years. The A.A. delegates felt splitting Kansas City and Milwaukee between the two leagues would weaken both leagues, as each would have to take in a smaller city. With K.C. and Milwaukee both in the American Association, this would allow the A.A. to remain a Class A minor league. The Western League could find two smaller cities to become a Class B league, which would save money for its backers. Watkins of Indianapolis pointed out that when the Western League had only smaller western towns in 1900, all teams made money. When the league expanded in 1901 to take in Kansas City, St. Paul and Minneapolis, the only club to make money was Omaha. The smaller cities of the league could not afford the salaries the larger cities were forcing on them in order to compete. Of course, the Western League was not in favor of this proposal.

At this point Pat Powers, president of the Eastern League, made this proposition: The American Association would enter the National Association as a full-fledged member, respecting contracts, reservation and territorial rights, with the Western League retaining its clubs in Milwaukee and Kansas City. Both leagues would play under conflicting or non-conflicting schedules in these two cities, as might be determined, until such time as one or the other club might have enough of the fight and retire voluntarily. In this event the territory would belong exclusively to the league whose club outlived the other. Powers' plan would let the clubs in Kansas City and Milwaukee fight it out without expense to the other franchises in the two leagues. It would also allow the Western League and American Association to fight their battle without driving up salaries in or tempting players to jump from other minor leagues. It was reported all parties were in favor of Powers' plan.

However, W.T. Van Brunt was not at the meeting at this point, as he had to leave to attend to important railroad business. When Van Brunt was contacted and informed of Powers' proposal, he instructed President Sexton to reject it and stand firm on the earlier Western League proposals, even adding a fourth two-prong proposal — that the Western League would vacate Milwaukee and Kansas City if paid $20,000, or the Western would pay the American Association $20,000 if the A.A. would vacate both cities. In either scenario the vacating league would turn over all property to the other league. This put the National Board in a bad position. It had to back Powers' proposal, which was endorsed and accepted by the American Association and the president of the Western League, or "to crawfish at the dictation of one man" and continue the disastrous war. The Board was said to be favoring Powers' plan when it was discovered a resolution had been passed earlier delegating the National Board the duty of conferring on all peace propositions and instructing it to make no settlement that would not be acceptable to the Western League. This left the Board unable to enact the plan. The American Association delegates' reaction was "better imagined than described." The National Board members, wanting some kind of peace, suggested negotiations not be called off but adjourned for all heads to cool off. Another meeting was called for November 15.[10]

Five. League Peace but Battle Continues in Two Cities

Sporting Life, claiming not to take sides, made solid arguments in "AN APPEAL TO REASON" editorial why the Powers' plan was needed to save not only the Western League and American Association, but the National Association of Minor Leagues "from a costly and intolerable position — acting as buffer in a Quixotic struggle in which it had little to gain and much, if not everything to lose."

> There is right and wrong on both sides, as usual; moreover, a great deal of the purely personal enters into the quarrel.... If the movement for peace — so disinterestedly started and fostered by 'Sporting Life'— fails every minor league interest in the country will suffer grievously. A continuation of the war positively means for the American Association another season of costly struggle to establish itself, with every man's hand against it. For the Western League it means the continuation of an expensive and futile battle for territory and class in which it is not naturally entitled or adapted. For the National Association it means a sure loss of prestige by reason of its inability to yield full protection to all its members under a state of war — a condition which must tend inevitably either to the disintegration of the Association or the creation of a rival body; in which event the minors' independence would soon be lost forever.
>
> Our chief concern in this situation is for the National Association, which in one short year has amply demonstrated its capacity for self government; its usefulness to its constituents; and its power for good, needing only the inclusion of the powerful American Association to make itself absolutely impregnable and imperishable. To have such an organization, with its splendid first-year record, its bright future and vast possibilities, impaired in strength, impeded in progress and, perhaps, imperiled in existence for a foolish quarrel over comparatively insignificant territory, aggravated by the personal feud of four men, and muddled by peanut politics, would be a blistering shame. The fall of such an organization, for such a quarrel, would be as melancholy as the fall of a lion under an ass' kick.[11]

The Philadelphia weekly hoped the Western League would re-think its position and accept the Powers compromise. It also urged the National Association to step forward and end the quarrel to protect its members. A continuation of the war would bring financial loss and probable ruin to the entire minor league world, *Sporting Life* warned.

While not all agreed on which solution was the best, everyone realized a settlement had to be reached. Thomas Burns of Colorado Springs advocated vacating Milwaukee if the American Association would leave Kansas City to the Western League, saying, "This arrangement will give us a little more of a compact league, as Milwaukee is a considerable distance. Milwaukee is a good ball town, but we will probably give it up to stop the fuss."[12]

The delegates of the Western League met at the Pacific Hotel in Chicago on November 15, 1902, and formulated their demands. The next day their American Association counterparts reached Chicago and made their headquarters at the Auditorium Hotel. That afternoon they gathered to prepare for the conference. Delegates from the National Association of Professional Base Ball Leagues also arrived in Chicago on November 16. The National Board was represented by Western League president Michael Sexton, James O'Rourke of the Connecticut League, William H. Lucas of the Pacific Northwestern League, and its newest member, William Kavanaugh of the Southern League. Kavanaugh was quickly assessed of the previous proceeding between the two warring leagues. Another board member failed to appear, but Sexton was given his proxy. However, because Sexton was a party of the litigation, he could not act, and he voluntarily withdrew. Then board president Pat Powers became so ill with pneumonia that he could not attend the conference. In his place Edward Mack of the Toronto Eastern League club was appointed temporary chairman of the Board. The meeting was remarkable in that there were at least as many non-delegates present as delegates. In addition to most of the club owners in both warring minor leagues, various team managers, players, and newspapermen from a number of Western League and American Association cities were in attendance. At least two National League magnates attended various sessions.[13]

On the afternoon of November 16, the Western League was first to submit its proposal to the National Board. Sexton, Packard and Burns presented the final Western League proposition with an amendment to give $20,000 to the American Association to vacate Kansas City and Milwaukee. The Western League further stated it would not accept any sum to vacate these cities. The American Association, represented by William Watkins, Thomas Bryce and Charles Havenor, then proposed to give W.T. Van Brunt a half interest in the Kansas City American Association club if the Western League would vacate Milwaukee and Kansas City. If this proposition failed, the American Association was willing to accept the Powers compromise. The American Association also made application to the National Board for admission to the National Association of Professional Base Ball Leagues at this time.

It was plain neither minor league had softened its position since October. It had been brought up at the New York meeting in October that there was a resolution in place that the National Board could settle the war only on terms satisfactory to the Western League. William Kavanaugh brought to light that after this resolution had been adopted, another was passed giving the National Board full power to settle the war without any qualification or condition whatever. Thus, the National Board had full power to do as it saw fit. But the Board, guided by Edward Mack, decided to use its power only to move the two parties along. The Board acted well. "It argued every proposition fairly, expostulated, conciliated and advised with both factions — all the time

Five. League Peace but Battle Continues in Two Cities

bringing a quiet, unobservable, but nevertheless, tremendous pressure for compromise to bear, which finally wore down all opposition."

These negotiations lasted four days, featuring bitter spirits and harsh words. In the first two days, as various propositions were placed on the table, the American Association delegates refused to budge, staying with the Association's original proposal to the Board. Some forward movement was made on the third day when the Board decided that, in the event of a peace settlement, all claims to reserved or contracted players up to October 29 would go as they lay, except Western League players of the 1902 reserve who had been signed by American Association clubs would be returned to the Western clubs. All other leagues, with the exception of the Pacific Northwest League, "generously waived all claims in the interest of peace."

With this player issue settled, the Western League proposed to accept the Powers compromise with the condition that ten players of the 1901 reserve list be returned to them. Of these players, three had signed with major league clubs, five belonged to St. Paul, one to Toledo and one to Louisville. The latter two clubs were willing to give up the players, but George Lennon of St. Paul objected to giving back five players. In addition to negatively affecting his team, Lennon had set Charlie Ferguson and William "Spike" Shannon up in business in St. Paul at great expense. The American Association initially balked at sending the St. Paul players to the Western League, but a comprise was worked out where Ferguson and Shannon stayed in St. Paul.

Van Brunt unexpectedly came to Chicago and went before the National Board. The St. Joseph owner announced the Western League was dropping all previous proposals and submitting a new one: "That the Powers' Compromise be accepted, provided the American Association would play on the Western League grounds in Kansas City under non-conflicting schedule at $3000 per annum rental for balance of lease, four years, under conditions assuring the Association Club equal treatment with the Western League club; and further, provided the Association give a $5000 bond that salaries in Kansas City and Milwaukee not exceed the salaries paid in other cities, and that no players be transferred to strengthen those two teams."

The National Board thought this a fair offer and urged the American Association to accept it. The Association asked for the night to mull it over. The A.A. men, too, thought the offer fair — so fair they suspected "a snake somewhere." They believed Van Brunt was attempting to tie them up in the Western League Kansas City park for four years, thus preventing them from moving into Chicago or Detroit if the opportunity arose, while the Western League would be free to transfer at will. It was explained Van Brunt's proposal was for real. He had been wired that his presence was needed if peace was to be had. The Western League "Angel" then immediately left New York for Chicago. If the American Association really wanted peace, which Van Brunt doubted, his offer could not be refused.

After discussing the offer, the American Association replied everything was acceptable except the ballpark situation. If the Kansas City Association club played in the Western League park, the Association would be paying rent in addition to paying for the grounds it already had. In addition, the small seating capacity at the K.C. Western League park — 2,500 people — would necessitate improvements at great expense, — improvements to be made with American Association money on Van Brunt's park. Since a non-conflicting schedule was almost impossible to establish, playing in the same park was out of the question. The bottom line was that it was estimated the American Association stood to lose from $20,000 to $30,000 a year if it accepted this offer. Thus the Association rejected this offer, stating it would fall back on the last Western League proposal before this, excepting only four St. Paul players from the claimed list of returnable players. The American Association delegates offered to withdraw from further negotiations so the National Board would not have to make a decision that might go against one of its own.

As it seemed peace was again slipping away, Thomas Burns of Colorado Springs stated he would be willing to waive the Kansas City ballpark stipulation if everything else was acceptable. D.C. Packard of Denver seconded this. With this, "Chairman Mack and the members of the Board leaped to their feet in a frenzy of enthusiasm, grasped the hands of Burns and Packard, and then began a veritable love feast."

The compromise accepted, the articles of agreement were published on November 19, 1902. First, a non-conflicting schedule would be made for Kansas City and Milwaukee, as far as was reasonable. Second, both leagues were to put up a bond of $5,000 that the salaries of the K.C. and Milwaukee teams would not exceed the salaries of the other clubs in their respective leagues; this salary limit was computed on the basis of the average salary of the other six clubs in the league, limited to 13 men each. Further, no player could be loaned by other members of either league during the season to strengthen Milwaukee or Kansas City. The third article stated the reserve lists and contracts of players who were under contract and played in the Western League in 1902 would be respected. However, if a player had signed with an American Association club before October 29, he would be property of the contracting team. If a player who was forced back to the Western League had received advance money, he had to return it within ten days of demand. The fourth article gave each league the right to use its own grounds in Kansas City and Milwaukee.

After the agreement was signed by representatives of both leagues and

Five. League Peace but Battle Continues in Two Cities

by National Board Secretary J.H. Farrell, the American Association was formally presented full membership in the National Association of Professional Base Ball Leagues.[14]

Ed Boynton, the *Sporting Life* correspondent from Columbus, summed it up correctly while commenting on the American Association's admission into the organized minor leagues: "It not only demonstrates their standing as a body, but proves, from the president down to the water boys, that this circuit is on the base ball map for keeps, and is sure to be a factor in the future of the greatest of American sports."[15]

There was indeed some type of peace agreement, but this quote from real estate tycoon D.C. Packard in the December 6, 1902, issue of *The Sporting News* shows the hatchet was not completely buried:

> You would think to read the accounts that Mr. Hickey and his men agreed to the propositions and not then until they had made every point they demanded. The fact is, that the Western did not concede any more than did the American, though at the opening of the conference the American fellows had us beaten. By the time we were through talking we secured an equitable arrangement, and I fully believe the Western secured a decided advantage. The American Association managers came, each with the representative of a newspaper from his town, and each got the sort of a report sent out that he most wanted.
>
> I take off my hat to the American Association men as base ball men. They have us of the Western League beaten all the way. We do not begin to be in it with them. But you must understand that these American magnates have nothing to do but handle base ball teams and they had a whole year to figure how to get the better of us.[16]

Upon admission to the National Association of Professional Base Ball Leagues, the American Association entered a claim to the Chicago and Detroit territories. Some believed Detroit was to be dropped by the American League, and Pittsburgh, where a group of investors was looking to purchase a franchise, would take its place to challenge Barney Dreyfuss' Pirates. There were also reports the American League was making overtures to Dreyfuss to come to the new circuit, to which Dreyfuss answered "nothing doing."[17]

Within days rumors swirled that the American Association was to drop St. Paul and Minneapolis and enter Chicago and Detroit. This was a turnabout from the previous year. Thomas Hickey had said in March 1902: "We are not in the same class as Chicago and it would be unwise for us to attempt to put a team in the city, for the same reason that it is unwise to mix large and small cities in any circuit. The real reason of the organizing of the American Association is the fact that the people of the larger towns in the Western League last year would not patronize the games where the teams from the smaller towns of the circuit played."[18]

George Lennon — The clothing store owner fought a battle with the city of St. Paul and other American Association owners to keep his team in St. Paul (*St. Paul Globe*, December 11, 1904).

George Lennon, owner of one of the largest retail clothing houses in St. Paul, was still trying to secure a new downtown park in St. Paul, claiming to have lost money at Lexington Park — which was four miles from the central city — over the past two seasons. Lennon had complained for almost a year that the Lexington Park grounds (located at Lexington and University avenues) were so far out that businessmen could not attend the weekday games. Lennon had threatened to move his club in the winter of 1902 if he was refused permission to build downtown. Even though a majority of the common council was in favor of a downtown site for the ballpark, the mayor had enough votes at that time to sustain his veto. The fears of what might happen at the new ballpark's location were outlined by the *St. Paul Globe*: "Ministers and other interested parties believed that Sunday ball was to be played at the downtown park, that a number of saloon men had rented buildings near the proposed site, and that with the team away from home the park would be rented to irresponsible parties for circuses, German villages and other objectionable purposes."[19]

After the 1902 playing season, the other American Association clubs had decided Lennon must secure more accessible grounds than Lexington Park or transfer his club. Lennon had a five-year lease on grounds located about five blocks from the center of the city. In an open letter he told the St. Paul public he wanted to erect a ballpark there at a cost of $10,000.[20] Lennon proposed to play weekday games at the new location but continue to play Sunday games at Lexington Park, as Sunday crowds were always big there. The Saints reported in late November that the situation looked dark because there was little likelihood of the city council permitting a park downtown.

Stories circulated that Lennon and Chicago politician Robert Burke would be the owners of a new Chicago club in the American Association, with Michael Kelley or former Chicago White Stockings star Jimmy Ryan managing the team. There was also a report out of Chicago that White Stockings owner Charles Comiskey was to leave the ballpark on the south side for a new park on the west side to better fight the National League team situated

Five. League Peace but Battle Continues in Two Cities 119

there. The American Association club would then take over the south side park, paying around $15,000 for it.[21]

Another report had the Indianapolis franchise transferring to Chicago. As Indianapolis did not have Sunday baseball, visiting clubs did not cover expenses in the Indiana city. George Tebeau told Louisville reporters if the Indianapolis club was not permitted to play Sunday ball in 1903, the American Association would request its transfer to Chicago. Indianapolis' William Watkins said this was news to him. With Indianapolis having a ten-year franchise agreement in the Association, any attempt to displace the city would be met with resistance.

President Hickey confirmed the American Association was considering the invasion of Chicago, and St. Paul would be the club to transfer if such a move occurred. He was careful to say that no definite plans had been made, and everything depended on what Comiskey did with his White Stockings. While Hickey was telling reporters this, Comiskey told *Sporting Life*:

> It's a pretty good bet that I will be on the South Side next season. [Chicago National League owner James] Hart has gone to the trouble of explaining to the public that it is a hard matter for me to get along in my present quarters, and for this reason it might be pleasant to show him how the American League might draw in his neighborhood. I don't care to always be building parks, however. I have my plant complete, and am thoroughly established on the South Side. My crowds have been getting better every year, and I believe that the South Side has a great future as a base ball center. Developments might change the situation, but at present it seems to me that I will remain in my present location. I have no lease or option on any West Side plant, and do not know that I will get any.[22]

In early December George Lennon said he would receive permission to build a downtown park in St. Paul, and would begin work on the new park in the spring. Perhaps sensing the city aldermen were against him, a day before the vote Lennon offered to give his baseball team to the St. Paul Commercial Club absolutely free for the nine years remaining in the American Association agreement if the Board of Aldermen would not grant him the downtown park privilege. This offer included the franchise, players and lease at Lexington Park. If after any year the Commercial Club did not find running the club a profitable business, it would be returned to Lennon. One condition Lennon placed on this proposed transfer gives some insight into player costs of that period. Lennon's condition was the money received for any player sold before the 1903 season would go to him. The Saints' owner said he had $12,220 invested in the franchise and players. He claimed he had been offered a good sum for some of his players, including $2,000 for Miller Huggins, $1,500 for Mike Kelley, and $1,000 each for Charlie Ferguson and Spike Shannon. Lennon claimed the franchise was worth $10,000, and he could receive that amount, provided the franchise would be transferred to another city. However, he claimed at this point he wanted the Saints to stay in St. Paul, thus the offer. The Commercial Club was in favor of this plan, and the vice president of the streetcar company in St. Paul stated he would not oppose a downtown park and would use his influence to help obtain a site.[23]

Within days the Committee on Streets of the Board of Aldermen, listening to protests of neighboring property owners, killed the ordinance by a vote of 5 to 2. Lennon's immediate reaction was to give up. The *St. Paul Globe* quoted the Saints' owner as saying:

> I am through working to hold the team here. I have been advised to look for another spot where the opposition might not be so strong. All the advice is a mere waste of words. Go any place in St. Paul even to the city limits and pick a plot for a ballpark and immediately some of the residents in the vicinity of the selected site will be at the council meeting ready to oppose my securing the place.... I offered to erect a modern up-to-date ballpark, paint the fence and stands white, to do everything to make the park one of the attractions of the Central park district and not an eyesore, and despite all this I am refused my request. There was not a single claim that the park would prove a nuisance to the neighborhood, and I guaranteed that it would not. I wanted to play but forty or forty-five games there during the summer and these games when the citizens in the few houses in the neighborhood would, at least the majority of them, be at the lake. I guaranteed to play only weekday games at the park and to hold the park for baseball purposes only, but I was refused permission, and now the American Association can take the team away from here if it wants to.[24]

Lennon soon changed his mind and decided he would still build a park. The clothing store owner said he would either find another site "where the property owners have enough public spirit to permit the ballpark in their neighborhood," or he would build a steel structure on the site where the council refused the wooden structure.[25] Lennon could build such a ballpark in the downtown district without securing an ordinance. However, this would require vacating a street, which seemed unlikely considering the political differences over the park.

As December continued, so did this dance. Comiskey was still toying with going to the west side of Chicago and Lennon was getting nowhere with his downtown St. Paul ballpark. The day before Christmas 1902, President Hickey announced there would be no American Association club in St. Paul in 1903. He said the franchise would be transferred to Chicago and would play either at South Side Park, if Comiskey moved, or locate on the north side of town if Comiskey did not move. In either case, "prominent Chicago politician" Robert E. Burke would make a satisfactory settlement to purchase the club from Lennon.[26] Burke was a former oil inspector and influential in Chicago's north side Democratic Party. He had managed the mayoral campaigns of Carter Harrison, Jr., in 1897, 1899 and 1901.[27] The Chicago correspondent to *The Sporting News* doubted a third team could make a go of it in Chicago, especially as National League owner James Hart thought two teams were too many. Another drawback would be the struggle for attention from the local press with the two major league teams getting the lion's share of newsprint. However, as major league Chicago teams had gone to a 50-cent admission, the American Association's one chance for success was its lower admission price. What's more, big name Adrian "Cap" Anson was said to be willing to invest in the new club.[87]

A week before Christmas Robert Burke traveled to St. Paul "armed with several bales of paper money and a few sacks of the gold" to buy Lennon's interest in the franchise. Something went wrong — Lennon, Burke nor Hickey would say what happened — and Burke went home in bad humor. There was a report that Charles Comiskey would head the new American League team being placed in New York, and Burke would succeed him in Chicago.[29]

It appeared the Saints would stay in St. Paul, but shortly before the first of the year Minneapolis manager Walter Wilmot said it was a done deal that St. Paul would be transferring to Chicago. Wilmot said this would hurt his revenue, as the rivalry between the two cities made money. He also felt if Detroit was to have a team in the American Association, it would be his Millers that transferred there.

If the American Association entered Chicago, where the team would play was certainly in doubt. If Comiskey left his park on Wentworth, the Association would play there. If Comiskey stayed on the south side, the American Association club would take the Congress Street field that Comiskey was considering. There was also the north side, where professional baseball had never been played. The last location was on Milwaukee Avenue, a slanting street that was the main artery of the northwest section of the city. The chances of these locations working was also doubtful to Chicago *Sporting Life* correspondent W.A. Phelon, Jr.:

> It seems to me that a team, a new team, in any of these locations, would have tough sledding. If Commy moved the new club would get nice grounds and big stands for a minor league organization — also a lot of expenses that would be pretty heavy for a minor league bunch. The real South Side cranks, wedded to the glories of the White Stockings, would either follow Commy to the West Side, or, disgusted at being deserted, fed for two years with major league ball, and unwilling to look at the minor league article, would stay home and never go near the park, not even on Sundays. If the new team went to the West Side, it would be between the devil and the deep sea. Small consideration would it get from either Hart or Comiskey in the arrangement of dates. The fans would go south or west each Sunday in a body, just as they have been doing right along;

the same on weekdays, and so where would the new team get off at? If the new club went to the North Side, it would have a vast population to draw from — but a population composed mainly of Germans, who do not care much for base ball, and would rather go to the Schnetzenfest and the picnic than to see any minor league tribe play the game. And if the new team located on Milwaukee avenue, a polyglot street of many nationalities — oh, mamma! The one and only chance the Hickey team would have to live would be this: that both the National and American League clubs would become tail-enders and play such rotten ball that the cranks would not care to see them. In this most unlikely event, a third team might on Sundays draw in enough coin to make a bare living.[30]

The editorial staff of *Sporting Life* thought a move to Chicago would be good "inasmuch as such a move will vastly enhance the dignity and importance of the rise and prosperous American Association." A move into Chicago would further the chances that the Association would then enter Detroit and would have an ideal circuit, with the smallest mileage of any important league in the country.[31]

To add more fuel to the Chicago American Association story, Western League "Angel" W.T. Van Brunt visited Charles Comiskey on December 30. Although neither man said what was discussed, a special dispatch out of Chicago reported the St. Joseph millionaire was contemplating establishing a club in Chicago as a counter attraction to Hickey's proposed club. It was thought Van Brunt was attempting to get an option on the White Stockings south side grounds, which would affect the American Association plans. Most doubted the Western League wanted to go into Chicago. D.C. Packard in Denver told the press: "What on earth would the Western League want of Chicago anyway? The Western has all the fights it can take care of just now, and will not dance around trying to get up any more scraps. We don't care about vaudeville baseball anyway, and that is what there will be in Chicago. All these stories of possible changes in the circuit of the Western are with a purpose. Don't you believe any of them."[32] It was likely Van Burnt was in Chicago to talk with Comiskey about taking over the reins of the American League's entry in New York.

On January 14, 1903, it was reported George Lennon had come to terms with the American Association, and his club would transfer to Chicago. The club would be owned by Chicago capital and play in a new ballpark on the north side. Complete details were to be given at the upcoming Association meeting. Two days later, president Thomas Hickey made a formal demand upon Lennon for the transfer of his club. Lennon claimed he now had a suitable downtown site for his team in St. Paul and wanted out of his verbal deal with the Association. The St. Paul owner instructed his attorney to notify Hickey that he would have to go through the courts to nullify the 10-year agreement St. Paul had with the American Association. The franchises moving

Five. League Peace but Battle Continues in Two Cities

to Chicago were now rumored to be Milwaukee's, with Burke and Charles Havenor as owners, or Toledo. Toledo was the smallest city in the circuit, and the town had not been a moneymaker. It was further said Charles Strobel, owner of the Toledo club, was in favor of such a change.

Of course, neither the American League nor National League Chicago owners wanted to see a third club in Chicago. If the American Association would put its club on the west side, Hickey would have to frame the Chicago schedule so as not to conflict with the James Hart's National League team, thus conflicting with Comiskey's south side team and robbing him of his west side patrons. It was felt with plenty of Saturday and Sunday games on the schedule Hickey would cut Comiskey out of the people who liked to see baseball but did not care to travel too far. Thus, if the American Association did come into Chicago, Comiskey would like to see the team north of the river, and the National League club would rather the newcomers remain as far away as possible from them.

The American Association was set to meet in Chicago on February 7 and settle the question of its invasion of Chicago. Hickey said despite reports to the contrary, the Association was moving the St. Paul franchise to the Windy City. In this he was backed by Thomas Bryce, William Watkins, Charles Havenor and George Tebeau. The Louisville owner gave notice to the Chicago owners before the meeting:

> The American Association will have a club in Chicago this year, notwithstanding the edict of Messrs. Hart and Comiskey, and if they attempt to shut us out of that city by an underhand business we will bring suit against both leagues in the United States Court, under the provision of the Sherman anti-trust law. We will ask for a restraining order against both these gentlemen and their associates if the American Association is willing to be good, but if they won't let us in we will create a small-sized disturbance in base balldom that may possibly enlarge into a battle royal, for we are not done. The owners of the American Association clubs are all practical base ball men. They are not novices, managerially or politically in base ball circles, and will stand up for their rights. If war is waged against them by the Base Ball Trust — for the two major leagues are nothing more than a Trust now — we will wage war in the "guerrilla" fashion against them: that is, we will take a shot at some of the big magnates from ambush, and, in the parlance of base ball warfare, that mode of fighting is always annoying to the enemy.[33]

The Chicago correspondent to *The Sporting News* was quick to respond to this American Association threat. In the February 7, 1903, issue he wrote:

> Tebeau's talk of coming in here and his hints at court proceedings under the anti-trust laws looks good to the uninitiated. But they won't stand washing in the sunlight of facts. The big leagues will make no open opposition to the transfer of

the St. Paul Club here if it is contemplated. They can not make any objection without a National Agreement. There will be nothing for the American Association to hang a court case on if it tries. The American and National leagues will simply decline to form a new National Agreement with the minors and there is certainly nothing in the laws which can compel anybody to combine into a trust against his will. Lennon knows this as much as anyone and there is nothing in the talk of putting a club here except as a sort of whip and spurs on Lennon.[34]

The correspondent said the National Association of Minor Leagues would not permit Hickey to draw them into a fight with the major leagues. President Thomas Hickey and his American Association gave the minors trouble enough in 1902, and there were few minor league owners willing to start a fight for Hickey. The newspaperman was certain all this talk was only a bluff to help Lennon get new grounds in St. Paul.

The Chicago correspondent to *Sporting Life*, W.A. Phelon, Jr., felt Hickey perhaps "fired by the past example of Ban Johnson, has the bee of ambition buzzing wildly in his bonnet, and wants to climb the ladder of base ball fame exactly as Johnson did." The parallels between Johnson and the old Western League of 1899 (that became the American League in 1900) to Hickey and his Western in 1903 were striking. Both men were baseball leaders who showed clever maneuvering and diplomacy. Hickey, as Johnson had been, was now at the head of a powerful minor league, and was taking the step of placing a club in Chicago, just as Johnson did for the 1900 season. "In view of the terrific convulsions which have been agitating the base ball world, should not the career of Johnson and his league be duplicated?"[35]

At its February meeting the American Association got the routine business out of the way immediately. Among other things, the Victor ball was adopted, the old claim list going back to 1901 was re-established, and each club was requested to place an additional $500 in the treasury for working capital. Another rule prohibited teams in the American Association from exchanging players after four months of the season had been played. This was enacted to do away with the loaning of players to teams to strengthen them at the end of the pennant race.

The Association then got down to the St. Paul/Chicago business. After two days of discussion, the matter was referred to a committee composed of Hickey, Lennon, Tebeau and Havenor to iron it out. After two sessions this committee decided that George Lennon and Robert E. Burke, the would-be Chicago owner, should work out an agreement. Although nothing official was done, it was reported Lennon and Burke would jointly operate the Chicago club, each having one-third ownership, and a third person — named by President Hickey — controlling the other third. The team would either be located

Five. League Peace but Battle Continues in Two Cities

"on a very accessible site" on the north side of Chicago or the Congress Street grounds would be leased for 10 years at a gross rental of $60,000. Improvements would probably cost another $20,000, but the new club would have a "first-class plant." It was felt a north side location for the club would not materially affect the attendance at either of Chicago's major league clubs, so neither Comiskey nor Hart would object to the American Association's entry into Chicago.[36] However, while Comiskey publicly said he was not opposed to a third club in the Windy City, James Hart announced he would oppose it, and would oppose any agreement between the major leagues and minor leagues if the American Association entered Chicago. Ban Johnson, president of the American League, was of the same opinion as Hart.

On February 17 the matter was settled. George Lennon announced he had secured an option on a downtown site in St. Paul where his team would play. Lennon said he had received "a most flattering offer" to transfer his club to Chicago, but he knew there were many people who wanted to keep the team in St. Paul, and he was deferring to their wishes.[37] It was also thought as Lennon had large business interests in St. Paul, he was naturally afraid his abandoning the city would have repercussions from the public.[38]

The American Association was to remain in St. Paul. Although it was never officially stated, it appears pressure was put on the Association not only by the National and American leagues, but also other minor leagues. An example was a dispute over a player the Detroit club signed from Providence of the Eastern League. When president Pat Powers of the Eastern League protested, Ban Johnson promised Powers the player would be returned. This was said to have been done with the expectation that the Eastern League would withdraw its tacit support of the American Association's plan to enter Chicago. As it was put in *The Sporting News*: "There is nothing in base ball law today to prevent the big leagues taking what players they please from the minors, any more than there is a rule preventing a third club in Chicago, and the minors can not expect to have their rights to players treated with any consideration while they are contemplating overlooking the territorial rights of other leagues. Neither 'right' is legal, but exists by mutual consent alone, and one can not exist without the other."[39]

In April, Lennon temporarily lost his chance to have a downtown park when property owners adjacent to the site near Rice and Como Avenue objected to two sections of street being vacated. One owner demanded $2,400 for his signature on the vacating proceeding, and refused to compromise. Lennon then turned his attention to the east of the south approach to the Wabasha Street Bridge. An ordinance to permit the building of a ballpark was prepared, but the Omaha Railway Company served notice that it intended to acquire the property in question for trackage purposes and the ordinance was not presented.[40] The Columbus correspondent to *The Sporting News*, James Andrew, was not complimentary of the St. Paul president: "Lennon and his bum town simply got in this year on a rain check, and by what looks now very much like misrepresentation about having a downtown grounds. What the Association should have done was to have enforced that option of his franchise and gone into Chicago when they had the chance. They would have been rid of a very poor town and a pigheaded magnate who apparently wants to boom his private business at the expense of the Association."[41]

Lennon would be forced to open the 1903 season again in Lexington Park, but finally secured grounds for a downtown park in the area between Robert, Minnesota, 12th and 13th streets. As usual, there were complaints from neighboring residents, but this time a representative of the Central Park Methodist Church came out in favor of the location, saying a ballpark would remove "a lot of shacks that now were a blot on the locality." The church representative was even in favor of Sunday games, thinking it would be better for young men than a saloon. George Lennon's attorney assured the nervous neighbors that there would be no Sunday games at the downtown park, and said advertising would not be permitted on the outside fences. The common council passed an ordinance permitting the baseball club to construct a park within the fire limits, and the ordinance was signed by Mayor Smith this time.[42] By early June all the contracts for the new park, to be known as Downtown Park, had been let out, and by mid-month work was progressing rapidly enough that Lennon announced the park would be ready when his Saints returned on July 7.[43]

However, in June an application for an injunction to prevent any ball playing or other amusements from being played in this downtown park was filed by a number of citizens residing in the neighborhood. The petitioners claimed they lived in "a quiet and secluded residence district of the city, which is thickly settled and inhabited by persons of refinement and culture." The neighbors alleged that the park would prove detrimental to their property values, as "players and spectators will, at frequent intervals, indulge in loud and deafening shouts, cheering, rings of bells, blowing of horns, whistling, catcalls and other noises, which will disturb the plaintiffs and their families and seriously injure their health."[44] On June 22 the judge in the district court denied the injunction, ruling the park would not necessarily be a nuisance.[45] Work again continued on the park that would open July 20 before a crowd of 4,200. Soon this new Downtown Park would be ridiculed, called "another cigar box." The catcher stood only about 10 feet from the grandstand, and the grounds were surrounded with telegraph poles with wire netting fastened to the top to keep the ball inside the park.[46] The fans, however, came out in big numbers, with attendance at Downtown Park in 1903 reportedly more than doubling the crowds that had attended games in Lexington Park.[47]

Prior to the Western League meeting in January, George Tebeau of the American Association's Louisville club met in Denver with Michael Sexton, Thomas Burns, D.C. Packard and Charles Nichols. Tebeau asked these Western League men if the Western would trade Milwaukee for Kansas City, a proposition Western League President Sexton was willing to do. A little later Sexton traveled to Chicago and learned "White Wings" Tebeau thought this switch could interfere with his Association's St. Paul/Chicago deal. Tebeau now wanted the Kansas City teams consolidated under one American Association club, with the Western League receiving half of the receipts. The Western League would enter St. Paul, or some other city, to complete its eight team circuit. Sexton would have nothing to do with this plan. It was reported the Western League had offered to withdraw from Milwaukee if the American Association would transfer its Kansas City club to Chicago, but this deal was declined by Tebeau. The Western League president said: "The Western League always has been ready to settle on a give and take basis, but we do not have to give anything away." It appeared there would be a fight to the finish in Kansas City and Milwaukee, and Sexton thought his clubs had the favorable advantage.[48]

Other intrigues involving franchises and cities were occurring in the American Association. Walter Wilmot, manager of the Minneapolis Millers, applied for a Grand Rapids franchise in the newly forming Central League. In addition to Wilmot, who held an option on the ballpark in Grand Rapids, a local stock company was seeking the franchise. It was believed Wilmot wanted to try Grand Rapids again, as he had managed there previously, in the less-expensive Western Association. If the team would be supported, he would abandon the Central League and move his Minneapolis club to the Michigan city. This was enough to deny him the franchise in the Central League.[49]

Next the Kansas City American Association club had a change of ownership. A.L. Buell left the club and George Tebeau, who had a financial interest in the Blues — some said the controlling interest — took over the club's business affairs. Dale Gear continued as team manager.

While all this was occurring, the American League and National League ended their two-year war after a conference in Cincinnati on January 9–10, 1903. The basics of this peace treaty were the recognition of territory for each league — including the American League in New York — recognition of player contracts, and the establishment of a reserve rule. The two leagues also decided to adopt uniform playing rules. Another provision in the peace agreement called for the president of the National Association of Professional Base Ball Leagues to be invited to "confer and advise" with the big leagues in the formulating of the National Agreement. Thus, the minor leagues would be represented at National Agreement meetings, although not as a voting member.

The Western League held its annual meeting in Kansas City on January 20–21, 1903, shortly after the major league peace agreement was reached. Representatives of all eight clubs were in attendance: Hugh Duffy of Milwaukee; William A. Rourke of Omaha; W.W. Sears of Des Moines; James Manning and Charles Nichols of Kansas City; D.C. Packard and R.R. Burke of Denver; J.J. Barton of St. Joseph; Thomas F. Burns of Colorado Springs; and George Simmons of Peoria. Michael Sexton, who had recently been re-elected president of the Three-I League, was re-elected as the Western League president, treasurer and secretary, at a salary of $3,000 a year, including expenses. W.T. Van Brunt was elected vice president, while he, Burns, Simmons and Rourke comprised the board of directors. No changes were to be made involving the cities in the circuit. The Western's financial report showed its "sinking fund" had a balance of $3,800 and all obligations had been paid. (*Sporting Life* of February 21, 1903, stated this sinking fund was $8,000, and was to be used in backing Kansas City and Milwaukee in "a friendly fight" with the American Association.)

Peoria had been a problem for the Western League in 1902, but even with a terrible team the franchise ended the season with $10,000 in the treasury. For

A handful of Western League owners and manager are pictured on left. Michael Sexton (center) served as president of both the Western and the Indiana-Illinois-Iowa League (members of which are pictured on the right). On left are (*top*) Charles Nichols, Thomas Burns, Geo. Simmons (*bottom*) W.H. Everitt, C.H. Myrick, W.A. Rourke (*Spalding Baseball Guide*).

Five. League Peace but Battle Continues in Two Cities   129

the upcoming season a stock company was organized with $15,000 in capital. George Simmons, a leading laundry man, was elected president. Although it had 18 players under reserve, the club had no manager signed and was looking for a new park to play in. It was said the team would not play again on the Central Railway grounds, owing to the arbitrary manner in which the streetcar company refused to allow the team to play whenever a circus or other attraction came to town. Nevertheless, the directors looked forward to a successful season, however.

In Des Moines James McKinnon gave the reasons why Des Moines was an important part of the Western League:

> Des Moines is one of the few towns that is always a paying proposition. No matter what kind of a team we have, the gate receipts are generally large enough to pay the expenses and leave a little for the promoters besides. We had only one day last season when we were compelled to turn over the $40 forfeit. That was one wet, muggy afternoon, when every one expected the game to be called off. Of course, we have not got rich, but we have always managed to pay expenses. The Western League isn't going to let a town that pays like that go unless there is a mighty good reason for it. Another thing, the Western League would lose money by skipping Des Moines. It's a long jump from Illinois to Colorado and costs money to make it. Des Moines, however, furnishes a convenient stopping place and an opportunity for the visiting team to turn in and clean up some money for its railroad fare and hotel bills.[50]

The president of the Des Moines club, Frank Clarkson, was forced to step down because of health reasons, and C.H. Myrick became president of the club.

As early as August of 1902 there were reports that William T. Van Brunt, owner of the St. Joseph franchise and "angel" to almost all the Western League, would move east, as he had sold his interest in the streetcar system in St. Joseph. It appeared Van Brunt was tiring of the baseball war. It was said he "had stuck with the Western League nobly, but he is no fool, as the chances are that he will not put his head against a stonewall unless he can see something to buck for."[51] Rumors were circulating that Van Brunt would be involved in the new team the American League was placing in New York, but he denied this, telling the press he would still be involved in the Western League. In November it was reported Van Brunt would be spending most of his time in the East running a railway company. The St. Joseph club for 1903 would be in the hands of club secretary Joseph J. Barton and manager Byron McKibben. By March 1903 Van Brunt said that since he was permanently located in New York, he was ending his active connection with baseball. In early April, Barton also resigned to become Van Brunt's private secretary in New York.

On April 4, 1903, the St. Joseph franchise was sold to Frank L. Sullivan and Bert P. Batson, both from Iowa, for a reported $4,000. On April 27

Batson disposed of his holdings to Sullivan. The next day the St. Joe players refused to take the grounds to play Milwaukee in the opening of the Western League season until they were assured their demands for salary would be promptly met. John H. Van Brunt, general manager of the street railway system and brother of former owner William T. Van Brunt, assured the players their money would be forthcoming. On the following day John H. Van Brunt bought back the club from Sullivan, who had been very unpopular with the players.

There were other interior changes in the Western League. Shortly after the first of the year *The Sporting News* reported "on good authority" that W.T. Van Brunt had disposed of his holdings in Kansas City and Milwaukee, and these clubs would be financed by D.C. Packard of Denver and Thomas Burns of Colorado Springs.[52] In Kansas City Charles Nichols was telling people he owned the club, but Packard and Burns said they had purchased a controlling interest in that Western League team from Van Brunt as far back as July of 1902. In Milwaukee Hugh Duffy was re-elected president of the Creams, in addition to retaining his on field manager chores. Porter Higby of Denver was elected treasurer of the Milwaukee club. Higby had been associated with the Denver team when George Tebeau owned the club, and was now said to be a representative of Western League owners R.R. Burke, Thomas Burns, and D.C. Packard, who owned a large share of stock in the Milwaukee club.

Before the 1903 season began the Western League lost another of its strongest men. In December it was reported that Kansas City owner James Manning was getting out of baseball to help build a company that manufactured explosives. On April 24 an announcement was made that Charles Nichols had bought the interests held by Manning and would be in full charge of the Kansas City club. However, other reports said the franchise had passed into the hands of Thomas Burns and D.C. Packard, and Nichols was to run the team on the field at a salary of $3,000 a year.

Six

American Association Interlude

While St. Paul waited to learn the fate of its Association franchise, trouble was brewing in Milwaukee, Indianapolis and Columbus.

The Milwaukee Ownership Mess

In Milwaukee there was a public legal fight over the ownership of the Brewers. Immediately after the close of the 1902 American Association season, president and co-owner of the franchise Harry D. Quin made an ultimatum to secretary and co-owner Charles S. Havenor to either buy or sell the club at a set price — the same price for either man. For some time there had been differences on how the ball club should be run, and these differences came to a head at the close of the season when Quin wanted to re-hire manager Billy Clingman. Havenor thought Clingman's salary demands were too high and looked for another manager.[1] The Brewers had been losing money throughout the season, and Havenor had been putting money into the club while Quin had stopped. Havenor now wanted to sell some unowned shares of stock to recover a portion of his losses.[2]

In October Harry Quin filed for and received an injunction against Havenor to prevent him from disposing of any stock in the Milwaukee Baseball Club. His suit claimed that on January 22, 1902, the Milwaukee Baseball Club was incorporated with $15,000 worth of stock: Quin subscribing to 7½ shares, Havenor 6½ shares, and Havenor's partner in a tailor firm, H.J. Bauman, one share. Over time Quin and Havenor each paid $6,000 and received six stock certificates. The suit further stated Havenor informed Quin of a September 19 meeting of the directors only the afternoon before, which Quin could not attend. At the meeting Havenor and Bauman passed by-laws providing for the calling in on the subscriptions of $2,000 of the outstanding capital stock. Quin claimed all the stock had already been subscribed, leaving

Harry Quin and Charles Havenor went to court over the presidency of the Milwaukee club, making public the club's internal problems (*Milwaukee Sentinel*, October 5, 1902).

nothing left to sell. Quin believed Havenor and Bauman's actions would prevent him from receiving his remaining one and one-half shares of outstanding Brewer stock. Also at this September 19 meeting Charles Havenor was appointed general manager of the baseball club. As Quin also owned Athletic Park where the Brewers played, he further claimed he was fearful Havenor and Bauman would dispose of the lease on the park and the franchise itself, selling it to a third party at the determent of his interest.[3]

Charles Havenor countered by having a hearing before a court commissioner, who examined Quin so that Havenor could elicit testimony on which to base his answer to the injunction.[4]

This hearing began on October 7, 1902. As Havenor's lawyer, W.J. Turner, questioned Quin on proceedings of the baseball club, Quin's attorney objected to the line of Turner's questioning. The court asked what the purpose of the questioning was. Turner answered that the club had lost money to the point of having no value, partly because Quin refused to put any more money into financing the ball club. He further stated Quin was making claims that were not shown to be in the minutes of the ball club's meetings. Turner then dropped this sensational statement: "We also expect to establish that Mr. Quin hoped to wreck the American Association by selling out the Milwaukee club to the Western League, its most bitter rival."

Quin responded to this accusation angrily: "It was no one connected with the Western League who offered to buy the club, and I told President Hickey of the American Association three weeks ago that I would still give my check for $4,500 for his [Havenor's] interest in the club. I did not tell Hickey who it was that wanted to buy, but said it was none of his business. Hickey then offered to loan me the money to pay my assessment, but I told him I was not a pauper."

Turner asked if the baseball franchise had any pecuniary value at the time it was turned into a corporation. Quin answered he believed it had a value of $15,000, but Havenor thought it was worth $20,000. To Turner's follow-up questions on the club's value, Quin would only say an offer had been made on the club about six weeks prior. The Brewer president testified the state of affairs between himself and Havenor was such that since July he had not been allowed to call meetings or be part of the management of the club. Quin related that on July 21 he gave Havenor $1,000 and told him he would not contribute more money to the club.

Harry Quin said he was notified of the meeting of the baseball organization on September 19 that was intended to call in subscriptions on stock. However, he decided not to attend because he had paid all his obligations and wanted to devote his time to his business and not baseball. Quin testified that on September 25 Havenor demanded money from him, and he answered by asking for the one and one-half shares of stock in the club he felt he was entitled to. Quin ended his testimony by saying he thought Havenor had mismanaged the club to the point where it had no value and he did not wish to continue business with his former partner.

The minutes of the meeting of September 19 were produced, showing the club lost $4,876.25 during the 1902 season. Of this, it showed Havenor put in an extra $2,926.25 and Quin $1,950. Havenor was looking for his partner to contribute $976 more to the fund. These amounts were to be considered as loans. As only $12,000 of the original stock subscribed had been paid, it was decided at the meeting new subscriptions were to be received for an amount not to exceed $2,000. According to the resolution passed, the stockholders present—Havenor and Bauman—were given the first privilege of subscribing for the stock at par. However, a further resolution was adopted calling on Havenor and Quin to pay $1,500 each upon their original subscription to stock, with the payment being required by September 30. At the meeting Havenor was given authority to borrow $5,000 to carry on business, in addition to hiring a manager and signing players for the 1903 season.[5]

The hearing was adjourned until the following week, during which time Charles Havenor announced he had signed Joe Cantillon as manager of the Brewers for 1903. That he was acting alone is confirmed in the newspapers, as neither Quin nor Bauman knew of the signing.[6]

The hearing continued on October 14, with Brewer president Harry Quin again on the stand. Havenor's attorney asked Quin if it was true he refused Havenor's request for money to meet obligations, and had told Havenor his stock was for sale at 50 cents on the dollar. Quin answered he never said his stock was for sale, but Havenor had told him it was. Quin said he asked Havenor to put a price on his stock. The attorney then asked Quin if he intended on putting any more money into the club. On the advice of his lawyer, Harry Quin refused to answer. Quin did say matters were so bad that communications from American Association President Hickey were going directly to Havenor, and he, as president of the club, was not even seeing them. When asked why he did not call a meeting of the stockholders to talk about the differences between himself and Havenor, the Brewer president said it would not have done any good, as Havenor ignored him completely.[7]

Attorney Turner asked Quin how Charles Havenor had mismanaged the club; Quin responded with a few examples. During the summer while Quin was on the road, he was informed Hugh Duffy's Western League Creams were doing much better in attendance than the Brewers, and Quin decided to admit ladies free to Athletic Park on weekdays to counter this. He sent word to Havenor and the press regarding the ladies' days promotion. Upon returning home, Quin went to the ballpark to find 15 or 20 women near the entrance at game time. When the Brewer president asked why they were not inside, the women said Havenor would not honor the report to admit them free of charge. Havenor said he would not allow these women into the park for free just because Quin wished it. Quin honored his free admission policy by paying for all the ladies that day. Another riff between the two men again concerned free passes. Havenor announced that for the 1903 season all people were to pay to get into the park to see games; this included reporters, police officers and city officials. Quin whole-heartedly disagreed with this policy. Yet another problem was with Havenor refusing Quin's wish to send a man east to sign some new players when the Brewers began falling out of the pennant race early.[8] [Havenor later denied this, saying there never was any suggestion to send a man east, for the simple reason there was no one to sign. No teams would sell a player to the outlaw American Association, and the Association refused to take contract jumpers.[9]]

The hearing ended with Turner asking Quin if the above disagreements happened only after Quin refused to put any more money into the club. Quin answered: "Well, it did start about that time. Havenor blamed me because the team was losing, and I told him to run it alone." Turner then inquired of the president: "Then you said you would not put any more money up to pay the debts of the club." Quin responded: "I said that I would not continue to do so unless Havenor sold out." "That is all I wanted to know," replied Turner, who folded up the papers spread out on the table before him and asked no more questions.[10]

Charles Havenor's attorney petitioned the court to have Quin's suit against his client dismissed, saying money from stock sale was needed to run the club. In his written statement to the court, Turner said Havenor had paid $6,000 for his stock over installments, and Quin $6,000. Of the twelve shares of stock paid for, six belonged to Quin and six to Havenor. Havenor claimed that over the next three months he advanced the corporation $3,700 to meet obligations; this sum was reduced at the September meeting to $2,926.25. From June 16 to August 1 Quin advanced $1,950. Quin believed he had now paid for his remaining one and one-half shares of stock, and demanded the stock be given to him. Havenor stated these sums were considered to be loans, not amounts paid on the stock subscription, as Quin believed they were. Havenor claimed there never was an authorization to issue more stock, and none but the 15 shares were ever authorized.

Havenor further claimed the Milwaukee baseball franchise had no material or pecuniary value. The American Association, in which the team played, was neither a corporation nor a partnership, only an arrangement whereby certain individuals who were engaged in the business of managing and operating baseball clubs had agreed with the other individuals to play games. It was held together by the goodwill of the various individuals, and if one or more of these persons withdrew, the organization would cease to exist. Thus the franchise could not be bought or sold, and could have no adequate consideration for the issue of the stock.[11]

Apparently as a show of good faith, Havenor told the *Milwaukee Sentinel* the next day that if the Brewers made a profit in 1903, Quin would be given an equal share of it, even though he refused to have anything to do with the club at this time. Havenor said he would not take advantage of the situation by voting himself and Bauman fat salaries.[12]

The injunction hearing to prevent Havenor from disposing of the stock was held on October 25, 1902. Dispositions were filed by James H. Turner, a partner in the law firm representing Havenor, and two stenographers from the firm, denying they attended any meeting of the Milwaukee Baseball Club held at the law offices on January 22, 1902, where a transfer of the American Association club to the Milwaukee Baseball Club for $15,000 was discussed. Quin had testified before the court commissioner that Havenor and Turner were in attendance and a stenographer was called in to draft a resolution authorizing the purchase at the price named.[13]

Judge Halsey listened to the testimony in his court. Havenor's lawyer, W.J. Turner, basically went down the same road as before, saying Quin would not pay into the club to liquate debts and pay the players' salaries. If his client had not loaned money to the club it would have been forced out of business. Quin's lawyer said if Havenor would be given approval to dispose of stock, his client would be put under a hardship and deprived of his position as president of the club. Judge Halsey dissolved the injunction preventing Havenor from disposing of stock, noting that in all stock companies it was usually necessary to keep buying stock in order to retain a controlling interest in the corporation. Notice of appeal to the state supreme court was immediately given by Quin's lawyer, and a stay of 30 days was granted, with the provision Quin post a $1,000 bond to indemnify Havenor against damages.[14]

On January 31, 1903, the Milwaukee Baseball Club held a meeting at the offices of Turner, Pease and Turner. Present were Charles Havenor and Henry Bauman; Harry Quin did not attend on advice of his lawyer. As Quin owned half the stock in the club, the stockholder's meeting was adjourned. However, a board of directors meeting was immediately called, as a majority of the board was present. A resolution was passed allowing the positions of president and treasury to be held by one man. Havenor was elected to the duel post. Bauman was elected vice president and Cornelius Corcoran, alderman of the city's third ward, elected secretary. The meeting was soon adjourned.

Quin maintained the election was not valid, as under state law a majority of stock was necessary for any election of officers. As he held 50 percent of the stock and was not at the meeting, he was still president, and Havenor was not entitled to the honor. Quin believed the law provided that stock could only be issued by authority of the president. As Quin stated he was still legally the president, that would not happen.

Havenor's lawyer said Quin's stand was entirely without any legal foundation. The attorney said the law Quin referred to read that the stockholders shall transact all the business except where otherwise specially provided by law, or by the articles of organization of the corporation. One of the articles in the Milwaukee Baseball Club's articles of corporation provided for the election of officers by the board of directors. Turner said Quin was still a stockholder and a director, but no longer an officer in the corporation.[15]

Harry Quin would lose this battle, and Charles Havenor became president of the Milwaukee Brewers. In May Quin lost his appeal to the Wisconsin Supreme Court. The high court held that the order for the sale of $2,000 in capital stock left 13 shares of the stock from which Quin could get seven and on-half shares, and that his interests were not prejudicial to his rights.[16]

However, the Milwaukee mess was not quite over. On July 2, 1903, Charles Havenor filed suit to collect damages for the enforcement of the injunction issued at the behest of Quin when it was in force during the appeal to the state supreme court.[17] Havenor continued his legal wrangling to get money from Quin but to no avail.[18] The *Evening Wisconsin* summed the situation up the best. "It has been a long inning game and when finished will have proved costly all around. Baseball and the courts do not go well together."[19]

Harry Quin would divest himself of interests in the Milwaukee Baseball Club, including Athletic Park, which he sold to Charles Havenor in June 1904.[20]

Sunday Baseball Issue in Indianapolis

The Indianapolis Hoosiers played their baseball games at Washington Park, located on East Washington and Gray streets, in the far eastern part of the city. A few years later the site would become the area where Wonderland Amusement Park would be located. Even though professional baseball was not allowed to be played on Sundays in Indiana, club owner William Watkins at first decided to play games on the Sabbath in Marion, Indiana, about 70 miles from Indianapolis. Only one game was played in this city, and for the rest of the season scheduled Sunday games in Indianapolis were either postponed or transferred to the opposing city's grounds.

In the spring of 1902 there had been talk in the state assembly of repealing the Sunday baseball law. Political managers said there was little chance it would come up, as no one from either party wanted it to be a campaign issue, thus delaying

William Watkins — The Hoosier owner fought a losing battle to play the team's Sunday games in Indianapolis.

the discussion until after the elections.[21] In December there was again talk of repealing or modifying the law.[22] The Methodist ministers of Indianapolis had come out against Sunday baseball, declaring it "one of the greatest sins of which men could be guilty." On the other hand, the local Retail Liquor Dealers' Association believed it a healthful and harmless enjoyment. Indianapolis mayor Charles A. Bookwalter, a Republican, said if he were nominated, Sunday baseball would be an issue, indicating he would be in favor of it.[23]

In February 1903 the bill to legalize professional Sunday baseball was due to come before the Indiana House. The original draft of the bill called for legalizing baseball only in the state's largest cities. But while the bill was pending, an amendment had been offered to drop this to cities with a population of more than 20,000. This alarmed some ministers and churches, and petitions were circulated calling for the bill to be voted down. It should be noted that several of the Catholic clergy were in favor of the bill, saying that Sunday was a day for healthful recreation, as well as worship, and that baseball furnished the best means of recreation to the largest percentage of people. Delegates from the towns of the Central League were even pushing for an amendment that would lower the city size to 17,000 to permit professional baseball on Sunday, which would then make it permissible in some of that circuit's cities. This would also enable Anderson and Muncie to host Sunday baseball. Many, including Watkins of Indianapolis, feared this proposed amendment would kill the entire bill.

On February 2 a Senate committee met to discuss the bill. Those in favor of the bill agreed to drop their opposition to population limitations, agreeing it should apply to all the cities in the Central League. Another senator thought the population limit should be 15,000, which would include his home territory, as well as Lafayette and Logansport.[24]

The bill legalizing Sunday baseball in cities with a population of more than 16,000, with a provision that games start after 2:00 P.M. and the sale of intoxicants forbidden on the grounds, passed the Indiana House of Representatives by a 60 to 21 vote.[25] However, the bill was defeated in the Indiana Senate by a vote of 24 to 23 on February 11. Two senators were absent, one, who was in favor of the bill, being ill. Senator O'Brien did not vote on the matter. He said he promised his wife, a good Methodist, he would never vote for the bill. Not being permitted to vote for it, and not wishing to vote against it, he declined to vote. "To Mrs. O'Brien, therefore, belongs the credit for the defeat of the bill." Even the senator who introduced the bill voted against it.[26] However, a story circulated that Indianapolis Owner Watkins and Central League president Charles W. Halderman had an understanding that the bill would include all the cities in the Central League, but at the last minute

Watkins lobbied so the bill was introduced in a way that it would only be for Indianapolis. The Central League owners then secured enough votes to kill the measure. When Halderman asked Watkins about this, the Indianapolis owner reportedly said he was "looking out for No. 1," agreeing to this late amendment rather than see the entire bill die.[27]

A new bill was immediately introduced calling for Sunday ball throughout the entire state of Indiana. A favorable report was made on February 16 to repeal the present law against Sunday baseball, but a motion to postpone the matter indefinitely was carried 23 to 16.[28] In March William Watkins was reported to be making another effort to have a Sunday baseball bill passed, again with no population limits. However, he soon gave up hope of any bill passing.[29]

In April the Sunday baseball issue came up yet again in Indianapolis. A petition by wage earners, who had no opportunity to see baseball games except on Sunday, was circulated through Indianapolis to allow Sunday ball. The petition finished with 32,000 signatures. It was hoped Mayor Bookwalter would instruct officers not to interfere with Sunday games.[30]

A Hoosier game was on the American Association schedule for April 26. When questioned if he would stop the game, Mayor Bookwalter answered in a political way. He said there would be no Sunday baseball in Indianapolis with his "consent," saying, "I could as easily consent to you murdering a man Sunday as I could to the playing of Sunday baseball." He was then asked if it was possible to play the game without his consent. The mayor answered: "You know, murders are committed without it." The mayor continued evasively: "Well, there may have been better hotel openings at French Lick than the one last week, but if there have I did not hear of it." The day before the scheduled Sunday game, the mayor said he had no personal objection to Sunday ball, but it was his duty to enforce the laws, and ordered police to stop the proposed game and arrest the players if the contest was started. When a judge issued a temporary restraining order prohibiting the Sunday game, filed by a property owner near the ballpark at the instance of the Indianapolis Ministerial Association, the game was transferred to Columbus.[31]

William Watkins continued transferring his scheduled home Sunday games to the opposing team's city. In May his lawyer filed a demurrer to the complaint, claiming if there was any nuisance, it was a public one for city officials to take on, not private individuals. The attorney for the property owners around the park, citing several cases, contended it was a private nuisance and therefore a cause for private action. The judge overruled the demurrer.[32]

The laws prohibiting Sunday ball and the rescheduling and shifting of games caused one major headache for the American Association at the end of

June. The scheduled Sunday, April 26, game was transferred from Indianapolis to Columbus with the understanding a game scheduled in Columbus would be transferred to Indianapolis. This game was to be April 30, but rain prevented play that day. It was agreed to reschedule the game for Tuesday, June 30. Looking forward, Columbus was scheduled to play a game in Indianapolis on Saturday, September 5, and two games on Sunday, September 6. The two teams agreed to play a double-header on September 5 and transfer the second game to Indianapolis on Monday June 29. A problem arose when the Columbus-Louisville game on June 28 was rained out in Louisville and rescheduled by the Louisville management for the next day. Columbus business manager Quinn told Louisville's George Tebeau of his team's arrangement with Indianapolis, but Tebeau insisted their rained-out game be played the next day. Quinn telegraphed American Association President Hickey for instructions but did not receive a reply. The Columbus team left for Indianapolis in the morning and the umpire forfeited the game to Louisville that afternoon. The Hoosiers and Senators did play in Indianapolis, the Hoosiers winning 4 to 3. To add to this, American Association President Hickey fined the Columbus club $500 for forfeiting the game, and ruled the Indianapolis-Columbus game did not count in the standings. Needless to say, neither Watkins nor Quinn were happy. After a meeting between Columbus president Thomas Bryce and Hickey, it was decided the forfeit would stand, but Bryce would not pay the fine.[33]

Watkins began to make arrangements to have his Sunday games played in Anderson, Indiana, a city about 40 miles northeast of Indianapolis. When the Anderson baseball franchise in the Central League was soon transferred to Grand Rapids, Watkins announced the scheduled Sunday games for Indianapolis would be played in Muncie.[34] The Muncie ministers were not happy about this and held a meeting to ask the Muncie police commissioner to visit the Indiana governor to find out whether Sunday baseball laws should be enforced.[35] Two games were played in Muncie in late June, with crowds of 2,500 and 1,300.[36] Watkins found rescheduling the Sunday games in Indianapolis into a double-header on Saturday more profitable. However, one more game was played in Muncie. On August 30 a Sunday crowd of 1,150 watched the Kansas City Cowboys beat Watkins' Hoosiers 9 to 6.

The Billy Clingman Contract Problem

The most interesting off-season item — which spilled into the 1903 playing season — in the American Association was the Billy Clingman situation, causing, as *Sporting Life* put it, "a peck of trouble, Methodist measure."[37]

Immediately after the 1902 season the Brewer skipper said he would not manage in Milwaukee again the next season, as management was refusing to pay him what he believed appropriate for a player-manager of his caliber. As discussed above, in late September the two Brewer owners, Harry Quin and Charles Havenor, were fighting over control of the club. Quin wanted to keep Clingman to manage for 1903, but Billy told him he wanted to go to a club where he did not have to manage. Quin gave him permission to negotiate with other teams. Havenor thought Clingman's salary demand was too high and wanted to hire another man to manage, while keeping him as a player. Havenor then offered Clingman a contract to play for the same salary he received in 1902. Then, without Quin's knowledge, Havenor hired Joe Cantillon as the 1903 Brewer manager.

Billy Clingman soon signed with the Columbus Senators, but Milwaukee insisted he was on its reserve list as a player, and demanded his return. Clingman claimed the Brewers had no legal claim to him because American Association contracts in 1902 had no reserve clause in them, and he had an agreement with Charles Havenor that his term of service with Milwaukee would only be for the 1902 season. Clingman said he felt honor bound to play with Columbus, having turned down a managerial job in Birmingham of the Southern League.[38] Havenor saw it differently. The Brewer co-owner replied that when he said he would not stand in Clingman's way to better himself after one year, it was with the understanding he would not sign with an American Association team.[39] Clingman's next move was to say he was not on the reserve list the Brewers sent to the American Association after the season. President Hickey's office produced the list and Clingman was indeed on the list, which had been written out by Clingman himself.[40]

Thus Clingman belonged to Milwaukee, according to the American Association, but Columbus claimed him for its team. In February a three-way trade was made in which the Minneapolis Millers secured pitcher Archie Stimmel from St. Paul for third baseman Billy Phyle, who was then traded to Milwaukee for Clingman. Phyle had jumped the Millers in 1902 to play in San Francisco, and had been placed on the suspended list. The trade had to be a three-way transaction because the infielder said he would return to California before dealing with Minneapolis. Milwaukee management had hoped the Millers would simply give up their claim so the Brewers could sign Phyle. However, president Edward A. Johnston of the Minneapolis club said: "Baseball is not a charitable institution, and as I did not notice any of the other clubs falling over themselves to help us out last season when we needed men badly, I do not see why we should drop our claim against Phyle or anybody else."[41]

Thomas Bryce in Columbus continued to claim Clingman belonged to him and said he would appeal to the National Board. For his part, Clingman said he would not go to St. Paul. Clingman began spring training with Columbus. At first American Association President Hickey decided not to intervene in the situation, letting George Lennon of St. Paul and Bryce work the matter out. But then Hickey notified all clubs in the American Association not to play Columbus should Clingman be part of the team.

Bryce threatened to take the case to court. On April 22 the Columbus club brought suit in Common Pleas Court of Franklin County against the other clubs of the American Association, President Hickey, the board of directors and umpires to restrain them in any way from interfering with his team playing Clingman. A temporary restraining order was granted and served on Toledo president Charles Strobel immediately. The Toledo-Columbus Opening Day game was scheduled for this same April 22. Hickey wired Columbus not to play the game. But with a large crowd in the park, Strobel decided to play the game, under protest. Columbus won the contest 2 to 0, Clingman at shortstop, collecting two hits.[42]

The Columbus management said Clingman would play even if they were forced to bring injunction proceedings in every city in the American Association. Hickey called a meeting of the clubs at his office in Chicago the next day, a meeting that Columbus management did not attend. After a discussion of the matter, it was decided the American Association would stand behind its president. Hickey ordered Columbus to refrain from playing Clingman, and a resolution was drawn up to notify Bryce that if he failed to comply with the constitution and by-laws of the Association, his franchise would be forfeited. Clingman played in Toledo on April 23, but remained out of the lineup after that.

On April 26 there was a meeting between Hickey, William Watkins, George Tebeau and Bryce. Hickey awarded the first Columbus-Toledo game to the Mud Hens. It was decided that Clingman would be awarded to St. Paul with the stipulation that St. Paul offer Clingman a contract within 15 days, at a salary equal to what he was contracted for in Columbus. Thomas Bryce said he would accept the decision, but Billy Clingman issued this statement: "Out of the many offers I have received I selected that of the Columbus Club as best suited in my needs. In the recent complications regarding my services I think my personal rights were entirely lost sight of. Rather than be compelled to fill an engagement to which I was never a part, and concerning which I was never consulted, I prefer not to obey the decree of the directors, and will go home to Cincinnati and stay there, with the hope that the directors will reconsider their action, which I am sure was not deliberative. I have no personal feeling against the officers of the St. Paul Club."[43]

St. Paul management sent Clingman a contract, but there was word he would be traded back to Columbus for two players. Clingman ended up staying with Columbus, as St. Paul waived its rights to him. On May 8 Walter Wilmot was fired as the Minneapolis manager, and arrangements made for Clingman to succeed him. However, Cincinnati of the National League, in addition to Detroit and Cleveland of the American League, wanted the shortstop. Columbus immediately traded Clingman and catcher Jack Slattery to Cleveland for 23-year-old Jack Thoney.[44]

Billy Clingman returned to Columbus later in the season. In late July the Senators needed to shore up their infield. Bryce secured waivers on Clingman from St. Paul, and started negotiations with Cleveland for the shortstop. Clingman had not played that well with the Blues, hitting .281 in 21 games while committing eight errors in the infield. Bryce soon purchased Clingman's contract from Cleveland, but it turned out deals had been made. Within weeks young Jack Thoney went back to Cleveland. It was reported as part of the deal that allowed Bryce to purchase Clingman (and pitcher Gus Dorner), the Columbus president would allow Cleveland to negotiate with third baseman Terry Turner — a player half of the major league clubs were after — for the next season. Cleveland soon signed Turner, putting a nice sum of money in Bryce's pocket.[45] Terry "Cotton Top" Turner would play in Cleveland the next 15 years.

Seven

♦ ♦ ♦ ♦

The 1903 Seasons

There were a number of managerial changes in both the Western League and American Association prior to the 1903 season.

In the American Association this changing began early. In August of 1902 Charles Strobel signed "Doc" Frank Reisling to a two-year contract at $350 a month to manage his Toledo Mud Hens for 1903. Reisling had started his minor league career in the Ohio–West Virginian League in 1897 before graduating to the Interstate League. In 1898 he pitched with Toronto in the Eastern League before joining Bristol of the Connecticut State League, where he also managed. After two more years in Bristol, Reisling played and managed in 1902 with the Hartford Senators of the Connecticut State League. At the 1902 winter meetings of this league, he was expelled for contract jumping and fined $100 for allegedly trying to induce Connecticut State League players to jump to the American Association. Reisling denied he was a contract jumper, saying his contract was voided with Hartford when that club failed to play him in July.[1]

In Columbus Thomas Bryce hired Frank J. Leonard of Lynn, Massachusetts, to manage his Senators for a $2,500 season salary. Leonard had extensive minor league managerial experience, having started his career in the New England Interstate League in 1888. In 1899 he began a four-year stint with Eastern League teams and managed in Worcester in 1902. Leonard was said to be an excellent judge of young players, having developed one or more for the big leagues every year he managed.

Billy Clymer was rehired in Louisville. William Johnston Clymer was entering his second year as manager of the Louisville team for George Tebeau. Clymer was born in Philadelphia in 1873, and played with the Athletics of the old American Association in 1891 for three games, going hitless in eleven at-bats. The young man found his niche in baseball, however, as a career minor leaguer. In the following years he played with Portland, Maine, of the New England League, before making the higher minors in Buffalo and Rochester of the Eastern League. He could be found at second base, shortstop

Seven. The 1903 Seasons 145

American Association leaders of the 1903 season. Players are as follows: 1. Hickey, 2. Bryce, 3. Watkins, 4. Strobel, 5. Gear, 6. Johnston, 7. Tebeau, 8. Havenor, 9. Leonard, 10. Clymer, 11. Cantillon, 12. Kelley, 13. Reisling, 14. Wilmot (*Spalding Baseball Guide*).

or center field. After a year with Wilkes-Barre, Clymer was sold to Kansas City of the old Western League, before returning to Wilkes-Barre to manage and play in 1900. In June of that year he again joined the Eastern League, this time in Toronto, and played the 1901 season in Buffalo of the Eastern. Tebeau picked Clymer to manage the Louisville Colonels in their first year in the new American Association. It was said Billy Clymer was a clever coach, resembling Arlie Latham in his glory days.[2]

Also rehired for a second season was Michael Kelley in St. Paul. The 27-year-old Kelley like Clymer, had also played only one season in the major leagues—1899 with Louisville of the National League, hitting .241 in 76 games as a first baseman. Kelley was also a career minor leaguer. A product of Maine, he started in the New England League in 1895 with the Augusta Kennebecs. After three years in this league he graduated to the Eastern League in 1898, playing with Rochester. In the years prior to signing on as

Michael Kelley—The career minor leaguer managed the St. Paul Saints to the 1903 American Association championship (Minnesota Historical Society).

Lennon's manager in St. Paul, Kelley played for Indianapolis in both the (minor) American League and Western Association, in addition to managing the Des Moines team in the Western League in 1901.

In Kansas City Dale Gear returned, also serving as a coach for the University of Kansas baseball team.[3] Walter Wilmot continued to manage his Minneapolis Millers, as did William Watkins in Indianapolis.

As covered in the previous chapter, Billy Clingman did not return to manage in Milwaukee, and Joe Cantillon was hired to skipper the Brewers. Cantillon, a former Western League and National League umpire, was currently managing an all-star team of major leaguers on a tour to the West Coast. Born in Janesville, Wisconsin, in 1861, Cantillon started his playing career in Green Bay in 1883. The next year, while still playing for Green Bay, he and a number of other players were arrested in that city for playing baseball on Sunday. Cantillion first appeared in the minor leagues in 1886 in Eau Clarie of the Northwestern League and played on teams in the Midwest before going to the West Coast to play in 1890. By 1894 he was back in the Midwest, playing with Western Association and Western League clubs, while playing in the winter in California. He managed the Dubuque club in 1895 and 1897. Joe had ties to Milwaukee in the 1890s, residing in the city for a while and having success operating a chicken farm in the suburb of Cudahy with Kid Speer and another player in 1899. In addition to having a reputation as a fine baseball man, Joe was a crowd pleaser. It was said he could amuse a crowd as well as anyone in the business with his many baseball yarns, which he had at his fingertips.[4] Cantillon would immediately begin signing players, as we shall see later in the chapter.

In the Western League Billy Hart resigned as Peoria's manager at the end of the 1902 season, saying he would stay with the Distillers as a player if the salary was satisfactory. Although he received some good offers from three American Association teams, in addition to the opportunity to manage in Birmingham of the Southern Association, he stayed with Peoria in 1903 to pitch. Former big league catcher Bill Wilson, who had caught for the Distillers in 1902, took over as manager/catcher for 1903. Wilson was a popular choice with the local fans, as it was said "if any man kin, Wilson kin" give Peoria an improved ball team for 1903.[5]

Hugh Duffy was rehired in Milwaukee to manage the Creams, but not before rumors floated that he would manage the new American League team in New York and another that he had been offered a job to manage the American League team in Washington. Duffy received an increase in his salary for 1903; he was making $3,400 for the season, a very good compensation for a minor league manager.

Charles "Kid" Nichols returned to manage the Kansas City Western Blue

Stockings after receiving a flattering offer to manage the St. Louis National League team. Billy Everitt also stayed at his job in Colorado Springs. Everitt was born in Fort Wayne, Indiana, in 1868. He first played professional ball with San Francisco of the California League in 1890. After a year with the Southern Association and one in the Western League, Everitt made it to the Chicago Colts in 1895, playing six years there in the infield and outfield, hitting .323. His time in 1901 was split between Washington of the new American League and Denver of the new Western League.

Joe Quinn stayed on for his second season as manager in Des Moines, and in Omaha William Rourke continued to manage his own club.

There was a managerial change in Denver. Parke Wilson left the Grizzlies, jumping to the Pacific Coast League and receiving one-third interest in the Seattle team. It was said there was little weeping upon his departure. He had never been popular in Denver, and was considered a failure as a field director.[6] Thomas Delahanty took over the Denver team. The 31-year-old second baseman was a popular choice since he was considered the best all-around player in the Western League and "a proven good general on the field."[7]

St. Joseph also lost its manager to the West Coast, as Bryon McKibben signed with Tacoma of the Pacific Northwest League. George Rohe would take over the reins of the Saints in 1903, while also continuing his job as the third baseman. There had been some dispute earlier over Rohe. It was reported that the St. Joseph third baseman had been signed by Joe Cantillon of the Milwaukee American Association Brewers, but it was unclear if he was signed before or after the peace agreement between the two minor leagues.[8] Rohe would be held in high esteem by his team and the St. Joseph fans, as he was a heads-up ball player and a thorough gentleman who believed the public wanted clean baseball and not the rowdy ball found in the league.[9]

On December 7, 1902, the *Milwaukee Sentinel* reported the eight American Association clubs had signed 136 players for 1903. Most clubs had more than enough players signed to fill a team. For example, pennant-winning Indianapolis had 17 players under contract. Toledo had 21 players signed, and Kansas City had 18 signatures on contracts. The 1902 pennant runner-up Louisville had 19, as did Minneapolis. New manager Frank Leonard in Columbus announced that he had 29 players signed for the 1903 season, most of the new players from the California, Eastern and New York State leagues. St. Paul tallied only nine players, and Milwaukee had none on the list.

One of the reasons so many players were signing was the impending peace between the National League and American League. As a *Sporting News* correspondent wrote in December: "The majority of players are out for the money and go after it strong. As a consequence high prices are the rule and not the exception. The man who has his name to a contract before peace comes will be to the good for the season of 1903. By the close of the playing season the magnates will be the dictators and will go the naming of salaries. It will surely come."[10]

A few American Association teams were beginning to make wholesale changes in their rosters. By mid–December Walter Wilmot announced that he had signed 26 players for his Minneapolis team, about 12 more than he could use. The list had many new players, with Wilmot saying the old players were not passed over because of their inability to play, but merely to get younger and new faces on the team. One name missing was Big Perry Werden, who had been a fixture on the Minneapolis team for many years.

Having fielded one of the stronger teams in the American Association in 1902, Louisville had been depleted of many of its star players by the major leagues. By late October it was reported that George Tebeau would lose up to nine players, mostly starters. Billy Clymer wasted no time getting players together to replace his lost stars for his 1903 team. He signed a "stonewall infield" with Bob Schaub, Peter Childs (1902 with Reading), Sutor Sullivan and Pete Cassidy (1902 in Providence).[11] However, Cassidy would return to the Eastern League to play in 1903.

In mid–December it was said Milwaukee's new manager Joe Cantillon — walking with a cane as a result of an accident in which the rig he and several players were in tipped over on a rough road one night in San Francisco[12] — had been very successful in signing players from the California League, where he was touring with an all-star team. One of the interesting cases of the California players Cantillon signed was that of Bob Unglaub. The 21-year-old infielder had been playing with Sacramento and signed with Cantillon in November. Three weeks later he "played the rubberleg," jumping back to the California League team. Two weeks after this, the same Unglaub decided to go back to the Brewers. Unglaub made a point to say he had signed with the Brewers before he made arrangements with the outlaw Sacramento club. If this were the case, he would evade the $1,000 fine he would face from the National Association for contract jumping.[13] To add to this situation, Unglaub was under reserve to Worcester of the Eastern League, where he had played before jumping to the California League. However, the Eastern League club waived all claims to the first baseman. Cantillon, meanwhile said he now had 14 men under contract, and within weeks that number jumped to 23.

* * *

As the American Association was not part of the National Agreement until January 1903, the two major leagues began taking players from American

Association teams at season's end. Most of these players were taken with no controversy. The Milwaukee Association Brewers lost ace pitcher Nick Altrock to the Boston Americans, the major league club paying him $600 a month. The Brewers also lost outfielder Bill Hallman to the Chicago White Stockings.[14]

Louisville lost shortstop Lee Tannehill, pitcher Patsy Flaherty, and 30-game winner Dave Dunkel to Chicago of the American League. The Association's top hitter, John Ganzel, who would contract smallpox at his home in Grand Rapids that offseason, signed with the new New York club of the American League.[15]

Some transactions were controversial. Frank Bonner, who had finished 1902 with Louisville, on September 29 signed with Boston of the National League. Bonner had jumped from the Toronto Eastern League club to play for the Philadelphia Athletics in 1902. After the second baseman was cut by Connie Mack in June, George Tebeau signed him on July 9 for the remainder of 1902 and 1903 for his Louisville club, giving him a $200 advance. Tebeau said he would be willing to sell the player to Boston for $1,000, a price deemed too high for the Beaneaters. Initially the Boston press and public were not in favor of Bonner in their town because of his contract-jumping status. However, in February National League president Harry Pulliam promulgated Bonner's contract, and he would start 1903 with the Beaneaters, even though Boston manager Al Buckenberger admitted the evidence showed the player belonged to Louisville. Perhaps as a matter of pride, Louisville suspended "the human flee" in May.[16]

The Western League also lost the usual amount of players that a minor league did to the major leagues through sales and drafting. The National League St. Louis club purchased Mordecai Brown from Omaha, and Frank Owen went to the Chicago White Stockings. Hugh Duffy in Milwaukee lost pitcher Merle Adkins to the New York Highlanders. Denver lost pitcher Henry Schmidt to Brooklyn. Schmidt had jumped Denver to the California League the previous year but now was back on Denver's reserve. Connie Mack had made arrangements to secure the pitcher for his Athletics from D.C. Packard "for favors," but Schmidt would pitch in the Bronx, winning 22 games.[17]

* * *

After the peace settlement between the Western League and the American Association, a number of the players who had signed contracts or were on the reserved lists of the American Association teams were either signed or on the reserve lists of other clubs in the National Association. It was soon obvious that many disputes would have to be settled by the National Association's board. Certainly not all the disputed cases can be discussed, but some of the more interesting and controversial will be given an outline here.

One of the first player disputes to arise after the American Association was admitted to the National Association was the case of Claude Berry. The catcher had signed a contract with Indianapolis on October 20, 1902, to play with the Hoosiers for 1903. However, Berry had signed a two-year contract covering 1902 and 1903 with Dallas. The Indianapolis argument was that the Texas League had been organized for only one year, and that Berry had requested and obtained his release by the Dallas manager on September 14, 1902. The National Board ruled that even though the Texas League had closed early, its membership had not lapsed, and Berry was awarded to Dallas, where he would play in 1903.[18]

The Columbus Senators lost Jack Toft to Toronto of the Eastern League in a deal perhaps not entirely above the table. Manager Frank Leonard signed the catcher on October 23 for a handsome salary, plus $100 in advance money, before the peace treaty between the minor leagues. Toft claimed he had not signed a contract with Toronto and would not because that club had not given him what he believed to be his share of receipts for some exhibition games played after the regular season. Then Toronto manager Ed Barrow claimed Toft had signed with the Maple Leafs on September 23. It was thought by American Association people "that the Barrow contract, like the marriage license in a certain case, was dated back to cover accidents." Despite an affidavit from President Bryce of Columbus relating the contract signing and advance money, the National Board awarded Toft to the Maple Leafs, based on the player's affidavit that he had signed with Toronto first.[19]

Another case before the National Board with controversy involving the Eastern League, this time involving Louisville, was that of Peter Cassidy. Louisville had submitted an affidavit claiming the player was under contract prior to October 29, 1902, but Providence produced an affidavit saying that the player had called the Eastern League offices asking that his services be transferred from the Providence club to another team other than Louisville. Providence also produced letters from Cassidy dated October 31 and November 5 seeking his release from Providence in order to sign with another club. Thus, the Providence club believed it showed from this affidavit and letters that Cassidy had not signed a contract with Louisville. Even though there was a signed contract from 1902 with Louisville, the player was assigned to Providence by the National Board in February. Louisville manager Billy Clymer was sure there had been "some lobby work done" in the case. Clymer suspected Cassidy wanted to be traded to Jersey City of the Eastern League, a club willing to pay the infielder what he wanted.[20] The decision in the Toft and Cassidy cases made some, observers, including people outside the American Association such as H.C. Merrill from Wilkes-Barre, suspect that the National Board was showing favoritism to the Eastern League.

Indeed, Cassidy did sign with Jersey City. In March the case took on a more sinister tone. Thomas Murnane of the National Association sent a letter to the *Chicago Record-Herald* claiming Cassidy told Secretary Farrell of the National Association that manager Billy Clymer coaxed him to swear that he signed a Louisville contract earlier than he actually did, when the contract was actually signed after the peace agreement between the minor leagues. It was said Cassidy produced evidence to prove this statement. *The Sporting News* was blunt in its opinion:

Pete Cassidy — His contract assignment created a good deal of friction between the American Association and National Association of Professional Base Ball Clubs in the 1902-03 offseason.

> If the confession of Cassidy ... establishes that Clymer was guilty of subornation of perjury he should not be permitted to play with a National Association club. If the investigation shows that a club owner of the American Association was privy to the conspiracy, he should be as severely punished as the agent whom he employed. The National Board can not do the game a greater service than by laying bare the facts in the Cassidy case and inflicting an adequate penalty on every one whose connection with the infamous transaction is proven beyond a reasonable doubt. After the National Association's highest tribunal has finished with the affair, a transcript of the evidence should be turned over to the prosecuting attorney of the county in which the affidavit was made by Cassidy.... Clymer stands high in base ball and business circles. He is a player and manager of ability and should take immediate steps to clear himself of the charge contained in the Cassidy confession.[21]

H.C. Merrill came to Clymer's defense. He wrote that he had talked to Clymer on October 25, and that the Louisville manager told him Cassidy had accepted terms and he was mailing his contract. At the time Clymer asked Merrill not to give out the names of the players Louisville had signed due to the still-outlaw status of the American Association. A few days later Clymer wrote a letter to Merrill saying that he had heard from Cassidy, who wanted to play for him. Further, in November Clymer had told Merrill the names of all the players on his team, which included Cassidy. Citing some other inconsistencies in the case, Merrill said Cassidy's story was "surely as full of holes as a sieve."[22] Louisville appealed to the National Board to reopen the case but was turned down.[23]

There was another dispute over pitcher-outfielder Hugh Hill, who had won 22 games with Nashville in 1902. After the season Hill was sold to Cleveland of the American League, but he said he would not recognize the sale and would play for Kansas City in the American Association, signing there. In May he was released from his Cleveland contract, and the Kansas City Blues of the American Association claimed he had previously signed with them. Hill, meanwhile, signed and played with Nashville of the Southern League. In fact, in his first game there he hit two balls over the fence for home runs. Hill was a very popular player in Nashville, as this account will tell: "When Hill made his second homer and was going to the bench, a perfect shower of coins fell on him from the bleachers and grand stand. He received by actual count $62.35, and more applause than was ever given any player in the history of the game around these parts."[24] Kansas City's Dale Gear claimed Hill belonged to him, and appealed to the National Board. Secretary Farrell of the National Board advised Nashville president William Kavanaugh the player belonged to K.C. and that he had to play there. Kavanaugh advised his manager not to play Hill until the matter was settled.

The matter went before the National Board in July. The testimony showed that on October 27, 1902, the Kansas City team signed and paid advance money of $25 to pitcher Hugh Hill, whose name appeared on the reserve list of Nashville of the Southern League. Hill signed in November with Nashville. Dale Gear gave a sworn statement that he saw a telegram from Nashville manager Newt Fisher dated November 14, stating that Hill accepted the Nashville offer. The Kansas City club also introduced a letter from Hill telling Fisher he had signed with Kansas City a month before he signed with Nashville. Nashville submitted no evidence at the hearing, and K.C. was awarded the player.[25]

This did not stop the controversy. Hill, who had been tearing up the Southern League and was hitting .416 in mid–July, refused to abide by the National Board's decision and reportedly signed with an independent team in Huntsville, Alabama. Kansas City next sold Hill's contract to Birmingham of the Southern League in late July. Nashville President Kavanaugh insisted the player was the property of Nashville, and he would play in Nashville or nowhere in organized ball. Farrell of the National Board advised Kavanaugh that Hill belonged to Kansas City. Kavanaugh then made arrangements to trade Hill to the Washington Senators, but the player went to Kansas City until the end of the season, when he was picked up by the Cincinnati Reds.

Charles Strobel in Toledo had among the most difficult situations with players jumping contract and disputes. First, he was forced to give up catcher Patrick O'Connor to Springfield of the Connecticut State League, where the young catcher had first signed. The Toledo owner also signed third baseman William O'Hara, but Syracuse claimed the player, saying Strobel signed him after the peace conference in New York. Strobel reported he had a signed contract from the player dated September 25. The National Board awarded O'Hara to Syracuse. Dissatisfied with the decision, O'Hara jumped to the outlaw Pacific Coast League. Pitcher Edwin Quick had pitched for Spokane in 1902, and the management there claimed he had instead signed a contract with them for 1903. The pitcher said he had signed no contract and signed with Toledo for $250 a month, transportation, and a bonus for every game he would win during the 1903 season. Quick's case went before the board of the National Association in January and the pitcher was awarded to Toledo.[26] Before the season started, Quick jumped the Mud Hens and signed with Portland of the Pacific Northwest League, claiming Strobel had refused to give him his stipulated advance money.

The most interesting case of jumping from the Toledo team was that of Jack Burns. In January it was reported the second baseman had jumped to the San Francisco club of the Pacific National League, a league in the National Agreement. Burns had been playing on the West Coast, and Strobel explained why: "Burns followed me for two nights to give him the privilege of going to the coast. The team was in bad shape and had no chance to win games, so I gave him permission to go if he would sign a contract for the season of 1903 at an increased salary over what he was getting. I received several letters from him thanking me for the favor of letting him go to earn the money he has, and he promised faithfully to return."[27] Strobel had been sympathetic to the player, whose brothers were out of work because of a coal strike in Pennsylvania, and advanced Burns money every month to send to his mother.[28] A little later it was reported that Burns married a girl in San Francisco whose father "has several varieties of money." Jack wrote that his father-in-law had purchased him a fine cottage in the city, and did not want to return from the West Coast to play baseball. Burns also said the Toledo owner had told him he could stay on the West Coast if he liked, which Strobel denied.[29] The case would go to the National Board, which ruled in favor of the San Francisco club, where Burns played the 1903 season.

Strobel even came out on the wrong side of a player dispute in a decision from his own league's president. Outfielder Dan Hoffman left the Philadelphia Athletics in July because he was "tired of warming the bench, and preferred active work." Hoffman had played the previous year with Springfield of the Connecticut League, and that club sold him to Connie Mack's Athletics in

February. Strobel claimed he had signed the outfielder in August of the previous year and thus had claim to him, but American Association President Hickey ordered Hoffman suspended from the Toledo team. The matter was settled when Hoffman voluntarily returned to Philadelphia.[30]

Of course, American Association clubs did not come out on the wrong end of player dealings every time. Elmer Meredith, who had jumped Denver in 1901 and played 1902 in California, accepted terms with Little Rock of the Southern League in December 1902. The Milwaukee Brewers claimed that Meredith had been signed by them prior to October 29, and the National Board awarded the pitcher to Milwaukee. However, it was thought odd by some that Meredith later said at that time he had been unsigned and was somewhat nervous as to his fate for 1903. No further claims were made, and Meredith went on to win 21 games with the Brewers.

Another case involving Little Rock and the American Association was that of Frank Martin. The second baseman had played with Little Rock in 1902 but was secured by Louisville from that club in the winter. After a few games with Louisville, Martin was turned over to Minneapolis. The terms of the peace agreement provided that if a player did not make good with his new team, he would be returned to his original team. National Association Secretary Farrell saw Martin going to Minneapolis as meaning he had not made good with the Colonels. Farrell thus awarded the player back to Little Rock. However, at a meeting of the owners of the American Association, it was decided that under no circumstance would Martin be returned to Little Rock, even if it meant the American Association would break away from the National Association of Professional Baseball Leagues.[31] Martin remained with the Millers, playing in 125 games and hitting only .178.

George Lennon in St. Paul signed catcher Elmer Pierce, pitcher W.J. Davis and pitcher Ted Corbett (real name Theodore Chapleske[32]), all of the Sioux Falls team, without the formality of drafting them. The Canary management filed a protest with the National Board. All three would play games with St. Paul in 1903.

Omaha asserted that it had first right to pitcher James Garfield Durham, born October 7 1881, and signed by the Kansas City American Association team. The National Board upheld the contract Durham had signed with Kansas City on October 21, 1902, and awarded the player to the American Association team. As Omaha had purchased Durham from Cedar Rapids, the National Board recommended that if the Cedar Rapids club had received any money from the sale, it had to be returned to the Omaha club.

The Milwaukee American Association club also signed outfielder Frank Hemphill, who had not been given his release from Colorado Springs. Thomas

F. Burns, owner of the Colorado Springs team, said there was a point to be made here: "I will not deny at all Hemphill doesn't stand much chance of playing with the local team next season, but he will wait until he gets my permission before he leaves. I have something to say where these men play that are on my reserve list, that is if they wish to remain in organized ball."[33] The National Board ruled Hemphill belonged to Colorado Springs, but the outfielder jumped to Seattle of the Pacific Coast League rather than report back to the Millionaires. Milwaukee gave up its claim to Hemphill, but after the season had started, Brewer manager Joe Cantillon persuaded him to return from the Pacific Coast, and the outfielder played the remainder of the 1903 season in Milwaukee.

One player contract the American Association won in dispute is noteworthy not for the playing of the player, but for his character. Ernest Crabill, a 26-year-old pitcher, was claimed by both Binghamton of the New York State League, where he had played the previous two seasons, and Columbus of the American Association. He was awarded to Columbus and signed with the Senators (wittily called the "Discoveres" by one newspaper man[34]) for $250 a

Frank Hemphill — This outfielder would jump to Seattle rather than play in Colorado but ended up in Milwaukee (Historic Photograph Collection/Milwaukee Public Library).

Ernest Crabill — The 26-year-old Columbus pitcher was an ordained minister. Rather than pitch on Sundays, he spoke to Y.M.C.A. and mission associations (*Milwaukee Sentinel*, July 26, 1903).

month. What set Crabill apart from other ball players was that he was an ordained minister. When spring training began, the Reverend Crabill resigned the pulpit at Halsted, Pennsylvania, where he had taken over some months earlier when the former pastor died. The Reverend Crabill told his congregation that under no circumstances would he play Sunday ball or even appear on the grounds. He would spend this day speaking for YMCA and mission associations in the cities his team was playing. Pitcher Crabill — sometimes referred to as "Deacon" or "Preacher" in the press — would finish with an 8 and 10 record with Columbus in 1903, and was able to "find his text in the troubles of Job the days he [got] his trimmings," according to *Sporting Life*'s light-hearted assessment of his season.[35]

The American Association also had disputes over players in its own league. In Milwaukee Joe Cantillon signed Andy Oyler, who had played 23 games with Baltimore in 1902. Minneapolis also had a signed contract with the player. The infielder explained he had received offers from both clubs on the same day. He relayed his acceptance to Walter Wilmot in Minneapolis by mail and telegraphed Cantillon the same day. American Association president Thomas Hickey awarded the player to the Millers after the Minnesota club presented affidavits that showed Oyler first agreed to play with the Millers.[36] In February the Brewers asked Hickey to reopen the case because they had additional evidence, but Oyler stayed in Minneapolis as the Millers' regular shortstop through the 1909 season.

Milwaukee was involved in yet another inter-league player dispute when the Brewers signed Bob Wood, recently released by Cleveland of the American League. George Tebeau in Kansas City apparently had some inside word that the veteran catcher was to be let go by the Cleveland Blues and claimed him before he was even released. The action violated the rules of the American Association, and Wood went on to play with Milwaukee.

In the Western League clubs also had problems with contract jumpers and losing reserve players. Des Moines lost veteran Jim "Ducky" Holmes, who jumped his reserve to sign with Washington of the American League. Holmes had not signed with Des Moines but had given his word to Joe Quinn that he would return to him. After the first of the year, word was about that Wally Hollingsworth of Colorado Springs would jump to California to play ball. Colorado Springs owner Thomas Burns said Hollingsworth probably would not be in a Colorado Springs uniform in 1903, but as he was on his reserve list, Hollingsworth could not leave without his consent, and Burns would see that the player was blacklisted from organized baseball. Hollingsworth went to play shortstop for Los Angeles of the Pacific National League, obtaining the sobriquet of "Hard Hitting Holly."[37]

It was reported that some questionable methods were being used to sign players away from the Western League. Reports later in the summer of 1903 detailed how two Denver players, Gus Dundon and Charlie Jones, were courted by the American League, with help from the American Association's Joe Cantillon. In the fall of 1902 Chicago White Stockings owner Charles Comiskey sent Cantillon out west to sign the two Denver Grizzly stars. The contracts called for $500 in advance money by November 1, or the contracts would be void. When the time came and the money had not, the two wrote to Cantillon looking for their money or their releases from the contracts. Cantillon told the players to wait and they would get their money. When Dundon and Jones had not received their advance money by November 20, they decided to sign with Denver. Later in the season Dundon jumped his Denver contract to finish the season with Comiskey's White Stockings. After the season both men would be awarded to Comiskey by the National Board.[38]

1903 American Association Season

The 1903 American Association baseball season was about to begin, and eight managers knew their club would win the pennant. A *Milwaukee Sentinel* baseball writer gathered what each manager had to say about his team.

MANAGER WATKINS, INDIANAPOLIS: We won the pennant last year and we are a whole lot stronger this year. When the end comes Indianapolis will be in her usual place in front. There will be no keeping us away.

MANAGER CANTILLON, MILWAUKEE: It's a cinch that Milwaukee is at last to have a pennant. I've got the pitchers, the hitters, and the fielders, and if we don't land first place it will be because the team drops dead from running so fast.

MANAGER KELLEY, ST. PAUL: This is the year that we don't break. By the middle of the season there will be no claimants in the field except St. Paul. I think any unprejudiced man will have to admit that the Saints are the strongest on paper and we will be just as strong on the diamond. There's nothing to it.

MANAGER GEAR, KANSAS CITY: It isn't a case of wanting to win the pennant this year; it's a case of having to win it, and what has to be will be, you know. No other place than first will do us.

MANAGER TEBEAU, LOUISVILLE: I am an old hand at winning pennants. I should have had the rag last season, but you can bet your little dish of breakfast food that I will win it this year. Indianapolis, or no other team, can slip ahead of us through an accident.

MANAGER LEONARD, COLUMBUS: With the team we've got here I would consider it a disgrace not to win the pennant. How you can figure any other club for first honors I don't see. We've got the goods and we are going to deliver them.

MANAGER REISLING, TOLEDO: Yes, Toledo is going to win the pennant and thereby furnish the surprise of the season. We were last, last year, and the order will be turned squarely around. No kidding; we will take the rag. People don't know how strong a team we have. But you bet they will find out.

MANAGER WILMOT, MINNEAPOLIS: This may be my last season as a manager, and I am going to make it memorable by winning one more pennant. The people up here want the pennant, and I haven't the heart to disappoint them. The Millers are a 3 to 1 shot for first place, and this isn't any bum steer.[39]

Seven. The 1903 Seasons

The 1903 American Association season opened on April 22. Despite very inclement weather, 3,000 attended an exciting game in Louisville, seeing the Louisville Colonels score two runs in the bottom of the ninth to tie the score, only to have the Indianapolis Hoosiers score two in the tenth inning to take the contest, 4 to 2.

George Tebeau had made a great number of improvements at Eclipse Park during the offseason. Even though attendance had been about 150,000 in 1902, he had to turn people away constantly due to a lack of grandstand seats. To increase seating Tebeau wanted to make a double-deck grandstand behind the plate area, in addition to extending it down the right and left benches. He soon found he could not add another story to the grandstand, but did extend it down the lines and also enlarged the bleachers. With these seating increases, rebuilding of fences, painting, new dressing rooms under the stands for both teams, and other improvements, it was estimated that Tebeau put $10,000 into the park.

Kansas City had an Opening Day crowd of 4,000 to witness the home team's 8 to 4 victory over the Minneapolis Millers. Dale Gear's Cowboys showed off their new uniforms, still the traditional blue, but now sporting stockings, caps and belts of steel gray, in addition to gray coats with blue trimming.[40]

George Tebeau had been forced to build a new park in Kansas City for the 1903 season. He had hoped to play again in Exhibition Park, but the rent was far too high — the rent on Exhibition Park and the grounds he had already leased would run to $5,000 a year. In addition the land was in litigation, and street improvements were being considered. Even if these obstacles could be overcome, it was thought the needed improvements would include more than building a new ballpark.

In November 1901 Tebeau had secured a 10-year lease on grounds at East 20th Street between Olive and Prospect Avenue. Much grading needed to be done at this location, as the land was as much as 30 feet higher on the west side than the east side of the grounds, where a gully also ran. When Tebeau first purchased the land, the western portion was a cornfield, while the eastern part of the grounds had some immense trees several little shacks on it. A new park was planned but not built at that time. In spring 1903 Tebeau decided to build at this location. He said he would make $10,000 in improvements, including bleachers that would seat 4,500, in addition to a single-decked grandstand seating 3,500. Tebeau's new park was only a few blocks from the Western League park, and both parks were a distance from the business center of Kansas City. However, both were easily reached by several streetcar lines, so it was thought neither had a distinct advantage.

Work progressed nicely on the new park, but one major change occurred during construction. It was decided to lengthen left field several feet by cutting off seven rows of bleacher seating. With this it would be harder to hit home runs out of the park. Before the new park opened for baseball in April, it was decided a popular vote by the fans would be taken to name the park. The *Kansas City Journal* ran the contest, with Association Park winning with 6,149 votes. Not far behind were Blue Field (5,938 votes) and Gear Park (4,764).[41]

About 1,800 attended Opening Day in Toledo, where the Mud Hens lost to Columbus 2 to 0; the game would be tossed out because Columbus played Billy Clingman, an ineligible player. (See previous chapter for details.) The American Association's fourth home opener was in Milwaukee, where very cold weather kept the attendance down to around 1,000. The Brewers won the contest 10 to 7, which featured eight doubles, two triples and a home run.

There would be a second forfeit in this opening week, as on April 25 Toledo refused to continue play in the third inning when a runner was allowed for an injured Columbus player. Incidentally, Toledo was leading the contest at the time, 4 to 2.

The circumstances around this second forfeit are interesting as they highlight some of the differences from the game in 1903 and today. Columbus second baseman Fred Raymer had reached first base on an error. He then stepped off the bag for a substitute runner. As Raymer stepped from the bag, Toledo first baseman Red Owens tagged him and claimed Raymer was out because he had not obtained permission from the Toledo captain to have a substitute runner. Raymer and John McMakin, who was umpiring the game, claimed there had been an understanding before the game that a runner could be substituted for Raymer each time he reached base, as the player had a lame knee. Toledo manager Doc Reisling denied such an agreement, although there had been no objection when George Fox ran for Raymer in the first inning. McMakin waited the allotted five minutes for Toledo to continue play, then forfeited the game to the Senators. John McMakin was a pitcher for the Columbus Senators who was, filling in as the game umpire. American Association President Hickey had ordered regular umpire Jack Haskell not to report to Columbus but instead go to Indianapolis, as the A.A. boss was upset over the Columbus handling of the Billy Clingman situation. Then, in another twist, the secretary of the Columbus club announced his team would not accept the forfeit and would give Toledo a chance to play the game over on an open date.[42]

The first managerial change in the American Association in 1903 came early, on May 8, when Walter Wilmot was fired from his position as the head of the Minneapolis Millers. The Millers had lost their first eleven games, and were now dead last with a 2 and 13 record. At first it was said Billy Clingman, still assigned to Columbus, would succeed Wilmot, and that St. Paul would waive its claim to Clingman. However, Detroit and Cleveland of the American League wanted Clingman and nixed this possibility. Club president and majority stockholder Edward Johnston, who had been taking a more active role in signing players for the Millers, placed catcher George Yeager in charge of the team on the field. Within weeks Wilmot was hired as manager of the Butte, Montana, club, where his team would be the champions of the Pacific National League.

The American Association adopted the foul-strike rule in 1903 (the Western League had adopted it in 1902). With this rule, balls hit into foul territory before the batter had two strikes on him counted as strikes. Prior to this, a foul ball hit with no strikes or one strike on the batter simply was not counted. Fans and a few managers were initially against the rule. George Tebeau was an outspoken critic of the new rule, echoing what others felt. The Louisville owner felt it was a good rule for the lower minor leagues, as the players in those leagues were "inclined towards football on the diamond" by booting the ball around. The foul-strike rule could help keep scores down in these leagues. But in the higher minors and major leagues, he thought it gave too much advantage to the pitcher. He felt people did not come to the park to see two-hit games when the pitcher was not deserving of the honor. Under the old rule, a two-hit game was something to be talked about; now the pitcher would have the two-hitter at the unjust expense of the batter.[43]

As the season rolled on, scores were not affected that much. In its June 6 issue, *Sporting Life* reported there had already been 18 games in which one team had scored 13 or more runs. A fine example of the rule not hurting the batter was the May 19 game in Minneapolis. The Millers beat the Toledo Mud Hens 24 to 2, rapping out 12 singles, 12 doubles, three triples and a home run. That same day across the river, Frank Leonard's Columbus Senators beat St. Paul 15 to 7, collecting 14 hits to the Saints' 16. The early batting averages of American Association players also showed that hitters were holding their own. Averages published on June 7 listed 25 players who had appeared in 15 games or more with averages higher than .300. Bob Wood of Milwaukee (.451), Tom McCreery of Minneapolis (.415) and Mike Roach of Columbus (.400) led the parade.[44]

There was one very sad incident to report in the early season of 1903. While the Milwaukee Brewers were in Kansas City, third baseman Bob Unglaub received a telegram that his wife of three months was at the point of death. Unglaub left the game in the fourth inning and rushed to the train depot, catching the first train for Milwaukee. His wife died at their home three hours before his arrival in Milwaukee. Unglaub no doubt found some inner peace in the fact that he was a devout Christian and in his spare moments essayed missionary work in an attempt to convert his teammates.⁴⁵

In an effort to cut costs, on May 20 President Hickey ordered the American Association clubs to reduce their rosters to 13 players by June 1. Some believed this was a mistake, as 14 players allowed for four pitchers, an extra catcher and a utility man. If someone got hurt or sick, a club now would be compelled to shove a pitcher or catcher somewhere in the field. It was thought the American Association should offer the best baseball it could to its patrons at all times.

On May 28 Milwaukee sat on top of the American Association standings with an 18 and 9 record, mostly due to a 12-game winning streak in mid-month. Indianapolis was close behind with 19 wins and 11 losses. St.

Bob Unglaub — A devout Christian who had a mean steak in games, he lost his wife during the 1903 season (Library of Congress).

Paul remained within striking distance with 16 wins against 13 losses. All five remaining teams in the Association were under .500. One drawback in this early season was wet weather, especially in the two cities with competing teams. The Milwaukee Brewers led the Association in rain postponements with five. Although Dale Gear's Kansas City team had only one postponement, the constant rain had made the grounds "in much better condition for a canoe race than base ball."⁴⁶

As the season rolled on, Minneapolis played great ball. Since changing managers, the team was playing superb ball, and on June 5 was up to 18 wins and 21 losses. The Millers were also drawing better crowds than any other team in the American Association.

On June 11 Frank Leonard was forced to resign as manager of Columbus, owing to friction with the players. Leonard was being blamed by the players for the team's poor showing, and his continued chiding of their shortcomings did not sit well with them. The Senators were in seventh place at the time with a 15 and 26 record. Team captain and center fielder Jimmy Bannon took charge of the players on the field. Bobby Quinn, who had been associated with Columbus baseball in the past, became the business manager of the club.⁴⁷

The Columbus Senators were having a rather disappointing season on the field, but owner Thomas Bryce did come up with an idea new to baseball that spring. Bryce created a room under the grandstand "for the accommodation of those of too tender years to know the exceeding joy of a home-run swipe or the fanning out of an opposing batsman with the bases full. While above there will be the noise of the leather-lunged and, also, of the velvet-lunged, the clapping of hands, both horny and fair, and the general pandemonium that results from an issue successfully met, below there will be color supplements, blocks, toy engines and nipples and a white-aproned governess to wipe away tears and furnish goo-goo talk." Baby rooms had been installed in churches, theaters and even the World's Fair, so Bryce thought that if mothers attended baseball games, the sport certainly could not fall by the wayside in Columbus.[48]

The St. Paul Saints came to Milwaukee on June 26, losing the opening game of the series 5 to 1. Off the field the two teams had a narrow escape from death that night when a fire started in a tailor shop and spread to the Davidson Hotel — "accompanied by a terrific explosion" — where the players stayed. Brewer catcher Bob Wood, who had been sitting in front of the hotel, telephoned in the alarm and then ran through the hotel rousing the players and guests. The players "had to dress and pack hastily and run for their lives." No doubt shook up, the two teams played the next afternoon. The Saints, who had lost their uniforms in the blaze, took the field in outfits borrowed from the Milwaukee players, and won the game 8 to 7.[49]

On the morning of June 30 the Milwaukee Brewers held first place in the American Association with a 35 and 21 record. This record had been obtained with some heavy hitting. First baseman Jiggs Donahue was hitting .403, with 83 hits in 206 at-bats. Not far behind was catcher Bob Wood at .378, with 79 hits. No fewer than five regulars were hitting above .300. Indianapolis and St. Paul were only two losses behind Milwaukee, with a 35 and 23 record. The remainder of the Association looked like this: Louisville, 30 and 28; Kansas City, 22 and 26; Minneapolis, 25 and 32; Columbus, 23 and 34; Toledo, 19 and 35.

Even though the Brewers were in first place, attendance was not good. In the *Milwaukee Journal* of July 14, Brewer president Charles Havenor said what was on his mind:

> Last season, when the team was losing, and the attendance was light, the cry was "Give us winning ball, and we will support it," and the attendance so far this season has shown how well that promise has been fulfilled. While I am not looking to make a barrel of money out of baseball, yet there is some satisfaction in knowing that one's efforts are being appreciated. The general public has but little idea as to what the cost of maintaining a baseball plant really is, and it

matters but little to them, but as long as the proper spirit is shown, a manager does not mind so much a slight deficiency. Last season when we closed, I made up my mind to have a winner, and I spared no expense to get a team together which, I think, has made good, but maintaining a pennant winning ball club for one's personal amusement is rather an expensive amusement, and is fast losing its charms, and unless something is done to relieve this sort of thing I shall feel inclined to accept some of the flattering offers made for several members of the team.

Havenor received offers in the next week for some of his better players from Charles Comiskey. But Havenor rethought the matter and decided not to sell off his team.[50]

In Toledo the Mud Hens played in Armory Park, so named because of its location next to the armory, just west of the river in the area now bounded by Speilbusch Avenue and Jackson, Erie and Orange Street, where the United States Northern District of Ohio Courthouse stands. The park, built in 1897, had many drawbacks. The park was too small to accommodate the large Sunday Toledo crowds. The right-field fence was low enough that people in wagons on Ontario Street could see the game without paying. The short low fence was an easy target, and fly balls that would have been outs in other parks were doubles in Armory Park. Charles Strobel had considered building a new park east of the river in the spring but did not have enough time before the season began. Another idea was to raise the right-field fence and build a double-deck grandstand. However, Strobel did not want to spend the money, as it was possible the railroads were to run track through this area and could gobble up Armory Park.[51] Any improvements or thought of new grounds before the 1903 season began ended in March when Strobel became seriously ill with typhoid fever. At first it was thought he might die, but his condition rapidly improved, and he left the hospital in April.[52]

On July 9 the grandstand and a portion of the bleachers at Armory Park burned down. Strobel had no insurance for the estimated $8,000 loss, so local businessmen took up a collection to help him rebuild. Strobel soon contracted to build a new double-decked grandstand, seating 4,000.[53]

As if Charles Strobel did not have enough troubles, he had been threatened with a peculiar boycott. The Metal Polishers' Union of Toledo claimed that at one time pitcher Bill Carrick acted as a spy for a company in a strike in Dayton. The union demanded that Toledo drop Carrick, on penalty of having the labor unions of the city boycott the team. Strobel released Carrick, who had won only two of 10 decisions. Carrick went to Philadelphia but then jumped to the Seattle team of the outlaw Pacific Coast League as labor union threats continued to plague him in both of those cities.[54]

Since June there had been talk in Toledo of a stock company forming to

Seven. The 1903 Seasons

run the Mud Hens. Strobel said he was downcast at the poor showing of the team and was willing to do anything to help the game in Toledo. He admitted that he had had several offers from reputable businessmen who wanted to go into partnership with him, and the idea of a stock company materialized. In July Strobel took in a partner. Harvey Wylie, an ex–city auditor, took full charge of the business end of the club, and Strobel spent his time trying to improve the playing strength of the team.[55]

St. Paul had been playing very good baseball and by July 9 had taken over first place with a 42 and 26 record, only a half-game ahead of Indianapolis. Saints outfielder Phil Geier was leading the way with his hitting, becoming the first player in the American Association to reach the 100-hit mark in mid–July. The Brewers had managed to win only four games in two weeks and dropped to third place. Tebeau's Colonels were also playing well, having improved their record to 37 and 31, good for a solid fourth place and back in the pennant hunt.

With Kansas City struggling a few games under .500, fans came up with a way to induce home players to hit home runs. Fans decided to give $5 to each Blues player who hit a home run in Association Park. In the July 15 game against Indianapolis, popular shortstop Ed Lewee hit a pitch squarely that sailed out of the ballpark. One fan offered to present Lewee with a box of cigars valued at $5, but instead a hat was passed around and $4.25 was collected. Two men immediately offered to give 50 cents each to get the donation to five dollars. However, only one was permitted to give that amount, the other only a quarter. The collector said: "We want $5, no more, no less." Lewee was presented the money, and he said Mrs. Lewee would place it in his bank account the next day.[56] This $5 reward perhaps had an effect on the players, as the next day both Lewee and Mike Grady hit home runs. Grady would hit 16 round-trippers in 1903, but Lewee only six for the season.

As July ended the Saints still held first place with a 59 and 31 record, with Milwaukee close behind at 56 and 33. Indianapolis was beginning to fade, failing to 49 and 43, not much better than the Louisville Colonels' 48 and 41 record. Kansas City (39–42), Minneapolis (38–53), Toledo (34–57) and Columbus (34–57) were non-factors in the pennant race.

St. Paul continued to play good ball, stretching its lead to 5½ games over Milwaukee by August 12. The Saints were combining good pitching and hitting to pull away from the rest of the Association. Infielder-outfielder Phil Geier was hitting .343 and had scored 80 runs, second in the league to teammate Spike Shannon's 93 runs scored. Shannon, hitting .314, was an all-around athlete. In addition to being considered one of the best football players in the country and captain of the St. Paul Athletic Association football team, he was an expert trap shooter, a splendid swimmer and a golfer of marked skill who could "swing a brassey with the same ease with which he wields a Louisville slugger."[57] Saints player-manager Mike Kelley was hitting at a .316 clip, and outfielder Jim Jackson was carrying a .303 average. Charlie Chech had racked up 20 wins against only six losses. Charlie Ferguson had a 16 and 9 record, with Joe Stewart not far behind at 12 and 8. An added incentive was a $2,000 team bonus from owner George Lennon if the Saints won the pennant. (This was later reported as only $1,000.)[58]

On August 9 Frank "Doc" Reisling resigned as the Toledo Mud Hens' manager. Reisling and Charles Strobel had not been getting along for some time, with the manager claiming the owner had been interfering with his running of the team. Matters came to a head when Reisling presented Strobel a contract under which he could leave at the end of the season, and the owner refused it. Strobel said he had a verbal understanding with Reisling that he could leave and no contract was needed. However, Doc remembered that Billy Clingman had a verbal release from Charles Havenor of the Milwaukee Brewers earlier in the year, and Havenor had broken faith.[59] Reisling then resigned. It was said he had offers to pitch for Detroit and Chicago in the American League the next year. Third baseman Bob Schaub temporarily took over the team.[60] Reisling held out, saying he would be in the big leagues by September, even if he had to go to court to accomplish that feat. Strobel said he would stop him, and it was thought in the press that the manager "has not a ghost of a show to make an appeal to the courts."[61] Strobel and Reisling soon came to an agreement, and Doc continued at the reins of the team for the 1903 season.

St. Paul continued to dominate the American Association as the last month of the season began, maintaining its 5½-game lead, but now over Louisville, the Colonels having won 27 of their last 30 games going into September. Milwaukee, hampered by injuries, had dropped to third place, more than ten games off the pace, and only two wins ahead of fourth-place Indianapolis.

Spike Shannon — An all-around athlete, Shannon was considered one of the best football players in the country (Library of Congress).

The day Louisville took over second place from the Brewers was a monumental day for pitcher Pat Bohannon. The Colonels came up in the last of the ninth inning down 3 to 1. His teammates scored three runs, including two with two outs, to give the 24-year-old Kentuckian the win. The large crowd was surprised to see Bohannon start game two of the double-header. A Louisville sportswriter compared the pitcher to the then-famous race horse Lou Dillon, commenting the further Bohannon went in the game the stronger he became. "Julius Caesar in all his glory never received the homage of his fellow men as spontaneously and as earnestly as the Louisville rooters gave to Bohannon" after the Colonels won a close, well-played game, 6 to 4.[62] Pat Bohannon would finish the 1903 season with a 19 and 19 record.

On September 21 the American Association ended its season. St. Paul never faltered and managed to hold off the late-season charge of the Louisville Colonels. The 1903 final standings:

St. Paul	88	46	.657	Kansas City	69	66	.511
Louisville	87	54	.617	Columbus	56	84	.400
Milwaukee	77	60	.567	Minneapolis	50	91	.355
Indianapolis	78	61	.561	Toledo	48	91	.345[63]

St. Paul won with a combination of good all-around play. *The Sporting News* correspondent summed up the club nicely on the day the season ended.

> There never was a more gentlemanly lot of players on any manager's payroll than Manager Kelley brought us this year, and each and every one was a star in his position. Probably what counted as much as anything also on winning the pennant was the fact that during the entire season there was not the least friction among the players. There has never been any jealous feeling among the men or individual record work. Every player has played to win and went after everything. They were not afraid of errors and, consequently made many difficult and sensational plays where other players would not take the chance. One feature that was a winner for them was their daring base-running. They took all the chances. Leading in stolen bases and batting tells the story of how the flag was won.[64]

Splitting time between third base and the outfield, Phil Geier hit .361, and five other regulars hit higher than .300. Future Hall-of-Fame manager, 25-year-old Miller Huggins, who would be sold immediately after the season to the Cincinnati Reds for $3,500, stole 48 bases. Outfielders Jim Jackson and Spike Shannon stole 42 and 41 bases, respectively. Three other Saints stole 30 or more bases in the 1903 season. Charlie Chech won 24 of 33 decisions, followed by Charlie Ferguson's 19 and 10 record, and Joe Stewart's 16 and 10 record Harvey Bailey won 15 games and Harry Allemang notched 12 victories. It was indeed a well-rounded team.

St. Paul Saints — The 1903 American Association champs (*Spalding Sporting Guide*).

Western League in 1903

In March president Michael Sexton made up a 1903 Western League schedule having no conflicting dates in Milwaukee or Kansas City. This schedule had each team traveling far too many miles, and Sexton was forced back to the drawing board, submitting four different drafts. The final schedule cut mileage by about 5,000 miles. Of course, the schedule did not suit everyone. Hugh Duffy complained that his Milwaukee team would travel to St. Joseph and Kansas City only twice, playing nine games there each trip. The Creams manager felt fans would tire of seeing two teams playing that many consecutive games against one another. He also was not happy about the eleven conflicting dates in Milwaukee with the American Association Brewers.

Opening Day, April 28, in Denver was postponed for the first time in the history of baseball in that city. It was cold, with rain and snow flurries, as the thermometer dipped to 22 degrees. Both games of the series were rescheduled for June. The first game in Denver this season took place on April 30, with 3,000 witnessing the home team beating Omaha 5 to 4. The other home openers were played according to the schedule.

Thomas Burns' Colorado Springs team started off strong, sitting nicely in first place on May 22 with a 17 and 4 record. Denver and Milwaukee, at 12 and 7, were the only other teams above .500 at the time.

The Western League continued to use the foul-strike rule in 1903. Fans were not entirely in favor of the rule. In Des Moines they were loud in their condemnation of the rule, calling for "more fireworks and less pitching dueling."[65] No doubt the Des Moines fans would see a lot of scoring whatever rule was in use, as the downtown ballpark, which was extensively repaired over the off-season, was the "smallest band-box" in professional ball.[66] The right-field fence was only 150 feet behind first base, and the distance to left field was the same. Scores in the Western League did not seem to suffer during the season, and there still were good pitching duels. One of the best early-season games in the Western League was played on May 23 at Des Moines. Both Tom Barry for Des Moines and Otto Hess for Kansas City pitched shutout ball for 13 innings. The Blue Stockings finally scored three runs in the 14th inning, the first on a dropped fly ball with two outs, to record the win. Hess gave up only four hits in his 14 innings of work.

Hugh Duffy, Milwaukee's center fielder-manager, had an exceptional series in Denver in late May, going 13-for-17, with two five-hit games, and at one point collected 12 straight hits. Returning home from this western swing, the Milwaukee team and the Peoria team (coming from Colorado Springs) were lost in floods that devastated the Topeka area. The trains the teams were traveling on reached Manhattan, Kansas, on May 28 and reportedly left twelve hours before orders were sent out to stop all eastbound trains. The trains did not reach Topeka, and not a word was received for days after that. It was feared the trains might have been caught by a washout in the road and had been swept away by the raging waters of the Kaw River. The number of men traveling with the two teams numbered around thirty.[67] As it turned out, the clubs were marooned for four days in Manhattan, getting out on June 2. At one point the men had to ascend a mountain to seek refuge from the flood in the buildings of the Kansas Agricultural College. They were forced to stay at Clay Center, Kansas, as the washouts were too numerous in the area for the train to proceed safely.⁶⁸ The Peoria Distillers finally played again at home on June 6, losing 5 to 3 to Kansas City. The Creams got back to playing baseball on June 7, before a large Opening Day crowd of about 8,000 at the Lloyd Street grounds in Milwaukee, winning both ends of a double-header from St. Joseph.

These rains and flooding that went through Kansas, Missouri and Nebraska played havoc with the Western League schedule. Numerous games in Omaha, Kansas City and St. Joseph were canceled because of the conditions. Understandably, in Kansas City the newspapers did not carry many baseball stories, and for a while "nobody knew whether the Blue Stockings or the Blues were leading their respective leagues in the standing or taking a jaunt in the caboose and until the last day or two nobody cared."⁶⁹

With things getting back to normal on the diamond, Hugh Duffy's Milwaukee Creams made a surge. With a double-header win on June 21 against Colorado Springs, the Creams took over first place in the standings with a .667 winning percentage (26 wins against 13 loses), overtaking the Millionaires' percentage of .652 (30 and 16). One of the reasons for the Creams' rise was manager-center fielder Hugh Duffy's hitting. He was on a rampage, hitting .490 at one point.

It was at this time that rumors began to swirl about the Kansas City club transferring to Sioux City, Iowa. At first buyers were not named, only reports that two men who represented the Business Men's Association of Sioux City were the purchasers. However, A.B. Beall, who had owned the Minneapolis franchise earlier, was being mentioned. It was reported that Beall had built a grandstand seating 2,500, erected a double fence, and staked out a diamond at his downtown park. He even was said to have employed a groundskeeper and ticket seller. The first game was to be played in Sioux City on July 6.⁷⁰

This rumor was taken up by Ed Kundegraber, *Sporting Life*'s Kansas City correspondent. He wrote: "The reports started in Milwaukee, the home of hot air and other famous products. So many false rumors are sent out from the brewery town that it is nearly a safe proposition to brand rumors from Milwaukee as untrue and far more amusing than interesting. The removal of the Western League team to some other city has never been considered, so the local managers say. The season will be finished without a change, though it is safe to guess that the club has made little or no money this year."⁷¹

Another rumor was circulating at the same time that suggested the Western League was to abandon Milwaukee, possibly moving to Sioux City if Kansas City did not. The Creams' business manager, Porter Higby, claimed that league President Sexton had recently secured a five-year lease on the Lloyd Street grounds, providing sufficient proof the team would remain in Milwaukee.⁷²

Milwaukee was in a unique position to discover which of the two teams calling the beer city home would receive better fan support. From June 24 to June 27 both the Western League and American Association teams played at home. As both were in first place at the time, it is interesting to look at the attendance figures. On the first date, a Thursday, the American Association Brewers drew 440, while the Western League Creams attracted 186. The next day the Brewers had an attendance of 578, the Creams 275. On Saturday 2,200 fans showed up for the Association game, only 800 for the Western League game. On Sunday, June 27 both teams drew very well — the Brewers 4,700 at Athletic Park and the Creams 4,000 at Milwaukee Park.

The standings of the Western League looked like this as of July 2:

Milwaukee	38	13	.745	St. Joseph	25	28	.472
Colorado Springs	38	19	.667	Peoria	23	31	.426
Kansas City	27	26	.509	Des Moines	19	34	.358
Denver	29	29	.500	Omaha	17	36	.321

The wide difference in games played was due to the numerous rain postponements in some cities of the Western League. One of the more noteworthy games in June was played on the 24th on a chilly day in Denver. The score stood tied after seven innings, 6 to 6. For the next ten innings neither Denver's Frank Barber nor Des Moines' Bill Morrison gave up a run. The Grizzlies had numerous opportunities to win the contest, but the Undertakers got out of tight places in almost every inning. Finally in the 18th inning Des Moines pushed a run across to win the contest 7 to 6, in two hours and 40 minutes!

Just as the American Association had cut down its rosters to 13 men in May, the Western League decided to do the same in July. The top teams were to lose at least one player; these extra players would be turned over to the league and assigned to the weaker clubs. Western League President Sexton also said a deal was pending with an unidentified baseball organization to give the league's weaker clubs some players. This gesture apparently never came to pass.

In late July Bobby Lowe became the Denver Grizzlies' new manager. The team had been a major disappointment, having perhaps the best team on paper, but hung around .500 for the season. He replaced Tom Delahanty, whose playing was thought to have been adversely affected by his worry over managing the team. It was felt that if Delahanty was allowed to concentrate on playing he would again become a star. Adding to Tom Delahanty's problems was the drowning death of his famous brother, Ed, of the Washington Senators, at Niagara Falls on July 2. Even under these difficult circumstances, Tom Delahanty would hit .310 in 113 games with Denver in 1903.

The death of Ed Delahanty and the relieving of Tom of his managerial duties produced thoughts of what might have been. In the spring of 1903 Ed Delahanty had been in the midst of a contract dispute with Washington of the American League and New York of the National League. The Denver management made an offer to Ed, who had hit .376 with Washington in 1902, to come to Colorado. The Grizzlies were willing to pay him the same $4,000 salary he had been offered by the Senators. Denver owner D.C. Packard said the offer was genuine, as he believed Ed Delahanty would draw more in attendance revenue than his salary would be in just the opening weeks of the season. The previous year Packard had signed such big names as Billy Everitt, Burt Jones and Tom Delahanty, and these players brought added thousands through the gates. It was even reported Ed Delahanty had come to terms with Denver, but the National Association of Minor League Baseball Clubs told Packard to stop the transaction, as the organization did not want to create any problems that could hinder the new agreement between the major and minor leagues. An agreement was soon reached between Washington and New York, and Ed Delahanty signed with Washington.[73]

The 38-years-old Bobby Lowe, was a former big leaguer with steady years as the Boston Beaneaters second baseman from 1890 to 1901. Lowe had played 1902 with the Chicago National League team, and was released by that club earlier in the 1903 season. In Denver he was given authority to hire, fire and discipline players.

By the end of July the Western League had turned into a two-team race. In late July the Milwaukee Creams lost four games in Omaha, while the Colorado Springs Millionaires put together a winning streak to move into first place. However, on July 30 Milwaukee was back in first place with 50 wins and 27 loses, for a .649 winning percentage. The Colorado Springs Millionaires had a .639 winning percentage (53 and 30). Third-place Kansas City was playing .500 ball (40 and 40). The five other teams were all under .500. Colorado Springs owner Thomas J. Burns was receiving offers on almost a daily basis from big league owners hoping to acquire some of his players, but he said he would not let any players go until after the season so his team could stay in the pennant race. Hugh Duffy's Milwaukee Creams were in a similar position. It was being reported that major league clubs were looking to sign his catcher, his top pitcher and three infielders.[74]

The Millionaires and Brewers seesawed between first and second place for another week, until the Creams finally took the top spot for good on August 5. The games that determined the leader were head to head in Milwaukee, and showed the attendance problem in the Wisconsin city. On August 4, the day Colorado Springs took over first place with a win, only 325 were in attendance. At the August 5 game, only 378 were in the stands. The next day the attendance was given as 600, and on Friday August 7 the same number attended. The small crowds were evident to everyone, especially those who were on the field everyday, as the *Evening Wisconsin* reported: "The players are no fools when it comes to sizing up crowds, and they are about convinced that two clubs for one town is a bad thing."[75]

The terrible attendance with the Creams on the top of a close pennant race again led to rumors of the team being transferred. The story was that the Milwaukee team would be transferred to Peoria, while the Distillers would play in Milwaukee. As Milwaukee's fans would not patronize a winning team, it was thought Peoria's fans would. Then when the season was over the new Milwaukee team would be transferred to Sioux City, Iowa. Management of both Peoria and Milwaukee immediately denied the report.[76]

However, Milwaukee was not the only team with attendance problems in the Western League. The *Evening Wisconsin* gave the attendance figures for weekday games in the last week of July for each city in the Western League and American Association. The figures showed the Western could not keep up with the Association in attendance.

Western League

At Peoria	(3 games)	1,800	At Milwaukee	(4 games)	1,125
At K.C.	(4 games)	2,000	At St. Joseph	(2 games)	1,600

Total 6,525

American Association

At Columbus	(4 games)	6,187	At Louisville	(3 games)	5,500
At Indianapolis	(3 games)	3,534	At Toledo	(4 games)	5,630

Total 20,871

Accepting these figures and estimating the known price of admission, including an estimate on how many occupied grandstand seats sold at an additional quarter, the Western League took in $2,446.75 in these 13 games, while the American Association took in $7,826.50 in 14 games. However, Sunday attendance was significantly higher in all cities. At the August 2 Sunday games Columbus drew 8,200, Louisville 3,700, and Toledo 3,000. Indianapolis's Saturday double-header (the Hoosiers had switched Sunday home games to become Saturday double-headers) drew 6,200. Thus, the American Association had a total of 21,100 on Sunday, more than 300 more than the combined attendance at the weekday games. The Western League had an even bigger difference. Milwaukee drew 2,500, Kansas City 4,000, St. Joseph 3,000 and Peoria 3,500. This 13,000 attendance was double the weekday total attendance.[77]

The Milwaukee Creams continued to play a little better ball than Colorado Springs, and by August 19 had a .670 winning percentage (65 and 32) compared to the Millionaires' .612 percentage (63 and 40).

An interesting situation arose in a game in Denver on August 21. Joe Wright of Peoria hit a ball that bounded through the open door of the Denver clubhouse in deep center field. Left fielder Charlie Jones followed the ball into the clubhouse and returned it to the diamond in time to hold Wright to third base. Peoria manager Bill Wilson argued that the ball should have been considered as having gone out of the field and Wright allowed to score. Wilson made the point that the ball had passed from the umpire's sight and therefore could not certify that it was the same ball that had been hit into the clubhouse. Umpire McCarthy disagreed and the triple stood. The Distillers won the game 3 to 0.

On August 23 Joe Quinn resigned his position as manager of the Des Moines club. The change was effective immediately so that whoever took the club in 1904 would be able to build his own team. The Undertakers had a 43 and 58 record at the time. Quinn claimed he wanted some more time to look after his business in St. Louis but wished to stay on with the club as its second baseman. Having the pressures of the managerial job taken off his shoulders did Joe some good, as in this August 23 game he hit a triple and a home run in a 10 to 8 victory over St. Joseph.

Hugh Duffy's Creams should have been in a position to pull away from Colorado Springs but could not. In Colorado Springs his team won two of three, and then took three of four in Denver. The Creams then dropped three in Kansas City to allow the Millionaires to stay in the race. Injuries were preventing Duffy from putting his best team on the field. Shortstop Frank Gatins had a broken finger, third baseman Jim Cockman a bruised finger, and catcher Fred Lucia a split finger. Duffy had broken his hand.

The standings on September 2 showed Milwaukee in first place and Colorado Springs only one win behind — although the Millionaires had lost eight more games. A schedule quirk had the Creams play thirteen games in a row against Peoria. The Creams won the first eight games, then turned around and lost the next five. Duffy's team then defeated Omaha and Des Moines three each to put the pennant out of reach of everyone else.

After the September 17 games Western League president Michael Sexton officially declared the season ended due to the unusually bad weather conditions in the league's cities, which made operating at a profit an impossibility. Sexton also said there was very little chance of any changes in the team's positions in the pennant race. The final 1903 Western League standings were:

Milwaukee	83	43	.659	Denver	61	70	.466
Colorado Springs	77	52	.597	Peoria	57	69	.452
Kansas City	65	61	.516	Des Moines	55	76	.420
St. Joseph	62	59	.512	Omaha	49	79	.388[78]

Sexton explained the closing of the Western League season ten days early: "This decision was arrived at only after conferring with the magnates by wire, and the ending of the season in the manner chosen by no reason means that the league has suspended. All regulations have been complied with, and all league rights will be protected. Each city will reserve the players of its present team for the season of 1904, and the circuit for next year will be maintained exactly as it closed."[79] Sexton advised all club owners to mail a written notice of reservation to each player's last known address prior to September 25 to keep the player on their reserve list.[80]

However, most saw the closing as a cost reduction at the expense of the players. *The Sporting News* was critical of the decision, believing it unwise because it resulted in a loss of prestige with patrons and an "outrageous injustice" to the players. The move was approved by the National Board, of which Sexton was a member. The St. Louis weekly reminded its readers that Sexton had repeatedly denounced players who jumped their contracts and helped declare them ineligible to play professional ball. The paper asked: "If the individual is deserving of punishment for failing to live up to an agreement, why should not the party with which he engages be held to strict accountability for its observance?" *The Sporting News* called on the Western League owners, President Sexton and the National Board to take steps to make sure the players were paid for their services for the 10 canceled days.[81] Francis Richter, editor of *Sporting Life*, also saw the move as a mistake and an injustice to the players that would have consequences for the league. One immediate consequence was the refusal of all the Denver players to sign contracts for 1904, preferring instead to await further developments in the situation.[82]

Some thought it was Thomas Burns and D.C. Packard, who had large financial interests in the Milwaukee Creams, that called for the early end of the season. Milwaukee was drawing crowds of 200 or less and obviously bleeding money. W.W. Sears in Des Moines was "much displeased" over Sexton's move,[83] as was William Rourke in Omaha. Rourke believed his club and a few others could have recouped some of their losses if they had played the last ten days.[84]

The players dispersed and returned home "in a disgusted and rebellious state of mind." Many considered themselves free agents.[85] The clubs deducted the ten days' pay from the players' salaries, causing some to talk of appealing to the National Board.

As after the 1902 season, the owners of the four clubs in Milwaukee and Kansas City negotiated for post-season series in their respective cities. This year Hugh Duffy accepted the challenge from the American Association Brewers. But when the Western League season ended prematurely, most of his players were in no mood to play and many had left town. The Brewers, joined by some players from the Minneapolis Millers, who were in town when the season ended, instead went on a short post-season trip. In Kansas City a series was again arranged. It was determined the first team to win six games would receive 60 percent of the gate receipts. The American Association team won six of the nine games played. The series was a financial success, with about 14,000 people witnessing the games.

Eight

◆ ◆ ◆ ◆

The War Ends

Before the 1903 playing season had ended, it was obvious that both the Western League and American Association were hurting financially. This situation led to talk of peace. In anticipation of a new National Agreement (the document that laid out the rules of organized baseball), minor league clubs began selling players to the National and American leagues before these stars could be drafted at lower prices.[1] In late August, in Buffalo, the major leagues agreed on a new National Agreement. The minor leagues, however, rejected the agreement as being "utterly unsuited to minor league needs, so conducive to major league aggrandizement, and so subversive of National Association interests, if not existence."[2] The major leagues made some concessions, mostly on drafting, and a new agreement was signed in September.

President Thomas Hickey said the American Association as a whole made money in 1903, with the losses of a few clubs more than offset by the profits of the majority. It was said that only Kansas City lost money. But shortly after the season George Lennon said his pennant winning St. Paul club lost in the neighborhood of $5,000, not including the $20,000 he spent on the new downtown park. He blamed this loss on the high player salaries he was forced to pay. Lennon complained that players he had paid $175 a month in 1902 were making $300 in 1903.[3] A report out of Toledo claimed it was doubtful any club in the American Association made money in 1903, with Louisville and Indianapolis probably coming as close to breaking even as any clubs.[4] At its stockholders meeting the Columbus club claimed to have made a little money, but complained it paid out $7,000 more to visiting clubs than it received when on the road. The Columbus Senators salary list for 1903 had been a little more than $27,000, an enormous amount for the times.[5]

The Toledo club was thought to have lost the most money. Frank Collison, *The Sporting News* correspondent from that Ohio city, wrote: "The days of high-priced men for minor leagues are numbered. The fact that such ruinously high prices were paid the past season has bankrupted fully one-third of the managers in the country." It was clear the American Association needed a salary limit to continue. It was thought $2,500 a month would be established, which would be nearly $1,000 a month less than the last-place Mud Hens had paid in 1903.[6]

Attendance figures vary, but a report out of Columbus said that team attracted 151,876. Louisville was second in home attendance, finishing about 4,000 short of Columbus. St. Paul drew 135,000. The Kansas City American Association club drew about 100,000. Indianapolis drew 88,000. In contrast to Columbus having the largest home attendance, the Senators drew the worst on the road, with Indianapolis attracting the largest crowds on the road.[7]

Financial figures in the Western League were also murky, and can only be estimated from various comments made at the time. Without citing any sources, the *Milwaukee Daily News* gave these profit-and-loss figures for the Western League clubs the day after the season was halted:

	Profit	Loss
Milwaukee	......	$2,500
Colorado Springs	$2,000	......
Kansas City	......	$6,000
St. Joseph	......	$1,700
Peoria	......	$3,200
Denver	$2,300	......
Des Moines	$4,000	......
Omaha	......	$4,500
TOTAL	$8,300	$17,900[8]

Other sources declared that Denver, Colorado Springs, St. Joseph and Des Moines had made money during the season, the last club $5,000 to the good. The other Western League clubs ended in the red.[9] Another report asserted that Des Moines realized another $3,500 in the sale of three of its players at the end of the season.[10] William Rourke of Omaha claimed he lost $9,000 on the season. He said home games paid expenses, but road contests were a loss. This is hard to believe, for it was reported that attendance in Omaha in 1903 was only 39,000, compared with 142,000 the previous season.[11] (It had been previously reported by Western League officials to have been 132,000 in 1902.) Peoria was in such bad shape that when the season ended the directors voted to dispose of the assets of the club, including the players, to pay off the club's debts.[12] In Denver attendance was less than in 1902, even though the team had lowered its general admission price by a nickel, to 25 cents, with 40 cents extra for grandstand seating. (Colorado Springs had also lowered ticket prices.)[13] The Denver correspondent to *The Sporting News*, using the pen name "Ping Pong," said what will forever be true: "The season showed that the people will pay to see winning ball, whatever the price may be, and can not be enticed into the grounds if the team is losing."[14]

After the season Thomas Hickey announced he would resign as president of the American Association and join George Lennon in business in St. Paul. Besides his large clothing store, Lennon was starting a gentleman's furnishing establishment, named The Wardrobe. It was said he had secured a lease on another large building, which he would remodel and also stock with clothing. Lennon was one of the most successful young businessmen in the country, and the fact that his team won the Association pennant had been the best advertisement his business could have had.[15]

Thomas Hickey — After his first retirement as president of A.A. in 1903, he would return to lead that Association again from 1917 to 1935 (National Baseball Hall of Fame Library, Cooperstown, New York).

Mentioned as candidates for Hickey's job were Cincinnati sporting writer Ren Mulford, Tim Murnane of Boston, secretary Ernest Barnard of the Cleveland club, Western League president Michael Sexton (who in October stepped down as president of the Three-I League), former sports editor of the *Milwaukee Sentinel* A.W. Friese, and the secretary of the National Association of Baseball Leagues, J.H. Farrell. This last candidate was said to be the man slated for the job.[16] However, Farrell, who was also president of the New York League, turned down the $3,000-a-year position. Next, Ernest Barnard, who had Hickey's strong endorsement, turned down the presidency.[17] Some in the Association were in favor of having Hickey stay while moving his headquarters to St. Paul so he could still work with Lennon and continue as president at a reduced salary. Others wanted "an up-to-date man" in the position.[18] Some believed the American Association might even be run by committee — no doubt consisting of Thomas Bryce, George Tebeau and William Watkins. The choosing of a successor to Hickey dragged on, as several owners clung to their personal favorite for the job.

It was said in Indianapolis that William Watkins was considering selling his baseball interests to Cincinnati pitcher Bill Phillips. Watkins would then pilot the Minneapolis club. Watkins initially would not confirm or deny the story.[19] However, on November 3 Watkins sold his entire interest in the Hoosiers to Charles Ruschaupt, his partner for the last three years. Watkins then purchased the interest of Edward A. Johnston in the Minneapolis ball club for $10,000.[20] Bill Phillips was later signed as the manager of the Indianapolis club for 1904.

There were reports of Charles Strobel selling his Toledo club around this time, as well. Strobel told the press he had been losing money for the past four or five seasons.[21] It was initially reported that a syndicate of Toledo capitalists and several fans were making an effort to purchase Strobel's interest in the team. In November there was a report that Strobel was negotiating a sale of the club to Addison Clark, of the Clark Coach and Transfer Company of Toledo.[22] But within weeks Strobel said his club was not for sale, and he would remain the owner for years to follow.

In the other league, trouble was brewing in Omaha. William Rourke had been against the early closing of the Western League season. In addition, he was displeased with the Western League magnates, mainly because Hugh Duffy and Thomas Burns would not supply his team with some players in the middle of the season when his team was losing.[23] Rourke was also attempting to get rid of Western League president Michael Sexton, contending he was "too arbitrary in conducting of the league affairs and too autocratic in his rulings." No doubt Rourke, like some others, thought Sexton was too close to Thomas Burns. Sexton would stay on as the Western League president.[24]

Rourke was considering accepting an American Association franchise for the Nebraska city. The Omaha owner-manager said he would like to see an American Association circuit of Omaha, Kansas City, St. Paul and Minneapolis in the west, with Indianapolis, Columbus, Louisville and Milwaukee in the east. It was said this circuit would save about 2,400 miles in travel a season. Rourke suggested a revised Western League could consist of St. Joseph, Sioux City, Des Moines, Lincoln, Denver, Colorado Springs, Pueblo and one other city. This would make for a more compact circuit, and with a lower salary limit would give the revamped Western League a good chance to make money. The Colorado Springs manager also spoke along these lines, giving the possibility of changes credibility.[25]

Out of Indianapolis came word that Omaha might enter the American Association in Milwaukee's place. The Indianapolis correspondent to *The Sporting News* wrote: "This would, no doubt, strengthen the circuit materially, for Beerland seems to care nothing for a winning team."[26] In mid–October Bobby Lowe was reportedly seeking the Omaha franchise. Soon, however, Rourke said everything was fine in the Western League and he would stay.[27]

The National Association of Professional Baseball Leagues was set to hold its third annual meeting. Word was the National Association had told the Western League and American Association to settle their differences because the continuing war was affecting baseball throughout the country. It was believed the Western was willing to compromise, but the Association was not in that mood. It was reported the Western League would withdraw from Kansas City and Milwaukee if the American Association would help the Western retain its Class A status, thus protecting its players from the draft. The Association refused when the Western also wanted $15,000 to leave Kansas City.[28]

At caucuses before the meeting, the Western League felt it was financially solid enough to go head-to-head with the American Association for another year. The Association decided to insist upon a representative upon the National Board and have the Board adopt a new constitution that would protect the rights of Class A leagues. However, the American Association wanted to push the Western League out of its Class A standing, on the grounds the league did not meet the population requirements, had violated the leagues' agreement on conflicting dates, and ended its season early.[29]

On October 22, 1903, the minor league representatives met at the Southern Hotel in St. Louis. After the usual preliminaries were conducted, Pat Powers was re-elected president and J.H. Farrell secretary. A hot debate then began on how a committee should be formed to revive the Board's constitution. Some wanted the president to appoint a committee of three, others wanted an election by all members. It was felt by many that the American Association and the Eastern League were combining to force a new constitution upon the National Board. It was even rumored the two leagues were contemplating a consolidation and would control the Board completely. Michael Sexton of the Western League charged the American Association with trying to break up his league by designing a drive to force the Western out of Milwaukee and Kansas City. Sexton pleaded for the majority to stand up against these two leagues. Others followed his lead, and in the uproar that followed all the delegates of the American Association and Eastern League left the meeting. This left Pat Powers in an awkward position, being president of the Eastern League and president of the National Association. He remained at the chair, and after the regular order of business was restored the old board was re-elected.

The next day the meeting continued without the American Association or Eastern League. After a long debate it was decided to present these leagues with a proposal, presented by D.C. Packard of Denver, that the Board be expanded to seven members, allowing the Association and Eastern to have a representative. The Association/Eastern caucus countered with a proposal to have the Board consist of five members, three of these coming from Class A leagues. The American Association/Eastern League duo also made demands regarding exhibition games played during the season, contracts previously signed, and a firm rule on Class A leagues taking over territory for a payment of $2,500 to the previous owners. This last demand would enable the American Association to come to terms with the Western League in Milwaukee and/or Kansas City. The National Board agreed to the last three demands but not on board representation. A compromise was reached where the present board would be in place until the next term, when the Class A leagues would have three of the five members.

The meeting continued with rules regarding salary limits and drafting approved. The demand of Class A cities taking over the territory of other leagues was then addressed. It was decided that in addition to the $2,500 for the territory, the Class A league would have to compensate the vacating club for all assets, including buildings and the value of players. If the two parties could not agree, the matter would go to a board of arbitration, consisting of a member of the National Association and a member of each club involved.[30]

After the meeting it appeared Sioux City and Pueblo would take the place of Kansas City and Milwaukee in the Western League. Both cities had been mentioned numerous times in the summer of 1903 as a replacement for the new season. During the summer several Pueblo businessmen had talked to Michael Sexton, and the streetcar company was said to be ready to put up $10,000 to back a ball club. As an added incentive, the new ownership said it would not compel visiting clubs to ante up the five percent assessment to support the weaker clubs in the league.[31]

However, W.T. Van Brunt announced that St. Joseph would leave the Western League if Milwaukee and Kansas City were not in the league. Another report had Victor and Cripple Creek, Colorado, being added to the Western League, along with Sioux City. This would drop Milwaukee, Kansas City and Peoria. Victor and Cripple Creek, a district embracing 60,000 people, would put up a $10,000 guarantee to go through the season and pay for games — rain or shine — in addition to charging a 50-cent general admission.[32]

A Lincoln, Nebraska, dispatch reported that city would become a member of the Western League, and a canvas was being made to secure the necessary backing.[33] A tighter circuit would reduce railroad mileage in addition to cutting down on off days needed to allow teams to make connections. However, Lincoln in reality did not stand a chance, as Sunday ball was not allowed there. Yet another report had the Western dropping to a six-club circuit consisting of Omaha, Denver, St. Joseph, Kansas City, Des Moines and Colorado Springs.[34]

There was little doubt the Western League would leave Milwaukee. The club lost money and the lease on the ballpark had expired. Reports had circulated since at least August that president-manager-outfielder Hugh Duffy was to leave. Initial reports had him returning to the Boston National League club. Another report said he was to manage the Chicago White Sox, taking the best of his Western League team to build a championship team there.[35] In September it was reported the Creams' manager had accepted an offer to manage the Philadelphia National League team. Duffy at first denied this, but as the season ended he admitted he would be elsewhere in 1904. His star pitcher, Ed Kenna, said he would follow his manager if he could.[36] Duffy would sign with the Phillies on September 24, drafting four Milwaukee players.

Most also expected Kansas City to be out of the Western League, but this would be a matter for the arbitration committee, as Packard and Burns owned the park there, which cost more than $12,000. Naturally, they were not willing to give this investment up without some compensation. However, George Tebeau in Louisville was not in a peacemaking mood. He stated there would be no arbitration between the two leagues, as there "is nothing to arbitrate." Tebeau said if there was to be any payment for the Western League's withdrawal from Kansas City and Milwaukee, it would be what the Association chose to give "in a liberal spirit."[37] This, of course, put a temporary stop to negotiations.

George Tebeau — Perhaps the most influential man in the 1902/1903 Western League/American Association war (National Baseball Hall of Fame Library, Cooperstown, New York).

The Western League struck back at Tebeau, spreading a report he would be frozen out of Kansas City. It was said the American Association and Western Kansas City teams would consolidate into one team and play in the Association. Local capital would be found, forcing Tebeau to sell. Kid Nichols would manage this team.[38] P.H. Saunders, the Louisville correspondent to *The Sporting News*, was certain these men did not know what they were getting into. He wrote:

> Maybe those Kansas City fellows know what they are talking about. But my experience has been that they might just as well try to "freeze out" a chunk of

radium as Uncle George. It will be less expensive and fully as successful. Tebeau has shown on more than one occasion that he is fully able to take care of No. 1, and when he gets ready to pull up stakes and move from Kansas City, he will do it and not before, especially if the matter is put that way. I think Tebeau has the interest of the sport enough at heart to make almost any sacrifice that would be of benefit if he were approached in a proper manner, but a bluff don't go.[39]

Western League president Michael Sexton spent two days in Sioux City in November looking into the situation. He left saying he would give a favorable report to the Western League's Circuit Committee. The Iowa town had a downtown park and another for Sunday ball. There were a number of willing backers, including A.B. Beall, who had owned the Minneapolis franchise a few years prior.[40] Sexton soon reported he was certain Sioux City would be awarded a Western League franchise. The franchise would be a stock company headed by W.E. Lockhart, former president of the Iowa and South Dakota League, and Dr. George B. Wood, who owned the Sioux City franchise in that league. Other prominent stockholders would be Charles E. Hughson, also of the Sioux City baseball club, and W.R. Nation, proprietor of the Vendome Hotel. Sexton explained the franchise was awarded to the Wood group, as he had the rights to this territory by his membership in the National Association of Minor Leagues. Also entering the decision was Beall's dealings in the Western League two years earlier. The new owners were required to have $5,000 in working capital and $2,500 for the purchase of the franchise. The prospective Sioux City owners even announced the team had a manager, Frank Genins, who had played in Omaha in 1903. Sexton asked William Rourke to release the outfielder so he could manage the new team, and Rourke agreed he would.[41]

The other cities that would have teams in the Western League remained uncertain. The Western reportedly lost nearly $50,000 in Kansas City and Milwaukee in the two years of war.[42] Milwaukee was considered to be a lost cause, and Peoria seemed certain to be out, as it could not operate under the high salaries being paid in the Western League. With Milwaukee out of the circuit, the long eastern trip to Peoria would be costly for travel expenses. There was thought that Peoria might land a club in the Three-I League, trading places with Davenport, but the Peoria owners were refused permission. If no league was found soon, the owners of the ballpark said they would begin booking other amusements for the season. Then the Central League said it would be glad to take Peoria into its circuit for 1904, and Billy Hart even made an offer to purchase the franchise and become a magnate in the Central League.[43] Lincoln was still hoping to join the Western League, and made plans to form a stock company with $10,000. Interested parties raised $3,050 within a short period of time. As Sunday games could not be played in Lincoln, it was proposed the club's Sunday games would be played in Omaha.⁴⁴

Michael Sexton said it was possible the Western would stay in Kansas City, however, as the situation was not intolerable. The talk of Cripple Creek was done with, its high altitude and rainy weather too much of a factor against it. With Cripple Creek out, Pueblo could not find a place in the league, as Sexton wanted both new clubs to be in either the eastern or the western geography of the league.⁴⁵

While all this talk about Western League cities was taking place, a movement in the east was afoot that was causing some concern. George Tebeau spoke of a scheme that would merge the best teams of the American Association and Eastern League into "the strongest minor league ever organized."⁴⁶ This would create a circuit that would be almost equal in importance to either the National League or American League. With player salaries 30 percent lower than the major leagues and teams charging 25 cents for admission, Tebeau was certain this would be a money maker. Plans for the league included Toronto, Buffalo, Jersey City and Baltimore from the Eastern League, with Louisville, Indianapolis, Toledo and Columbus from the American Association. Current Eastern League cities that were not in this new league would go to the New York State or New England League, while the discarded American Association cities would no doubt find a berth in a re-organized Western League. The plan was endorsed by Arthur Irwin, manager of the Toronto club.⁴⁷ George Lennon in St. Paul was not concerned about this talk, saying he would stop the process if it got that far.⁴⁸ At the December meeting of the Eastern League the plan was discussed and met with favor. However, it was decided to recommend holding off on the plan until 1905.⁴⁹ At a meeting on January 25, 1904, this proposed league was killed when five owners of the American Association—Havenor of Milwaukee, Watkins of Minneapolis, Lennon of St. Paul, Dale Gear of Kansas City, and surprisingly Tebeau of Louisville (who also owned Kansas City)—signed an agreement that these five charter clubs of the American Association would remain in the Association for at least eight more years, and could not be dropped.⁵⁰

With no solution to the Western League–American Association situation on the horizon, P.H. Saunders, the newspaperman from Louisville, gave readers some insightful words:

> There is no other sport that appeals to the American people as base ball does. They give it lots more attention than all other forms of sport put together, watch closely the minutest detail and are very quick to see injustice and to resent it. If all the magnates were to get together and form a compact to deal squarely with each other and with the public, to make no claims without good cause and to

put base ball on the high plane that the average fan, in his enthusiasm, imagines it occupies, everybody would be vastly benefited and none more so than the magnates themselves.[51]

The Western League's decision to close its season early was brought before the National Board while all this talk was going on. Frank Lucia, the catcher of the Milwaukee Creams, appealed to the Board that he should be taken off the Milwaukee reserve list, because the Western League did not pay his 1903 salary in full. J.H. Farrell, secretary of the National Board, issued a statement that Lucia's contract set no dates for the Western League schedule, only April 1903 to September 1903. As the contract called for semi-monthly payments to the player on the 1st and 15th of each month during the season, the Western League club only had to pay him until it finished playing. Thus, the Milwaukee club fulfilled its contract and Lucia was still under reserve. It was thought this ruling would cover any players fighting the reserve.[52]

The National Board heard a similar case involving Morris Jacobs of Kansas City. Jacobs was also paid semi-monthly, through September 15. As the Western League ended on September 17, thus past his last payday, he argued he should receive ten days' pay or be released from Kansas City's reserve. The Kansas City club paid him only two days' pay, as his contract read he should be paid from May 21 (the starting date on his contract) until the "closing of the season."

Frank Lucia — The first player to take the case of the Western League closing its 1903 season early to the National Board. He lost the case, setting the precedent for others (*Milwaukee Sentinel*, May 31, 1903).

The National Board favored the club.[53] In the courts, however, the Western League did not fare as well. Ed Holly and Joseph Wright obtained a judgment against the Peoria Baseball Club for $150 and $100, respectively, money owed them from the early closing.[54]

In early December George Tebeau went to Denver to work out a settlement with D.C. Packard and Thomas Burns over that city's franchise situation. It was reported that Packard was ready to leave the game. An option on the Denver club had been given to Julius Alchele, on behalf of mining millionaire James Doyle, but due to a misunderstanding the arrangement fell through. The club was valued by Alchele, the clerk of Denver County, at $20,000.[55]

The Western League was set to

meet on December 15, 1903, to determine its future, but the meeting was postponed when President Sexton was called to Texas on personal business. The Lincoln promoters took this time to raise the $2,500 cash guarantee to enter the Western. Lincoln was certainly being looked upon as the new franchise, as the people in Sioux City were failing in their efforts to raise the necessary cash. The future of the Kansas City franchise was being held up, as the Western League men were not sure if the American Association–Eastern League proposed merger would take place. If it did go through, Kansas City would no doubt be given to the Western League.[56]

The American Association held its annual meeting in Chicago on December 28 and elected J. Edward Grillo as its president. Grillo was born in Germany in 1872 and came to America five years later, growing up in Cincinnati. He was a newspaper man, working on the same newspaper American League president Ban Johnson had, succeeding him as sporting editor. Thus, Grillo had a close relationship with Johnson and Cincinnati Red Stockings owner Garry Herrmann, both of whom were also on the National Base Ball Commission.[57]

George Tebeau was appointed to a committee of one to settle the differences between the American Association and the Western League. The Association was not willing to pay much to the Western, but it was expected to take care of the leases on the parks in Kansas City and Milwaukee.[58] *The Sporting News* saw this as a mistake, as the Western League, and D.C. Packard in particular, regarded Tebeau "as a trickster and a schemer."[59]

The pro–Western League *Sporting News* thought the Western League should stay in Kansas City and not give in to Tebeau and his tactics. The paper felt Tebeau's thinking was that the proposed American Association–Eastern League merger was going to happen after the 1904 season, and he would then acquire the Kansas City territory by confiscation. Tebeau would then have two valuable baseball properties. The Western League's baseball park, with three years left on its lease and an option of a five-year extension, generated income. The ballpark cost about $2,500 to run, but this amount was reduced greatly from the revenue brought in from football and other sources. The Thanksgiving Day rugby game between Kansas and Missouri, for instance, brought in $1,300 for the club. It was felt the revenue from the park could be $10,000 a year. *The Sporting News* thought if the Western League did abandon K.C., it should sell the park to Tebeau for at least $25,000, instead of the $1,000 a year in rent he had offered.[60]

The Western League owners were prepared to meet on January 12, 1904, in Lincoln, Nebraska, for their postponed annual meeting. However, the day before, George Tebeau secured an injunction against the Western League from doing business unless he was admitted as a full member, claiming he was still the lawful owner of a franchise in the league. Tebeau asserted he was granted a four-year membership with the Denver club in the Western League in 1901 and was wrongly voted out in favor of D.C. Packard prior to the 1902 season. Tebeau claimed that as the rightful owner of the Denver franchise he should receive his one-eighth share of the league's sinking fund, which he believed to be in excess of $3,500. D.C. Packard said he had the papers to prove he had purchased the franchise from A.B. Beall. Of course, president Sexton of the Western saw this as a move to coerce his league out of Kansas City. Sexton again stated the Western League would not leave Kansas City without a fair settlement.[61]

A week later George Tebeau purchased the Denver franchise, including the ballpark, from D.C. Packard and Richard R. Burke for $20,000. Burke however, would still own a portion of the club. Packard retained the refreshment privileges at the park for two years. Tebeau also purchased Packard's interests in the Kansas City club, thus clearing the way for the withdrawal of Kansas City from the Western League. Tebeau dropped his lawsuit in the Lincoln court against the Western League, as the Western League delegates admitted Tebeau had been wrongfully deprived of the Denver franchise.[62]

Now that George Tebeau controlled four franchises in two leagues, *The Sporting News* Kansas City correspondent wrote: "The Napoleon of the base ball world has yet to meet his Waterloo. Surely there are more worlds for him to conquer and it might be well to bid [American League President] Ban Johnson and [National League President] Harry Pulliam to beware, for if the Denver-Kansas City-Louisville magnate takes a notion to invade major league territory, the time is not far distant when he will become the supreme dictator, the main mogul of the base ball world." The K.C. newsman was happy to have a baseball club in Kansas City but thought Tebeau would be devoting most of his time and money on his other teams. Louisville was Tebeau's prize team, and Denver was his hometown, and no doubt he wanted to see a good team in that city. The correspondent sadly concluded: "It remains for Kansas City to be the boneyard for Denver and Louisville castoffs."[63]

William Rourke of Omaha saw trouble for the entire Western League, and was open about his feelings for George Tebeau. In a *Sporting News* column he was quoted as saying: "George Tebeau always has been noted for his business and his crafty maneuvers, and nothing he can do will surprise me much, for I notice that Tebeau is not given to the love of his fellow creature to any noticeable extent.... I have only this to say, and that is it will be a sorry day for the Western League when Tebeau once more gets his think tank into operation in connection with our affairs."[64]

Eight. The War Ends

The war finally came to an end when the Western League met in Chicago on January 28, 1904. Michael Sexton was re-elected president of the Western and C.H. Myrick of Des Moines was tabbed vice-president. George Tebeau, representing both the Denver and Kansas City clubs, was appointed to the board of directors, along with William Rourke and Thomas Burns. The 1904 Western League was to consist of six clubs: Denver, Colorado Springs, Omaha, Des Moines, St. Joseph and Sioux City. The Peoria franchise had been transferred to Sioux City, under W.R. Nation. The Milwaukee franchise was transferred to Pueblo, Colorado, and the Kansas City franchise to Lincoln, Nebraska. It was decided Pueblo and Lincoln would not become active members or have owners for 1904, but the territorial rights would be maintained, thus allowing the Western to keep its Class A minor league status.[65]

It was reported that the Western League–American Association war had cost the Western $75,000 and the Association at least $20,000. To pay for the cost of the war the American Association set aside three percent of gate receipts from each game in a general fund.[66]

Although both the American Association and Western League were classified as Class A minor leagues, it was clear the Association was the stronger league. As a matter of fact, the eight cities represented in the league since 1902 would remain until 1952 (with a two-year exception when Toledo was transferred to Cleveland to hinder the Federal League), when in June of that year the owners of the Toledo franchise moved the team to Charleston, West Virginia. The club operated as an independent barnstorming team within the American Association but retained the Toledo Mud Hens name.[67] After the 1952 season Milwaukee would leave the American Association, as Louis Perini transferred his Boston Braves to the Wisconsin city, and Toledo would reappear again in the A.A. as a farm team of the Milwaukee Braves.

The Western League would remain the same until July 15, 1905, when Colorado Springs transferred its team to Pueblo. Lincoln would replace St. Joseph the next season. In 1909 the Western expanded to eight teams and remained in various cities until its demise in 1937. Although the Western League would retain its Class A status until 1937, the American Association, International League and Pacific Coast League were elevated at Class AA in 1912, dropping the Western League to a lesser status in the minor league world.

Appendix A. American Association 1902 and 1903 Statistics

American Association 1902

The statistics vary for this season in different sources, including contemporary sources. I have decided to give the reader the differing statistics, when available. The statistics in the *1903 Reach Guide* are identical to those found in *Sporting Life* of April 11, 1903, thus the official stats of the day. The *Spalding Guide* is the 1903 edition. Baseball-Reference reflects updated research.

Team	Runs Scored	Batting Average (*Reach Guide*)
Louisville	876	.293
Indianapolis	832	.278
Kansas City	777	.280
St. Paul	696	.283
Minneapolis	638	.244
Columbus	630	.264
Toledo	622	.255
Milwaukee	601	.252

.300 Hitters (Minimum 200 At-Bats)

	Reach Guide			*Spalding Guide*		Baseball-Reference		
	AB	Hits	Avg.		Avg.		AB	Hits	Avg.
John Ganzel, Lou	521	194	.370	Ganzel	.367	Ganzel	530	194	.366
Bill Shannon, St.P	472	159	.337	Shannon	.344	Shannon	471	162	.344
Miller Huggins, St.P	466	153	.326	Hallman	.334	Huggins	466	153	.328
Phil Geier, St.P	512	167	.326	Kerwin	.332	Knoll	379	126	.332
Mike Grady, K.C.	502	163	.324	Grady	.329	Kerwin	521	171	.328
Lee Tannehill, Lou	296	96	.324	Huggins	.322	Grady	505	164	.325
Bill Hallman, Mil	587	189	.322	Tannehill	.322	Geier	524	170	.324

Appendix A

	Reach Guide			Spalding Guide		Baseball-Reference		
	AB	Hits	Avg.		Avg.	AB	Hits	Avg.
Julius Knoll, Col	438	140	.319	Geier	.319	Hallman	587 190	.324
Dan Kerwin, Lou	538	171	.318	Schriver	.319	C. McFarland, Col.	346 112	.324
Bill Schriver, Lou	295	93	.315	Knoll	.317	Tannehill	295 98	.322
Pat Dillard, St.P	510	160	.314	Smith	.310	Schriver	303 96	.317
Mike Smith, K.C.	408	127	.311	Coggswell	.309	Coggswell	276 86	.312
Vincent Maney, Col/Tol	448	139	.310	Maney	.308	Dillard	515 160	.311
Charles Coggswell, Tol	280	87	.310	Clingman	.305	Maney	468 145	.310
Jim Hart, Col	468	144	.307	Hart	.305	Hart	470 145	.309
Dan Turner, Tol	511	156	.305	Beville	.302	J. Rothfuss, K.C.	511 158	.309
Monte Beville, K.C.	517	156	.301	Dillard	.302	Beville	522 161	.308
Billy Clingman, Mil	540	161	.300	J. Flournoy, Lou	.301	Clingman	530 163	.308

Players Scoring More Than 100 Runs

Reach		Spalding	
John Ganzel, Lou	135	Hogriever	124
George Hogriever, Ind	124	Ganzel	119
Dan Kerwin, Lou	114	Kerwin	116
Bill Nance, K.C.	110	Nance	113
Bill Hallman, Mil	110	Hallman	104
Billy Clymer, Lou	105	Rothfuss	104
Jack Rothfuss, K,C.	104	Clymer	103
Monte Beville, K.C.	102		

Top Fielders (300 chances)

	Reach Guide					Spalding Guide			
Catchers	PO	Asst	Error	Pct.		PO	Asst	Error	Pct
George Speer, Mil	365	73	10	.978	Harry Spies, Louis	252	66	14	.946
Harry Spies, Louis	352	67	14	.968	Mike Heydon, Ind	440	100	20	.945
Bill Graffius, Tol	355	98	16	.966	Speer	365	66	12	.945
First Basemen									
George Kilm, Ind	1375	46	20	.986	John Ganzel, Louis	714	52	9	.988
Jack Grim, Col/Ind	674	34	11	.985	Kilm	1407	58	19	.987
Bill Myers, Col	610	27	12	.982	Grim	668	84	10	.985
Second Basemen									
Bill Fox, Ind	314	438	45	.944	Miller Huggins, St.P	342	384	41	.946

American Association 1902 and 1903 Statistics

	Reach Guide					Spalding Guide			
Catchers	PO	Asst	Error	Pct.		PO	Asst	Error	Pct
Frank Sheibeck, Tol/Mil	238	336	35	.943	Sheibeck	199	302	29	.945
Rony Viox, Col	162	211	23	.942	Fox	310	414	45	.941
Third Basemen									
Charlie Kuhns, Ind	278	91	27	.932	Turner	155	250	33	.924
George McBride, K.C./Minn	150	243	33	.923	Jud Smith, Tol	176	250	42	.912
Terry Turner, Col	187	311	42	.922	Bob Schaub, Louis	184	284	56	.910
Shortstops									
Tannehill, Lou	198	276	35	.931	Tannehill	193	274	35	.930
Billy Nattress, Col	159	210	29	.927	Nattress	160	211	31	.922
Ed Lewee, K.C.	379	460	72	.921	Lewee	360	432	68	.921
Outfielders (Minimum 250 chances)									
Sam Dungan, Mil	725	45	24	.970	Gilks	293	38	4	.988
Bob Gilks, Tol	319	52	13	.966	Dan Lally, Col/Minn	272	5	6	.978
Julius Knoll, Col	282	18	11	.965	Knoll	276	176	10	.966

Top Pitchers (Minimum 20 decisions)

	Reach Guide			Baseball-Reference
	Wins	Losses	Pct.	
Davey Dunkle, Lou	30	10	.750	Same
Frank Killen, Ind	16	6	.727	Same
Win Kellum, Ind	25	10	.714	Same
Perry Coons, Lou	24	10	.705	24–9
Ralph Gibson, K.C.	19	9	.678	Same
Charlie Ferguson, St.P	21	10	.677	Same
Nick Altrock, Mil	28	14	.667	Same
Tom Williams, Ind	24	12	.667	Same
Jack Sutthoff, Ind	24	13	.649	Same
Pat Flaherty, Lou	26	16	.619	Same

American Association 1903

The 1903 statistics are also from the *1904 Reach Guide*, and are the same as published in *Sporting Life* of January 16, 1904, the *1904 Spalding Guide* and Baseball-Reference.com. Nevertheless, these stats are probably not very accurate. In *The Sporting News* of January 16, 1904, it was stated the official statistics released by league president Thomas Hickey were totally unreliable, and a number of discrepancies were noted. For example, Jiggs Donahue was listed as playing in only 76 games; he actually played in 107. The Indianapolis correspondent to the St. Louis weekly called Hickey's averages "the biggest joke that was ever perpetrated by a league president. Perhaps he gave the job to the office boy and told him to make the hits, chances, etc. for the first month of the season only and then multiply by five to get figures for the final result. Hickey's stats show Hogriever's batting average as .330. Now, with all due respect to the scrappy right fielder's clouting ability he could not hit .330 if they played with a solid rubber ball and he used 'Home Run Hagerty's' famous lead-filled bat." The correspondent said Hogriever actually hit .272. Win Kellum's win total of 23 games was also challenged, it being claimed he won at least 26 and perhaps 27 games. *Sporting Life* (January 30, 1904) admitted there were some typographical errors, but stated that most data were correct.

Team	Runs Scored	Batting Average
Kansas City	896	.275
St. Paul	803	.281
Louisville	739	.260
Indianapolis	701	.261
Minneapolis	666	.257
Toledo	658	.275
Columbus	647	.257
Milwaukee	611	.266

.300 Hitters (Minimum 200 At-Bats)

	AB	Hits	Avg.
Phil Geier, St.P	518	187	.362
Mike Grady, K.C.	425	151	.355
Billy Clymer, Lou	345	121	.350
Jiggs Donohue, Mil	524	179	.341
Tom McCreery, Min	286	97	.338
George Hogriever, Ind	445	147	.330
Bill Nance, K.C.	526	171	.325
Mike Smith, Min	300	97	.323
Bob Wood, Mil	481	156	.322
John Kleinow, Tol	403	129	.320
George Kihm, Ind	463	148	.319
Fred Odwell, Lou	538	171	.317
Dan Turner, Tol	394	128	.312
Terry Turner, Col	503	156	.310
George Yeager, Min	371	115	.309
Mike Kelley, St.P	252	78	.309
Suter Sullivan, Lou	533	165	.309
Curt Bernard, Tol	431	133	.308
Miller Huggins, St.P	444	137	.308
Billy Shannon, St.P	535	165	.308
Jim Jackson, St.P	520	160	.307

	AB	Hits	Avg.
Germany Shaefer, St.P	480	147	.306
Bob Schaub, Tol	395	122	.306
Bob Unglaub, Mil	480	146	.304

Players Scoring More Than 100 Runs

Billy Shannon, St.P.	132
Jack Rothfuss, K.C.	116
Dan Kerwin, Lou	114
Phil Geier, St.P	113
Bill Nance, K.C.	111
Jim Jackson, St.P	102

Top Fielders (Minimum 300 chances)

Catchers	PO	Asst	Error	Pct.	Passed Balls
John Butler, K.C.	247	75	12	.994	7
George Speer, Mil	264	55	2	.993	5
Wood, Mil	536	122	7	.989	6

First Basemen					
Harry White, Lou	544	23	6	.989	
Mike Grady, K.C.	901	61	11	.988	
Mike Kelley, St.P	667	31	9	.988	

Second Basemen					
Pete Childs, Tol	186	237	13	.979	
Fred Raymer, Col	224	369	24	.961	
Larry Schlafly, Mil	302	387	47	.949	

Third Basemen					
Suter Sullivan, Lou	277	270	32	.944	
Terry Turner, Col	169	193	27	.930	
Charles McIntyre, Min	197	262	42	.916	

Shortstops					
Ed Lewee, K.C.	258	364	39	.940	
Roney Viox, Mil	171	220	30	.928	
Tom Owens, Tol	279	378	58	.918	

Outfielders					
Billy Shannon, St.P	305	19	8	.976	
Dan Lally, Minn	330	12	11	.868	
Fred Odwell, Lou	293	15	13	.859	

Top Pitchers (Minimum 20 decisions)

	Wins	Losses	Pct.
Tom Walker, Lou	26	7	.788

Appendix A

	Wins	Losses	Pct.
Charley Chech, St.P	24	9	.727
Claude Elliott, Mil	24	10	.705
Win Kellum, Ind	23	10	.697
Charlie Ferguson, St.P	19	10	.655
Elmer Meredith, Mil	21	13	.618
Joe Stewart, St.P	16	10	.615
Mal Eagan, Lou	24	16	.600
Doc Reisling, Tol	14	11	.560
Perry Coons, K.C./Lou	14	11	.560
Jim Durham, K.C./Ind	22	18	.550

Appendix B.
Western League 1902 and 1903 Statistics

Statistics from 1902 are from the *1903 Reach Official American League Baseball Guide*, *1903 Spalding Baseball Guide* and *Sporting Life* of December 27, 1902. Statistics from 1903 are from the *1904 Reach Guide*, *1904 Spalding Guide* and *Sporting Life* of January 4, 1904.

Western League 1902

Team	Batting Average
Denver	.287
Kansas City	.262
Milwaukee	.261
Colorado Springs	.260
Des Moines	.251
Omaha	.246
St. Joseph	.245
Peoria	.233

.300 Hitters (Minimum 200 At-Bats)

	AB	Hits	Avg.
Emil Frisk, Den	450	168	.373
Tom Delahanty, Den	554	194	.350
George Stone, Peo/Oma	573	193	.346
Jack O'Brien, Mil	560	191	.341
Bill Congalton, ColSp	313	106	.339
Irv Waldron, K.C.	553	178	.322
Bill Everitt, ColSp	504	159	.315
Fred Ketchum, K.C.	552	168	.304
Gus Dundon, Den	509	154	.303
Charlie Jones, Den	549	165	.301

Players Scoring More Than 100 Runs

Jack O'Brien, Mil	125
Charlie Jones, Den	120
Tom Delahanty, Den	118

Top Fielders (Minimum 300 chances)

Catchers	PO	Asst	Error	Pct.	Passed Balls
Johnny Gonding, Oma	676	165	18	.971	7
Joe Lohbeck, DesM	297	60	9	.962	5
Tom Messitt, K.C.	701	116	23	.959	12

First Basemen	PO	Asst	Error	Pct.	
Dan Stearns, DesM	403	15	4	.991	
David Calhoun, Oma	654	31	10	.983	
Charlie Hanford, Mil/Peo	380	61	9	.980	

Second Basemen	PO	Asst	Error	Pct.	
John O'Brien, Peo	241	297	17	.969	
Joe Quinn, DesM	256	375	26	.960	
Ace Stewart, Oma	336	478	39	.951	

Third Basemen	PO	Asst	Error	Pct.	
George Rohe, St. Joe	181	264	25	.947	
Gus Dundon, Den	201	291	37	.930	
Jim Cockman, Mil	125	177	34	.923	

Shortstops	PO	Asst	Error	Pct.	
Wally Hollingsworth, ColSp	225	335	44	.927	
Charley O'Leary, DesM	366	444	66	.927	
Joe Dolan, Oma	317	384	57	.927	

Outfielders (Minimum 275 Chances)

	PO	Asst	Error	Pct.
Josh Clarke, DesM	247	22	8	.971
Hugh Duffy, Mil	302	12	11	.966
George Stone, Peo/Oma	261	16	10	.965

Top Pitchers (Minimum 25 Games)

Neither *Reach's 1903 Guide* nor *Spalding's 1903 Guide* gives number of wins/losses, only percentage. Number of games pitched will provide only a guide to how many games a pitcher might have won and lost.

	Games	Winning Pct.
Charles Nichols, K.C.	37	.794
Ed Kenna, Mil	27	.739
Frank Parvin, St. Joe	38	.703
Frank Owen, Omaha	40	.703
Al Whitridge, Den	37	.676
Elwood Eyler, Den	41	.650

	Games	Winning Pct.
Mordecai Brown, Oma	43	.643
Charles McCloskey, Den	37	.627
Jake Weimer, K.C.	43	.625

Western League 1903

Team	Batting Average
Colorado Springs	.281
Des Moines	.265
St. Joseph	.265
Milwaukee	.265
Kansas City	.262
Denver	.257
Omaha	.255
Peoria	.250

.300 Hitters (Minimum 200 At-Bats)

	AB	Hits	Ave
Bill Congalton, ColSp	507	184	.363
Tom Fleming, ColSp	533	180	.338
John O'Neill, Mil	442	147	.333
Charley O'Leary, DesM	547	170	.311
Irv Waldron, K.C.	503	156	.310
Tom Delahanty, Den	461	143	.310
George Nill, ColSp	472	142	.301
John McConnell, St. Joe	229	69	.301
High Duffy, Mil	257	77	.300

Players Scoring More Than 100 Runs

Tom Fleming, ColSp	107
John O'Neill, Mil	107
Otto Thiel, Peo	101

Top Fielders (Minimum 300 chances)

Catchers	PO	Asst	Error	Pct.	Passed Balls
Fred Lucia, Mil	562	132	22	.963	5
Johnny Gonding, Oma	409	115	14	.963	6
Bill Wilson, Peo	386	84	9	.959	11
First Basemen					
Bill Everitt, ColSp	1099	87	14	.988	
Julius Streib, K.C.	1198	22	21	.983	
Jay Towne, DesM	1329	42	25	.982	
Second Basemen					
Joe Quinn, DesM	284	359	14	.976	

Second Basemen	PO	Asst	Error	Pct.
George McBride, St. Joe	266	332	24	.961
Tom Delahanty, Den	184	200	18	.955

Third Basemen

	PO	Asst	Error	Pct.
Peter Tibald, ColSp/Peo	137	176	26	.923
Jim Cockman, Mil	154	198	32	.917
George Rohe, St. Joe	169	286	42	.915

Shortstops

	PO	Asst	Error	Pct.
Charley O'Leary, DesM	330	429	60	.927
Frank Gatins, Mil	258	251	40	.927
Ed Holly, Peo	316	287	66	.914

Outfielders (Minimum 200 Chances)

	PO	Asst	Error	Pct.
Bob Carter, Oma	186	17	7	.967
Ira Belden, St. Joe	235	11	10	.961
Charlie Jones, Den	230	20	11	.958

Top Pitchers (Minimum 20 decisions)

	Games	Winning Pct.
Ed Kenna, Mil	39	.757
Frank Cable, K.C.	31	.643
Charles Nichols, K.C.	35	.636
Harris McNeeley, ColSp	42	.663
Len Swormstead, Mil	31	.631
Fred Glade, St. Joe	32	.600
John McPherson, Mil	32	.600
Bill Morrison, DesM	30	.600

Chapter Notes

Chapter One

1. *Sporting Life*, September 21, 1901, p. 6.
2. *The Sporting News*, October 5, 1901, p. 4.
3. *The Sporting News*, October 5, 1901, p. 3.
4. *Sporting Life*, July 19, 1902, p. 18.
5. *Sporting Life*, September 28, 1901, p. 6.
6. *Sporting Life*, October 19, 1901, p. 6; *The Sporting News*, October 19, 1901, p. 4.
7. *The Sporting News*, November 16, 1902.
8. *Sporting Life*, February 6, 1904, p. 6; *Portland Morning Oregonian*, March 6, 1896; *Chicago Daily Inter Ocean*, July 25, 1896.
9. *New York Times*, June 6, 1915.
10. *The Sporting News*, January 16, 1902, p. 5; *New York Times*, July 13, 1908; *St. Paul Globe*, December 13, 1901.
11. *Sporting Life*, July 18, 1908, p. 4.
12. *The Sporting News*, May 9, 1935, p. 2, September 26, 1956, p. 18.
13. *Sporting Life*, December 7, 1901, p. 3.
14. *Sporting Life*, December 14, 1901, p. 11.
15. *Sporting Life*, December 7, 1901, p. 6.
16. *The Sporting News*, December 7, 1901, p. 4.
17. *The Sporting News*, December 7, 1901, p. 4.
18. *The Sporting News*, December 14, 1901, p. 3.
19. *Sporting Life*, January 25, 1902, p. 1; *Milwaukee Sentinel*, February 9, 1902; *The Sporting News*, December 12, 1907, p. 5.
20. *Sporting Life*, September 13, 1902, p. 16.
21. *Sporting Life*, December 14, 1901, p. 2.
22. *The Sporting News*, December 14,, p. 3,4, December 21, 1901, p. 7.
23. *Sporting Life*, January 18, 1902, p. 8.
24. *The Sporting News*, April 5, 1902, p. 2.
25. *The Sporting News*, December 14, 1901, p. 3.
26. *Milwaukee Sentinel*, February 3, 1902.
27. *Sporting Life*, April 12, 1902, p. 5.
28. *Milwaukee Sentinel*, January 18, 1902.
29. *Minneapolis Journal*, December 23, 1901.
30. *The Sporting News*, January 18, 1902, p. 4.
31. *Minneapolis Journal*, December 21, 1901.
32. *The Sporting News*, September 28, 1901, p. 1.
33. *Minneapolis Journal*, December 5, 1901.
34. *Sporting Life*, December 28, 1901, p. 3.
35. *The Sporting News*, December 28, 1901, p. 7.
36. Some background from Nebaseballhistory.com, accessed July 15, 2010.
37. *Milwaukee Sentinel*, February 25, 1902.
38. *St. Paul Globe*, January 9, 1902.
39. *Sporting Life*, January 4, 1902, p. 5; *Milwaukee Sentinel*, January 3, 5, 1902.
40. *Sporting Life*, September 19, 1903, p. 21.
41. Clifford A. Brown. "Biography of Humphrey B. Chamberlin — Patron of the University of Denver's historic Chamberlin Observatory," *Sporting Life*, February 8, 1902, p. 2; *The Sporting News*, December 12, 1907, p. 5.
42. *The Sporting News*, February 1, 1902, p. 3.
43. *Milwaukee Sentinel*, March 1, 1902.
44. *Milwaukee Sentinel*, February 3, 1902.
45. *Milwaukee Sentinel*, February 21, March 1, 1902.
46. *Milwaukee Journal*, April 10, 1902.
47. *Milwaukee Sentinel*, February 27, 1902.
48. *The Sporting News*, January 25, 1902, p. 2.
49. *Colorado Springs Gazette*, March 17, 1902.
50. *Milwaukee Sentinel*, January 9, 1902.
51. *Milwaukee Sentinel*, January 31, 1901, January 9, 1902.

52. *The Sporting News*, November 23, 1901, p. 7, November 30, 1901, p. 4.
53. *The Sporting News*, March 1, 1902, p. 7.
54. *Milwaukee Sentinel*, February 3, 1902.
55. *Milwaukee Sentinel*, February 26, 1902.
56. *Milwaukee Sentinel*, February 25, 1902.
57. Information kindly provided by Ralph J. Christian of the State Historical Society of Iowa.
58. *Milwaukee Sentinel*, March 25, 1902.
59. *The Sporting News*, March 15, 1902, p. 4.
60. *Milwaukee Sentinel*, March 18, 1902.
61. *St. Louis Republican*, July 20, 1902; *New York Times*, July 29, 1905; Walter Williams, ed., *A History of Northwest Missouri* (Chicago: Lewis, 1915), 3:1798.
62. *Milwaukee Sentinel*, January 1, 1903.
63. *Milwaukee Sentinel*, March 25, 28, April 10, 1902.
64. *The Sporting News*, March 22, 1902, p. 2.
65. *The Sporting News*, March 22, 1902, p. 2.
66. *Milwaukee Sentinel*, March 25, 1902.
67. *Milwaukee Sentinel*, March 29, 1902.
68. *Milwaukee Sentinel*, March 14, 1902.
69. *Evening Wisconsin*, April 23, 1902.
70. *Sporting Life*, October 26, 1901, p. 2.
71. *Milwaukee Sentinel*, February 26, 1902; *Sporting Life*, March 8, 1902, p. 7.
72. *St. Paul Globe*, March 25, 1902.
73. *Sporting Life*, May 17, 1902, p. 18.
74. *Sporting Life*, April 26, 1902, p. 14.
75. *The Sporting News*, April 26, 1902, p. 4.
76. *The Sporting News*, January 21, 1937.
77. *St. Paul Globe*, August 3, 1902.
78. *Sporting Life*, April 26, 1902, p. 17.
79. *The Sporting News*, April 12, 1902, p. 2.

Chapter Two

1. *The Sporting News*, December 14, 1901, p. 7.
2. *The Sporting News*, March 15, 1902, p. 4.
3. *Milwaukee Sentinel*, December 10, 1901.
4. *Evening Wisconsin*, April 26, 1902.
5. *Sporting Life*, January 18, 1902, p. 8; *The Sporting News*, January 18, 1902, p. 5.
6. *Sporting Life*, February 8, 1902, p. 3.
7. *St. Paul Globe*, February 23, 1902.
8. *The Sporting News*, January 11, 1902, p. 2.
9. *The Sporting News*, January 25, 1902, p. 3, February 15, 1902, p. 5.
10. *Sporting Life*, February 15, 1902, p. 8.
11. *Sporting Life*, February 15, 1902, p. 13.
12. *The Sporting News*, February 22, 1902, p. 4.
13. *The Sporting News*, March 1, 1902, p. 4.
14. *The Sporting News*, March 18, 1902, p. 1,2.
15. *Sporting Life*, February 22, 1902, p. 10, March 8, 1902, p. 7, July 5, 1902, p. 25; *Evening Wisconsin*, April 23, 1902.
16. *St. Paul Globe*, April 13, 1902; *Milwaukee Journal*, July 10, 1902.
17. *St. Paul Globe*, March 5, 1902; *Sporting Life*, March 1, 1902, p. 7, March 8, 1902, p. 5.
18. *Milwaukee Sentinel*, March 7, 1902.
19. *Sporting Life*, April 5, 1902, p. 5; *The Sporting News*, April 12, 1903, p. 3.
20. *St. Paul Globe*, April 1, 1902; *Sporting Life*, April 5, 1902, p. 5.
21. *The Sporting News*, January 4, 1902, p. 4.
22. *Oakland Tribune*, March 22, 1902.
23. *Oakland Tribune*, March 22, 1902.
24. *The Sporting News*, May 3, 1902, p. 3.
25. "Roy Evans" by Brian McKenna, SABR Biography Project.
26. *Milwaukee Sentinel*, March 22, April 3, 1902; *Sporting Life*, April 5, 1902, p. 9, April 26, 1902, p. 17.
27. *Milwaukee Sentinel*, March 16, 1902.
28. *Sporting Life*, April 26, 1902, p. 17.
29. *Milwaukee Sentinel*, April 17, 1902.
30. *Milwaukee Sentinel*, April 12, 1902; *Sporting Life*, April 26, 1902, p. 17, 18.
31. *Milwaukee Sentinel*, April 12, 1902.
32. *Sporting Life*, October 12, 1901, p. 10.
33. *Sporting Life*, April 10, 1902, p. 9.
34. *Sporting Life*, April 26, 1902, p. 18; *The Sporting News*, April 26, 1902, p. 6.
35. *The Sporting News*, July 12, 1902, p. 4; *Sporting Life*, May 3, 1902, p. 13, July 19, 1902, p. 17, August 30, 1902, p. 6, 15.
36. *Milwaukee Sentinel*, May 7 1902.
37. *Evening Wisconsin*, April 22, 1902.
38. *Sporting Life*, June 7, 1902, p. 5,17.
39. *Sporting Life*, June 7, 1902, p. 18, June 14, 1902, p. 6.
40. *Sporting Life*, July 19, 1902, p. 15.
41. *Milwaukee Sentinel*, April 8, 9, 13, 1902.
42. *The Sporting News*, April 12, 1902, p. 5.
43. *The Sporting News*, May 24, 1902, p. 7.
44. *Sporting Life*, June 14, 1902, p. 4.
45. *The Sporting News*, August 9, 1902, p. 6.
46. *Milwaukee Sentinel*, June 11, 1902; *Sporting Life*, June 21, 1902, p. 15.
47. *The Sporting News*, June 21, 1902, p. 1, June 28, 1902, p. 4; *Sporting Life*, June 28, 1902, p. 15.
48. *Sporting Life*, August 16, 1902, p. 4.
49. *St. Paul Globe*, July 17, 1902.
50. *Sporting Life*, June 28, 1902, p. 15.
51. *Sporting Life*, August 9, 1902, p. 2, 21, August 30, 1902, p. 15.

52. *Sporting Life*, May 10, 1902, p. 9; July 5, 1902, p. 25.
53. *Milwaukee Sentinel*, June 10, August 9, 1902.
54. *Milwaukee Sentinel*, April 2, 1902.
55. *Des Moines Daily Capital*, March 6, 1902.
56. *Sporting Life*, January 25, 1903, p. 3.
57. *Milwaukee Sentinel*, April 13, 1902.

Chapter Three

1. *Sporting Life*, February 1, 1902, p. 10.
2. *Sporting Life*, February 15, 1902, p. 8.
3. *Milwaukee Sentinel*, February 9, 1902.
4. *The Sporting News*, March 1, 1902, p. 3; *Sporting Life*, March 1, 1902, p. 5, March 8, 1902, p. 2.
5. *Milwaukee Sentinel*, February 28, 1902.
6. *The Sporting News*, March 15, 1902, p. 5; *Sporting Life*, March 8, 1902, p. 7.
7. *Milwaukee Sentinel*, February 28, March 8, 9, 1902.
8. *Sporting Life*, March 22, 1902, p. 3, April 26, 1902, p. 10; For a detailed description of the events involving the building of Eclipse Park see Rex Hamann, ed., "The American Association Almanac: A Baseball History Journal," vol. 8, no. 1.
9. *Pittsburgh Post Gazette*, November 9, 1904.
10. *The Sporting News*, May 3, 1902, p. 6.
11. *Sporting Life*, May 17, 1902, p. 17.
12. *The Sporting News*, June 17, 1937, p. 2.
13. *The Sporting News*, April 26, 1902, p. 6.
14. *Milwaukee Sentinel*, March 29, April 11, 26, 1902.
15. *Milwaukee Sentinel*, February 26, 1902; *Milwaukee Journal*, April 14, 1902.
16. *Milwaukee Sentinel*, April 27, October 16, 1902; *Sporting Life*, May 24, 1902, p. 17; *The Sporting News*, June 14, 1902, p. 1; *Milwaukee Journal*, October 16, 1902; *St. Paul Globe*, October 17, 1902.
17. *Sporting Life*, May 17, 1902, p. 15.
18. *Milwaukee Sentinel*, May 12, 1902.
19. *The Sporting News*, May 24, 1902, p. 7.
20. *St. Paul Globe*, May 23, 1902.
21. *Colorado Springs Gazette*, March 31, 1902.
22. *The Sporting News*, January 18, 1902, p. 7, February 1, 1902; *Sporting Life*, March 20, 1902, p. 4; John Heney, "John's History Corner," Newsletter of the Pikes Peak Historical Street Railway Foundation, Winter 2001, vol. 10, no. 2.
23. *Colorado Spring Gazette*, December 9, 1902.
24. *Colorado Springs* Gazette, April 24, 1902.
25. *Milwaukee Journal*, May 3, 1902.
26. *Milwaukee Sentinel*, May 10, 1902.
27. *Valentine* (Nebraska) *Democrat*, June 12, 1902.
28. Omaha Public Library, Digital picture file http://digital.omahapubliclibrary.org/early omaha/buildings/millardhotel.html.
29. *St. Louis Republic*, May 14, 1902; *St. Joseph Gazette-Herald*, May 14, 1902; *The Sporting News*, May 24, 1902, p. 1; *Sporting Life*, May 24, 1902, p. 18, May 31, 1902, p. 18.
30. *Milwaukee Sentinel*, May 23, 1902.
31. *Milwaukee Sentinel*, May 24, 1902.
32. *Milwaukee Sentinel*, May 9, 1902.
33. *Milwaukee Sentinel*, May 29, 1902.
34. *The Sporting News*, May 17, 1902, p. 4.
35. *Des Moines Ledger*, May 25, 1902; *Sporting Life*, June 21, 1902, p. 18; *The Sporting News*, May 31, 1902, p. 7, June 7, 1902, p. 7.
36. *The Sporting News*, June 28, 1902, p. 4, July 12, 1902, p. 1.
37. *The Sporting News*, July 12, 1902, p. 1.
38. *Sporting Life*, April 26, 1902, p. 10.
39. *Sporting Life*, June 28, 1902, p. 18.
40. *Sporting Life*, July 5, 1902, p. 18.
41. *Milwaukee Sentinel*, June 26, 1902.
42. *Sporting Life*, June 28, 1902, p. 15.
43. *The Sporting News*, February 8, 1902, p. 2.
44. *Sporting Life*, July 12, 1902, p. 18.
45. *Sporting Life*, July 12, 1902, p. 6.
46. *The Sporting News*, July 26, 1902, p. 20.
47. *Sporting Life*, July 12, 1902, p. 20.
48. *Sporting Life*, July 12, 1902, p. 6.
49. *Milwaukee Sentinel*, July 2, 1902; *The Sporting News*, July 12, 1902, p. 4.
50. *The Sporting News*, July 12, 1902, p. 7.
51. *Sporting Life*, July 12, 1902, p. 5.
52. *The Sporting News*, August 9, 1902, p. 5.
53. *Sporting Life*, August 2, 1902, p. 13, 17; August 23, 1902, p. 1.
54. *St. Paul Globe*, September 22, 1902; *The Sporting News*, September 27, 1902, p. 1; *Omaha Daily Bee*, September 22, 1902.
55. *St. Paul Globe*, September 23, 1902.
56. *The Sporting News*, November 1, 1902, p. 6.
57. *Sporting Life*, January 25, 1902, p. 3; *Milwaukee Sentinel*, May 9, 1902.
58. *Milwaukee Sentinel*, June 12, 1902.
59. *The Sporting News*, August 2, 1902, p. 4.
60. *Kansas City Star*, August 26, 1902; *St. Joseph Daily News*, August 26, 1902.
61. *Peoria Evening Star*, August 26, 28, 1902; *Peoria Journal*, August 26, 28, 1902.
62. *Milwaukee Sentinel*, September 22, 1902; *Milwaukee Daily News*, September 22, 1902; *Omaha Daily News*, September 22, 1902.

63. *Omaha World-Herald*, September 22, 1902.
64. *Milwaukee Sentinel*, September 23, 1902.
65. *Omaha World-Herald*, September 23, 1902.
66. *Sporting Life*, October 18, 1902, p. 4,10.
67. *The Sporting News*, October 11, 1902, p. 1.
68. *The Sporting News*, October 4, 1902, p. 3, 7.
69. *Sporting Life*, September 27, 1902, p. 12, October 18, 1902, p. 4, 10, November 1, 1902, p. 8.
70. *Milwaukee Sentinel*, October 26, 1902.
71. *The Sporting News*, September 13, 1902, p. 1.
72. *The Sporting News*, October 4, 1902, p. 3.
73. *The Sporting News*, October 4, 1902, p. 7.
74. *Sporting Life*, September 27, 1902, p. 1.
75. *Milwaukee Sentinel*, October 7, 1902.
76. *The Sporting News*, September 13, 1902, p. 4; *Sporting Life*, December 6, 1902, p. 4.
77. *Milwaukee Daily News*, September 25, 1902.
78. *St. Paul Globe*, September 23, 1902.
79. *Milwaukee Sentinel*, August 3, 1902.
80. *St. Paul Globe*, February 4,1903.
81. *Sporting Life*, September 6, 1902, p. 7.
82. *The Sporting News*, October 18, 1902, p. 5.

Chapter Four

1. *The Sporting News*, February 22, 1902, p. 5.
2. *Milwaukee Journal*, April 23, 1902.
3. *The Sporting News*, May 3, 1902, p. 1.
4. *Milwaukee Sentinel*, May 28, 1902.
5. *Sporting Life*, June 21, 1902, p. 3.
6. *Milwaukee Sentinel*, June 18, 1902.
7. *Milwaukee Sentinel*, June 20, 1902.
8. *St. Paul Globe*, May 23, 1902.
9. *The Sporting News*, June 28, 1902, p. 6.
10. *Sporting Life*, July 19, 1902, p. 18.
11. *Salt Lake Herald*, July 26, 1902.
12. *The Sporting News*, July 19, 1902, p. 1.
13. *The Sporting News*, July 26, 1902, p. 7.
14. *Sporting Life*, December 13, 1902, p. 5.
15. *The Sporting News*, July 19, 1902, p. 1.
16. *Salt Lake Herald*, July 18, 1902.
17. *The Sporting News*, July 19, 1902, p. 4.
18. *Milwaukee Sentinel*, September 28, 1902.
19. *Sporting Life*, July 19, 1902, p. 18.
20. *Sporting Life*, August 23, 1902, p. 14.
21. *Colorado Springs Gazette*, August 31, 1902; *Milwaukee Sentinel*, August 31, 1902; *Sporting Life*, September 6, 1902, p. 1, September 20, 1902, p. 14.
22. *Milwaukee Sentinel*, August 8, 1902.
23. *Milwaukee Sentinel*, July 8, 10, 1902.
24. *St. Paul Globe*, August 1, 1902.
25. *Sporting Life*, August 30, 1902, p. 7.
26. *The Sporting News*, September 13, 1902, p. 1.
27. *The Sporting News*, October 11, 1902, p. 5.
28. *Sporting Life*, April 18, 1903, p. 12.
29. *The Sporting News*, April 25, 1903, p. 3.
30. *Sporting Life*, May 23, 1903, p. 19.
31. *Sporting Life*, May 23, 1903, p. 10.
32. *The Sporting News*, September 27, 1902, p. 4, January 3, 1903, p. 6.
33. *The Sporting News*, January 31, 1903, p. 1.
34. *Colorado Springs Gazette*, July 10, 1903; *Cedar Rapids Evening Gazette*, July 10, 1903; *The Sporting News*, July 18, 1903, p. 4; *Sporting Life*, July 25, 1903, p. 21.
35. *Milwaukee Sentinel*, July 27, 1903.
36. *St. Paul Globe*, September 22, 1903.
37. *Sporting Life*, May 9, 1903, p. 11.
38. *The Sporting News*, May 23, 1903, p. 7.
39. *Milwaukee Sentinel*, May 17, 1903.
40. *Sporting Life*, May 6, 1903, p. 23.
41. *Mansfield* (Ohio) *News*, June 13, 1903.
42. *Milwaukee Sentinel*, June 13, 1903, *Fort Wayne Morning Journal-Gazette*, June 13, 1903.
43. *Milwaukee Sentinel*, June 13, 1903.
44. *Milwaukee Sentinel*, June 14, 1903.
45. *Milwaukee Sentinel*, June 14, 1903.
46. *Milwaukee Sentinel*, June 15, 18, 19, 1903.
47. *Sporting Life*, July 4, 1903, p. 16.
48. *The Sporting News*, June 27, 1903, p. 1.
49. *Sporting Life*, July 11, 1903, p. 15.
50. *Sporting Life*, September 26, 1903, p. 15.
51. *Sporting Life*, July 18, 1903, p. 5.
52. *Mansfield* (Ohio) *News*, August 1, 1903.
53. *St. Paul Globe*, July 26, 1903; *The Sporting News*, August 11,1903, p. 4.
54. *Sporting Life*, September 5, 1903, p. 5.
55. *Milwaukee Sentinel*, September 8, 1903.
56. *Milwaukee Sentinel*, September 7, 8, 1903.
57. *Milwaukee Journal*, September 8, 1903.

Chapter Five

1. *The Sporting News*, September 27, 1902, p. 4.
2. *Milwaukee Sentinel*, June 28, 29, July 2, 1902.
3. *Sporting Life*, July 12, 1902, p. 7, August 30, 1902, p. 7.

4. *The Sporting News*, October 4, 1903.
5. *Evening Wisconsin*, September 1, 1902; *Sporting Life*, September 6, 1902, p. 7.
6. *The Sporting News*, October 18, 1902, p. 3, 4.
7. *St. Paul Globe*, October 28, 1902.
8. *The Sporting News*, November 1, 1902, p. 1.
9. *The Sporting News*, February 14, 1903, p. 6.
10. *Sporting Life*, November 8, 1902, p. 4.
11. *Sporting Life*, November 8, 1902, p. 6.
12. *Colorado Springs Gazette*, November 14, 1902.
13. *Sporting Life*, November 29, 1902, p. 4, December 6, 1902, p. 4.
14. *Sporting Life*, November 29, 1902, p. 4; *The Sporting News*, November 29, 1902, p. 5.
15. *Sporting Life*, December 6, 1902, p. 4.
16. *The Sporting News*, December 6, 1902, p. 2.
17. *Sporting Life*, December 13, 1902, p. 5.
18. *Sporting Life*, March 15, 1902, p. 7.
19. *St. Paul Globe*, December 7, 1902.
20. *St. Paul Globe*, November 30, 1902.
21. *Sporting Life*, November 29, 1902, p. 7, December 6, 1902, p. 4; *Milwaukee Sentinel*, December 18, 19, 1902.
22. *The Sporting News*, November 29, 1902, p. 2.
23. *Milwaukee Sentinel*, December 2, 9, 1902.
24. *St. Paul Globe*, December 12, 1902.
25. *Sporting Life*, December 20, 1902, p. 7.
26. *St. Paul Globe*, December 22, 1902; *Sporting Life*, December 27, 1902, p. 7.
27. *St. Paul Globe*, December 18, 1902; *Chicago Eagle*, December 20, 1902.
28. *The Sporting News*, January 3, 1903, p. 1.
29. *St. Paul Globe*, December 18, 19, 1902; *Milwaukee Sentinel*, December 24, 1902.
30. *Sporting Life*, January 17, 1903, p. 1.
31. *Sporting Life*, January 17, 1903, p. 6.
32. *Milwaukee Sentinel*, January 4, 1903.
33. *Sporting Life*, February 7, 1903, p. 4.
34. *The Sporting News*, February 7, 1903, p. 1.
35. *Sporting Life*, February 7, 1903, p. 4.
36. *Milwaukee Sentinel*, February 13, 1903; *Sporting Life*, February 21, 1903, p. 3.
37. *St. Paul Globe*, February 18, 1903.
38. *Milwaukee Sentinel*, February 10, 1903.
39. *The Sporting News*, February 21, 1903, p. 1.
40. *St. Paul Globe*, April 8, 1903.
41. *The Sporting News*, April 25, 1903, p. 7.
42. *St. Paul Globe*, May 6, 1903.
43. *St. Paul Globe*, June 14, 1903.
44. *St. Paul Globe*, June 17, 1903.
45. *St. Paul Globe*, June 23, 1903.
46. *Sporting Life*, August 29, 1903, p. 13.
47. *Sporting Life*, January 31, 1903, p. 2, February 7, 1903, p. 2; *The Sporting News*, January 24, 1903, p. 2.
48. *Sporting Life*, February 7, 1903, p. 8.
49. *The Sporting News*, January 24, 1903, p. 2.
50. *Sporting Life*, August 30, 1902, p. 7.
51. *The Sporting News*, January 10, 1903, p. 6.

Chapter Six

1. *Evening Wisconsin*, September 25, 1902; *Milwaukee Journal*, September 25, 1902; *Milwaukee Daily News*, September 25, 1902, October 8, 1902.
2. *Milwaukee Sentinel*, October 4, 8, 1902; *Milwaukee Journal*, October 4, 1902; *Milwaukee Daily News*, October 4, 1902.
3. *Milwaukee Sentinel*, October 7, 9, 1902; *Milwaukee Daily News*, October 7, 1902.
4. *Milwaukee Sentinel*, October 23, 1902.
5. *Milwaukee Sentinel*, October 7, 8, 9, 1902; *Daily Milwaukee News*, October 7, 1902.
6. *Milwaukee Daily News*, October 10, 1902.
7. *Milwaukee Sentinel*, October 15, 1902.
8. *Milwaukee Daily News*, October 13, 1902; *Evening Wisconsin*, October 14, 1902; *Milwaukee Sentinel*, October 15, 1902.
9. *Milwaukee Sentinel*, October 16, 1902.
10. *Milwaukee Sentinel*, October 15, 1902.
11. *Milwaukee Sentinel*, October 18, 1902; *Milwaukee Daily News*, October 18, 1902; *Milwaukee Journal*, October 18, 1902.
12. *Milwaukee Sentinel*, October 19, 1902.
13. *Milwaukee Sentinel*, October 23, 1902.
14. *Evening Wisconsin*, October 27, 1902; *Milwaukee Sentinel*, October 28, 29, 1902.
15. *Milwaukee Sentinel*, February 1, 1903.
16. *Evening Wisconsin*, May 9, 1903.
17. *Milwaukee Daily News*, July 2, 1903.
18. *Milwaukee Journal*, September 18, 1903; *Milwaukee Sentinel*, September 18, 1903.
19. *Evening Wisconsin*, July 7, 1903.
20. *Milwaukee Sentinel*, June 19, 1904.
21. *The Sporting News*, May 17, 1902, p. 1.
22. *Sporting Life*, December 27, 1902, p. 7.
23. *Sporting Life*, January 3, 1903, p. 7.
24. *The Sporting News*, February 7, 1903, p. 4.
25. *Sporting Life*, February 7, 1903, p. 7.
26. *Sporting Life*, February 21, 1903, p. 3.
27. *The Sporting News*, February 14, 1903, p. 2.
28. *Sporting Life*, February 21, 1903, p. 6.

29. *Sporting Life*, March 7, 1903, p. 3, March 14, 1903, p. 6.
30. *Sporting Life*, April 25, 1903, p. 13, 14; *Milwaukee Sentinel*, April 26, 1903.
31. *Milwaukee Sentinel*, April 26, 1903; *Sporting Life*, May 9, 1903, p. 10.
32. *Sporting Life*, June 6, 1903, p. 5, June 13, 1903, p. 12.
33. *Sporting Life*, July 11, 1903, p. 15.
34. *Sporting Life*, July 18, 1903, p. 1.
35. *Sporting Life*, June 27, 1903, p. 12.
36. *Milwaukee Sentinel*, June 22, 29, 1903.
37. *Sporting Life*, May 2, 1903, p. 10.
38. *Milwaukee Sentinel*, November 29, 1902.
39. *The Sporting News*, November 29, 1902, p. 5.
40. *Milwaukee Sentinel*, December 4, 1902.
41. *Milwaukee Sentinel*, January 30, February 7, 1903; *The Sporting News*, January 31, 1903, p. 1; *Sporting Life*, February 14, 1903, p. 2.
42. *Milwaukee Sentinel*, April 23, 1903; *Sporting Life*, May 2, 1903, p. 10.
43. *Sporting Life*, May 2, 1903, p. 10, May 9, 1903, p. 11.
44. *Milwaukee Sentinel*, May 9, 1903; *Sporting Life*, May 9, 1905, p. 14, May 23, 1903, p. 15; *The Sporting News*, May 30, 1903, p. 1.
45. *Sporting Life*, August 22, 1903, p. 4, 6; *The Sporting News*, August 15, 1903, p. 7.

Chapter Seven

1. *Sporting Life*, December 6, 1902, p. 9.
2. *Milwaukee Sentinel*, May 23, 1902.
3. *Sporting Life*, February 21, 1903, p. 3.
4. *Milwaukee Journal*, June 3, 1884, December 17, 1896; *Milwaukee Sentinel*, November 9, 22, 1899; *Chicago Daily Inter Ocean*, July 13, 1895.
5. *Sporting Life*, April 11, 1903, p. 15.
6. *The Sporting News*, January 10, 1903, p. 1; *Sporting Life*, January 31, 1902, p. 6.
7. *The Sporting News*, February 14, 1903, p. 6.
8. *Milwaukee Sentinel*, December 19, 1902.
9. *Sporting Life*, August 22, 1903, p. 1.
10. *The Sporting News*, December 20, 1902, p. 5.
11. *The Sporting News*, December 20, 1902, p. 5.
12. *The Sporting News*, December 13, 1902, p. 4; *Sporting Life*, January 31, 1903, p. 9.
13. *Milwaukee Sentinel*, December 4, 13, 20, 13 1902.
14. *Milwaukee Sentinel*, September 10, 1902; *The Sporting News*, October 25, 1902, p. 2.
15. *The Sporting News*, January 31, 1903, p. 2.
16. *Sporting Life*, April 25, 1902, p. 14, May 9, 1903, p. 11.
17. *Sporting Life*, November 1, 1902, p. 3, February 21, 1903, p. 9.
18. *Sporting Life*, December 20, 1902, p. 7; *The Sporting News*, April 4, 1903, p. 2.
19. *The Sporting News*, January 24, 1903, p. 3; *Sporting Life*, February 7, 1903, p. 8.
20. *Sporting Life*, February 14, 1902, p. 6, February 21, 1903, p. 2.
21. *The Sporting News*, March 14, 1903, p. 4.
22. *The Sporting News*, March 28, 1903, p. 7.
23. *Sporting Life*, March 28, 1903, p. 8.
24. *Sporting Life*, May 30, 1903, p. 4.
25. *Sporting Life*, July 11, 1903, p. 19.
26. *Salt Lake Herald*, December 16, 1902, January 31, 1903.
27. *The Sporting News*, January 24, 1903, p. 5.
28. *The Sporting News*, March 14, 1903, p. 7.
29. *Sporting Life*, February 14, 1903, p. 2; *The Sporting News*, March 14, 1903, p. 7.
30. *Philadelphia North American*, July 19, 1903.
31. *Milwaukee Sentinel*, May 21, 1903; *Sporting Life*, May 30, 1903, p. 2.
32. *Sporting Life*, October 25, 1908, p. 8.
33. *The Sporting News*, January 17, 1903, p. 4.
34. *St. Paul Globe*, July 17, 1903.
35. *Washington* (D.C.) *Times*, March 25, 1903; *St. Paul Globe*, May 22, June 7, 1903; *Sporting Life*, August 15, 1903 , p. 17.
36. *The Sporting News*, January 10, 1903, p. 1; *Milwaukee Sentinel*, January 25, 1903; *Sporting Life*, January 31, 1903, p. 9, February 7, 1903, p. 4.
37. *Sporting Life*, May 23, 1903, p. 11.
38. *The Sporting News*, August 22, 1903, p. 7; *Sporting Life*, August 22, 1903, p. 6, November 28, 1903, p. 5, 6.
39. *Milwaukee Sentinel*, March 22, 1903.
40. *Sporting Life*, March 28, 1903, p. 8.
41. *Sporting Life*, April 18, 1903, p. 14.
42. *Toledo Bee*, April 26, 27, 1903.
43. *Sporting Life*, April 25, 1903, p. 12.
44. *Milwaukee Sentinel*, June 7, 1903.
45. *Sporting Life*, May 23, 1903, p. 5; *Daily Kennebec* (Maine) *Journal*, July 8, 1903.
46. *Sporting Life*, June 6, 1903, p. 23.
47. *Milwaukee Sentinel*, June 12, 1903; *Sporting Life*, June 20, 1903, p. 22, 23.
48. *Sporting Life*, April 18, 1903, p. 13.
49. *Evening Wisconsin*, June 27, 1903; *Mil-

waukee Journal*, June 27, 1903; *Milwaukee Daily News*, June 27, 1903.
50. *Milwaukee Sentinel*, July 14, 21, 1903.
51. *The Sporting News*, March 7, 1903, p. 1; *Sporting Life*, March 21, 1903 , p. 1.
52. *Sporting Life*, March 14, 1903, p. 6, March 21, 1903, p. 9, April 25, 1903, p. 14.
53. *Sporting Life*, July 18, 1903, p. 5, 17, July 25, 1903, p. 3, 17.
54. *Sporting Life*, June 6, 1903, p. 23, June 13, 1903, p. 18, June 20, 1903, p. 7, July 4, 1903, p. 12, July 25, 1903, p. 7; *Washington* (D.C.) *Times*, June 15, 1903.
55. *Sporting Life*, June 27, 1903, p. 22, July 25, 1903, p. 3.
56. *Sporting Life*, July 25, 1903, p. 17.
57. *St. Paul Globe*, August 3, 1902; *The Sporting News*, September 5, 1903, p. 5.
58. *The Sporting News*, August 22, 1903, p. 1; *Sporting Life*, September 5, 1903, p. 16.
59. *Mansfield* (Ohio) *News*, August 18, 1903.
60. *Milwaukee Sentinel*, August 11, 1903.
61. *Mansfield* (Ohio) *News*, September 2, 1903.
62. *Sporting Life*, September 12, 1903, p. 15; *The Sporting News*, November 21, 1903, p. 3.
63. *Reach 1904 Base Ball Guide. Sporting Life* of October 3, 1903, p. 10 gives different win-loss totals, but team positions remain the same.
64. *The Sporting News*, September 26, 1903, p. 7.
65. *Sporting Life*, April 25, 1903, p. 10.
66. *Sporting Life*, May 2, 1903, p. 14.
67. *Sporting Life*, June 6, 1903, p. 5.
68. *Milwaukee Sentinel*, June 2, 3, 5, 1903; *Sporting Life*, June 13, 1903, p. 11, June 20, 1903, p. 21.
69. *The Sporting News*, June 13, 1903, p. 1.
70. *Milwaukee Sentinel*, June 20, 23, 24, 1903; *Sporting Life*, July 4, 1903, p. 15, 16.
71. *Sporting Life*, July 25, 1903, p. 17.
72. *Milwaukee Sentinel*, June 20, 24, 1903.
73. *The Sporting News*, April 11, 1903, p. 3, April 18, 1903, p. 5; *Sporting Life*, May 2, 1903, p. 4.
74. *Sporting Life*, August 1, 1903, p. 17, August 8, 1903, p. 21.
75. *Evening Wisconsin*, September 8, 1903.
76. *Milwaukee Sentinel*, July 28, 1903; *The Sporting News*, August 1, 1903, p. 1; *Sporting Life*, August 8, 1903, p. 21.
77. *Evening Wisconsin*, August 4, 1903.
78. These standings from *Reach 1904 Base Ball Guide* and *Sporting Life*, September 26, 1903, p. 18. *The Sporting News* of September 26, 1903, p. 6 and *Spalding 1904 Base Ball Guide* give different win-loss records, but the same team positions in the race.
79. *Sporting Life*, September 26, 1903, p. 18.
80. *Sporting Life*, October 3, 1903, p. 4.
81. *The Sporting News*, September 26, 1903, p. 4.
82. *Sporting Life*, October 3, 1903, p. 4.
83. *Sporting Life*, October 3, 1903, p. 4.
84. *St. Paul Globe*, September 22, 1903.
85. *The Sporting News*, September 26, 1903, p. 4.

Chapter Eight

1. *Milwaukee Sentinel*, August 16, 1903.
2. *Sporting Life*, September 5, 1903, p. 4.
3. *Sporting Life*, October 17, 1903, p. 12, 13.
4. *The Sporting News*, October 10, 1903, p. 1.
5. *Sporting Life*, November 21, 1905, p. 4, 5.
6. *The Sporting News*, October 10, 1903, p. 1.
7. *Sporting Life*, October 17, 1903, p. 13.
8. *Milwaukee Daily News*, September 18, 1903.
9. *Sporting Life*, November 7, 1903, p. 4.
10. The Sporting News, October 31, 1903, p. 3.
11. *St. Paul Globe*, September 19, 22, 1903.
12. *Milwaukee Sentinel*, September 26, 1903; *Sporting Life*, October 3, 1903, p. 4.
13. *Colorado Springs Gazette*, November 23, 1902; *The Sporting News*, November 29, 1902, p. 4; *Sporting Life*, January 10, 1903, p. 4.
14. *The Sporting News*, September 19, 1903, p. 5.
15. *Sporting Life*, October 3, 1903, p. 4; *The Sporting News*, October 3, 1903, p. 1, October 24, 1903, p. 8.
16. *Sporting Life*, October 17, 1903, p. 1, October 24, 1903, p. 9; *St. Paul Globe*, December 27, 1903.
17. *Sporting Life*, November 7, 1903, p. 4, November 21, 1904, p. 4.
18. *Sporting Life*, November 28, 1903, p. 7.
19. *The Sporting News*, October 24, 1903, p. 2.
20. *Milwaukee Sentinel*, November 4, 1903; *The Sporting News*, November 14, 1903, p. 1; *Sporting Life*, November 21, 1903, p. 9.
21. *Sporting Life*, January 2, 1904, p. 10.
22. *Sporting Life*, November 7, 1903, p. 9, November 21, 1903, p. 4.
23. *Sporting Life*, October 3, 1904, p. 4.
24. *Milwaukee Sentinel*, October 16, 1903.
25. *Evening Wisconsin*, September 8, 1903.
26. *The Sporting News*, October 24, 1903, p. 2.
27. *Sporting Life*, October 17, 1903, p. 13, November 7, 1903, p. 4.

28. *Sporting Life* January 23, 1904, p. 7.
29. *Sporting Life*, October 31, 1903, p. 6.
30. *Sporting Life*, October 31, 1903, p. 6.
31. *Sporting Life*, November 7, 1903, p. 4, August 29, 1903, p. 17.
32. *The Sporting News*, October 31, 1903, p. 1, 3; November 7, 1903, p. 1; *Sporting Life*, November 7, 1903, p. 6.
33. *Sporting Life*, November 14, 1903, p. 6.
34. *The Sporting News*, October 31, 1903, p. 3.
35. *Milwaukee Sentinel*, August 11, 17, 1903; *The Sporting News*, September 26, 1903, p. 4.
36. *Sporting Life*, September 12, 1903, p. 6, September 26, 1903, p. 5, 19.
37. *The Sporting News*, October 31, 1903, p. 3; *Sporting Life*, November 14, 1903, p. 6.
38. *Milwaukee Sentinel*, November 3, 1903.
39. *The Sporting News*, November 14, 1903, p. 4.
40. *Sporting Life*, November 21, 1903, p. 7.
41. *Milwaukee Sentinel*, November 12, 1903; *Sporting Life*, December 5, 1903, p. 2; *The Sporting News*, December 5, 1903, p. 7.
42. *Sporting Life*, November 14, 1903, p. 6.
43. *Milwaukee Sentinel*, January 11, 1904; *Sporting Life*, December 5, 1903, p. 11, December 26,.
1903, p. 5; *The Sporting News*, December 19, 1903, p. 6, 7.
44. *The Sporting News*, November 28, 1903, p. 2, December 19, 1903, p. 7.
45. *Sporting Life*, December 5, 1903, p. 2; *The Sporting News*, December 5, 1903, p. 7.
46. *Sporting Life*, December 5, 1903, p. 1.
47. *The Sporting News*, November 7, 103, p. 1, November 14, 1903, p. 1, November 28, 1903, p. 4; *Sporting Life*, December 5, 1903, p. 1.
48. *Sporting Life*, January 2, 1904, p. 10.
49. *Sporting Life*, December 19, 1903, p. 8.
50. *The Sporting News*, February 6, 1904, p. 2; *Sporting Life*, February 6, 1904, p. 6.
51. *The Sporting News*, November 14, 1903, p. 4.
52. *Sporting Life*, December 12, 1903, p. 4.
53. *Sporting Life*, December 19, 1903, p. 6.
54. *Sporting Life*, December 12, 1903, p. 8.
55. *Colorado Springs Gazette*, September 5, 1903; *The Sporting News*, December 19, 1903, p. 6; *Sporting Life*, December 19, 1903, p. 7, January 2, 1904, p. 10.
56. *Sporting Life*, December 26, 1903, p. 5, January 2, 1904, p. 9.
57. *Sporting Life*, January 9, 1904, p. 5.
58. *The Sporting News*, January 9, 1904, p. 1; *Sporting Life*, January 9, 1904, p. 5.
59. *The Sporting News*, January 9, 1904, p. 3.
60. *The Sporting News*, January 9, 1904, p. 3.
61. *Sporting Life*, January 23, 1904, p. 7; *The Sporting News*, January 16, 1904, p. 1, January 23, 1904, p. 5.
62. *Milwaukee Sentinel*, January 19, 1904; *Sporting Life*, January 23, 1904, p. 7, January 30, 1904, p. 6, February 6, 1904, p. 5.
63. *The Sporting News*, January 23, 1904, p. 1.
64. *The Sporting News*, January 30, 104, p. 2.
65. *Milwaukee Sentinel*, January 29, 1904; *Sporting Life*, February 6, 1904, p. 5; *The Sporting News*, February 6, 1904, p. 1.
66. *Sporting Life*, January 30, 1904, p. 6, 7.
67. Baseball-reference.com/bullen — Toledo Mud Hens and Charleston Senators.

Bibliography

Newspapers

Cedar Rapids (Iowa) *Evening Gazette*
Chicago *Daily Inter Ocean*
Chicago *Eagle*
Colorado Springs *Gazette*
Des Moines *Daily Capital*
Des Moines *Ledger*
Daily Kennebec (Maine) *Journal*
Evening Wisconsin (Milwaukee)
Fort Wayne *Morning Journal-Gazette*
Kansas City *Star*
Mansfield (Ohio) *News*
Milwaukee *Daily News*
Milwaukee *Journal*
Milwaukee *Sentinel*
Minneapolis *Journal*
New York *Times*
Oakland (California) *Tribune*
Omaha *Daily Bee*
Omaha *Daily News*
Omaha *World-Herald*
Peoria *Evening Star*
Peoria *Journal*
Philadelphia *North American*
Pittsburgh *Post Gazette*
Portland *Morning Oregonian*
St. Joseph *Daily News*
St. Joseph *Gazette-Herald*
St. Louis *Republican*
St. Paul *Globe*
Salt Lake *Herald*
Sporting Life
The Sporting News
Toledo *Bee*
Valentine (Nebraska) *Democrat*
Washington (D.C.) *Times*

Books and Journals

The American Association Almanac: A Baseball History, vol. 8, no. 1 and 2.
Brown, Clifford A. "Biography of Humphrey B. Chamberlin, Patron of the University of Denver's Historic Chamberlin Observatory." Dec. 16, 1980. Available online at http://www.denverastrosociety.org/dfiles/chambio.pdf.
Reach Base Ball Guides
Spalding Base Ball Guides
Williams, Walter, ed. *A History of Northwest Missouri*. 3 vols. Chicago: Lewis, 1915.

Internet Resources

American Association almanac: almanacpark.blogspot.com
Baseball-reference.com
Nebaseballhistory.com
Pikes Peak Historical Street Railway Foundation newsletter: coloradospringstrolleys.com
Omaha Public Library Digital Collection: http://digital.omahapubliclibrary.org
SABR Biography Project: bioproj.sabr.org
SABR Encyclopedia: sabrpedia.org

Index

Abbott (umpire) 97
Adkins, Merle 80, 149
admission prices 18, 21, 121
Alchele, Julius 186
alcohol, players use of 68
Alleman, Harry 167
Alloway, Arthur 64, 80, 94, 106
Altrock, Nick 37, 91, 96, 149, 193
American Association 7, 8–10, 15, 17–18, 22–24, 26, 28, 31–32, 34, 38–42, 44–46, 49–54, 56, 57, 66–69, 72–78, 86–88, 91–92, 97, 103–104, 108–109, 111–125, 133, 135, 139–142, 147, 148–149, 154, 159–168, 173, 177–178, 180–183, 185, 187–189
American League 3, 10, 33–34, 89, 125, 127, 147, 157
Anderson, Indiana 138, 140
Andrew, James 126
Anson, Adrian "Cap" 7, 8, 121
Armory Park (Toledo) 57, 164
Armour, William B. 37, 48
Association Park (Kansas City) 159–160, 165
Athletic Park (Des Moines) 24, 98, 169
Athletic Park (Milwaukee) 15, 27, 62, 64, 110, 132, 134, 137, 171
attendance at league's games 57–62, 64, 66–68, 71, 73, 75–76, 82, 84, 85, 86–87, 159–160, 163–164, 169–173, 175, 178
Auditorium Hotel (Chicago) 114

Babb, Charles 52, 53
Bailey, Harvey 45, 63, 167
Ball, Artie 65–66
Baltimore (Eastern League) 185
Bandle, Frank W. 19
Bannon, Jimmy 162
Barber, Frank 66, 78, 171
Barnard, Ernest S. 77–78, 179
Barrow, Ed 45, 150
Barry, Tom 66, 78, 169
Barston, Charles 95, 110
Barton, Joseph J. 85, 128, 129
Batson, Bert P. 129–130

Bauman, H.J. 131–136
Beall, A.B. 7–8, 15–16, 38, 170, 184, 188
Bean, Joe 39
Belden, Ira 200
Beloit College 47
Bernard, Curt 194
Berry, Claude 150
Beville, Monte 192
Binghamton (New York State League) 155
Birmingham (Southern League) 141, 146, 152
Bohannon, Pat 167
Bone, George 94, 96
Bonner, Frank 149
Bookwalter, Mayor Charles 59, 138, 139
Boston Beaneaters (National League) 13, 149, 183, 189
Boston Red Sox (American League) 29, 149
Boulevard Park (Colorado Springs) 63–64, 70
Boylan (Indianapolis police sergeant) 101
Boynton, Ed 117
Brain, Davy 40
Brashear, Norman 41, 50
Bresnahan, Roger 110
Broadway Park (Denver) 15–16, 20, 38, 63, 82
Brooklyn Superbas (National League) 36, 47, 109, 149
Brown, Mordecai 35, 78, 80, 82, 149, 199
Brush, John T. 60
Bryce, Thomas J. 6–7, 8, 23, 45, 51, 53, 59, 62, 68, 111, 114, 123, 140–143, 145, 150, 163, 179
Buckenberger, Al 149
Buell, Arden L. 19, 21, 22, 46, 67, 127
Buffalo (Eastern League) 24, 39–40, 43, 54, 185
Burke, Richard A. 110
Burke, Robert 118, 120–121, 123, 124
Burke, R.R. 128, 130, 188
Burns, Jack 37, 74, 153
Burns, James F. 4, 64
Burns, Thomas F. 4, 8, 15, 19, 23, 25, 26, 63–64, 70, 85, 96, 108–110, 113–114, 116,

211

127, 128, 130, 155, 157, 172, 175, 180, 183, 186, 189
Butler, John 195
Butte (Pacific National League) 161

Cable, Frank 200
Cable Building (Chicago) 23
Calhoun, David 198
California League 33, 34, 36, 38, 55, 147, 148
Cantillon, Joe 101–105, 134, 141, 145, 146, 148, 155, 157–158
Carrick, Bill 164
Carter, Bob 65, 82, 200
Cassidy, Pete 148, 150–152
Cedar Rapids baseball team 154
Central League 127, 138–140, 184
Central Park Methodist Church (St. Paul) 126
Central Railway Co. 81, 128
Chapleske, Theodore 154
Charleston, West Virginia 189
Chase, W.P. 20
Chech, Charles 40, 63, 76, 166, 167, 196
Chicago, Illinois 3–4, 7, 8, 117–125, 127
Chicago baseball parks 119–122, 125
Chicago Colts (National League) 42, 45, 119–123
Chicago White Sox (American League) 56, 118–119, 121–123, 149, 158, 183
Childs, Peter 148, 195
Churchill Downs 58, 59
Cincinnati, Ohio 8
Cincinnati Reds (National League) 39, 42, 56, 143, 152
Clark, Addison 180
Clark, Charles 26–27
Clark Coach and Transfer Company 180
Clarke, Josh 78, 198
Clarkson, Frank P. 25, 129
Cleveland (American Association) 189
Cleveland (American League) 37, 47–48, 143, 152, 157, 161
Cline, Ed 52–53
Clingman, Billy 23, 37, 54, 72, 131, 140–143, 146, 160–161, 166, 192
Clymer, Billy 39, 53, 90, 97, 100, 105, 144, 148, 150, 151, 192, 194
Cockman, Jim 99, 174, 198, 200
Cogan, Dick 40, 69
Coggswell, Charles 192
Cole (umpire) 94
Collison, Frank 177
Colorado Iron and Fuel Co. 108, 109
Colorado Springs Millionaires (Western League) 3–4, 9, 11, 14, 19, 21, 25, 36, 37, 55, 70, 78–79, 81, 83, 85, 86, 94, 96, 98, 108–109, 147, 154–155, 157, 174, 178, 180, 182, 189, 197, 199
Columbus (Western Association) 3, 5–6, 10
Columbus Senators (American Association) 8, 23, 34, 37, 45, 51, 57, 59, 62, 67, 68, 74, 77, 86, 101, 140, 141–143, 144, 147, 150, 155, 160, 162, 168, 177–178, 185, 191, 194
Comiskey, Charles 34, 73, 118, 120–122, 125, 158, 164
Congalton, Bill 197, 199
Connecticut State League 144
Coons, Perry 69, 193, 196
Corbett, Joe 154
Corbit, Joe 57
Corcoran, Cornelius 19, 21, 22, 136
Coulter, Arthur 39
Council Bluffs, Iowa 8
Cox, Chester 63
Cox, Eugene 78–79
Crabb, J.R. 16
Crabill, Ernest 155–157
Cripple Creek, Colorado 4, 182, 185
Cunningham, Ellsworth 100, 101, 103–104, 105

Dallas (Texas League) 150
Dammann, Bill 68
Davenport (Three-I League) 184
Davidson Hotel (Milwaukee) 22, 163
Davis (umpire) 94
Davis, Ira 70
Davis, W.J. 154
Dayton (Western Association) 37
Delahanty, Ed 171–172
Delahanty, Tom 79, 93, 147, 171–172, 197, 198, 199, 200
Denver, Colorado 109
Denver Grizzlies (Western League) 3–4, 11, 14, 15–16, 19, 25, 41, 43, 52, 55, 65, 68, 70–71, 78–79, 81–83, 85, 92–93, 147, 149, 157, 169, 171–175, 178, 180, 182, 186, 188–189, 197, 199
Des Moines Undertakers (Western League) 3, 9, 11, 14, 18, 20, 24–26, 36, 55–56, 65, 68, 78, 83, 85, 97, 98, 108, 129, 147, 157, 171, 174, 178, 180, 182, 189, 197, 199
Detroit (American League) 125, 143, 161
Detroit, Michigan 109, 117, 121, 122
Devereaux, William 54
Dillard, Pat 192
Dolan, Joe 198
Donahue, Jiggs 104, 163, 193–194
Dorneer, Gus 143
Dowd, Tommy 19, 20
Downtown Park (St. Paul) 118–120, 122, 125–127
Doyle, James 186
Dreyfuss, Barney 117
Dubuque, Iowa 14
Duffy, Hugh 20, 25, 26, 28–29, 30, 32, 40, 55, 72, 74, 82–84, 86, 94–97, 110, 128, 130, 146, 168–170, 180, 182–183, 198, 199
Dulaney, W.H. 58
Dundon, Gus 41, 79, 157–158, 197, 198
Dungan, Sam 193
Dunham, Wiley 51, 57
Dunkel, Dave 149, 193

Index 213

Dunleavy, Bill 105
Durham, Jim 105, 154, 196

Eagan, Mel 196
Eastern League 39–40, 53, 181–182, 185, 187
Ebbets, Charles 47
Eclipse Park (Louisville) 59, 159
Egan, Aloysius 105
Elk's Club 36
Elliott, Claude 105, 196
Evans, John 52
Evans, Roy 42–43
Evansville, Indiana 74, 110
Everitt, Bill 4, 25, 37, 49, 80, 98–99, 128, 147, 172, 197, 199
Evers, Jack 83
Exhibition Park (Kansas City) 14, 116, 159, 183, 187
Eyler, Elwood 71, 78, 198

Farrell, J.H. 35, 117, 151–152, 154, 179, 181, 186
Federal League 189
Ferguson, Charlie 115, 119, 166, 167, 193, 196
Figgmeier, Frank 76
Fisher, M.E. (Detective) 55
Flaherty, Patrick 39, 53, 69, 149, 193
Fleming, Tom 65, 80, 199
Flood, Tim 36
floods (Kansas area) 169–170
Floto, Otto 11
Flournoy, John 53, 69, 75, 192
Flynn, Frank 8, 20, 24
Foreman, Frank 80, 95, 96, 100, 101, 105, 106
foul-strike rule 161, 169
Fox, Bill 36, 192
Fox, George 74, 160
Francis (umpire) 96
Francks, Buck 54–55, 98–99
Frank, Charles 74
Friese, A.W. 66, 95, 179
Frisk, Emil 79, 197

Ganley, Bob 100, 105
Ganzel, John 69, 149, 191, 192
Gatins, Frank 83, 174, 200
Gatto, Larry 22
Gavin, Joseph 29
Gear, Dale 22–23, 38, 41, 44, 46, 77, 96, 101, 127, 145, 146, 152, 158, 185
Geier, Phil 165, 167, 191, 194, 195
Genins, Frank 65, 184
Gibson, Norwood 70, 80
Gibson, Ralph 193
Giddings, E.W. 64
Giljohan, Rudolph 21
Gilks, Bob 193
Glade, Fred 80, 200
Gonding, Johnny 65, 198, 199
Grady, Mike 96–97, 101, 105, 165, 191, 194, 195
Graffius, Bill 192
Grand Rapids, Michigan 73–74, 109, 127, 140

Grand Rapids (Western Association) 17
Granville, Art 80
Grillo, J. Edward 187
Grim, John 23, 34, 53, 74, 192
Griswald, Sandy 30
Gross, Fred C. 14–15, 20, 25, 28, 30
Grossert, George 37
Gunnels, J.W. 6

Haldermann, Charles W. 60, 138–139
Hallman, Bill 149, 191, 192
Halsey (Judge) 136
Halsted, Pennsylvania 156
Hanford, Charlie 66, 198
Hardesty, George D. 23
Harriman, E.H. 25
Harris, Ira 64
Hart, James A. 45, 119, 121, 125
Hart, Jim 192
Hart, William 24, 25, 35, 55–56, 146, 184
Hartford (Eastern League) 39–40
Hartman, Billy 41, 50
Haskell, Jack 105, 160
Havenor, Charles S. 4, 8, 15, 26, 50, 84, 103–104, 109, 114, 123, 131–137, 141–143, 145, 163–164, 166, 185
Hemphill, Frank 103, 154–155
Herman, Art 92
Hess, Otto 169
Heydon, Mike 192
Hickey, Mike 68
Hickey, Thomas 3, 7–9, 10–11, 18–19, 23, 26–27, 32, 33, 39, 44–46, 49–51, 54, 67, 86, 97, 100, 103, 105–107, 109, 117, 119–120, 122–124, 133, 140, 142, 145, 154, 157, 160, 177, 179, 193–194
Higby, Porter 130, 170
Hill, Hugh 152
Hill, "Still Bill" 68
Hoffman, Dan 153
Hogriever, George 76, 192, 194
Hollingsworth, Wally 157, 198
Holly, Ed 186, 200
Holmes, Jim "Ducky" 157
Hoops, S.E. 16
Hotel Baltimore (Kansas City) 18
Huggins, Miller 40, 119, 167, 191, 192, 194
Hulen, William 4
Huntsville, Alabama 152
Hurley, Jeremiah 43
Husting, Pete 72

Indiana-Iowa-Illinois League 30, 31, 128, 179, 184
Indianapolis (Western League) 20, 23–24, 60
Indianapolis Hoosiers (American Association) 8, 23–24, 34, 39, 59–61, 67, 74–77, 84, 86, 97, 101, 103, 105, 109, 119, 137–140, 147, 150, 168, 177, 179, 185, 191, 194
Indianapolis Ministerial Association 139
Interstate League 38

Index

Iowa Hotel (Des Moines) 99
Irwin, Arthur 185
Ivywild, Colorado 63–64, 70

Jackson, Jim 166, 167, 194, 195
Jacobs, Morris 186
Jersey Club (Eastern League) 29, 150–151, 185
Johnson, Ban 11, 12, 23, 29, 34, 89, 124, 125, 188
Johnston, Edward A. 16, 141, 145, 161, 180
Jones, Burt 172
Jones, Charles 43, 79, 157–158, 197, 198, 200
Joss, Addie 37, 47–49
jumping of player contracts 31–32, 33–56, 68, 77, 116, 134, 144, 148, 149, 150–158

Kansas City (National League) 12
Kansas City Blue Stockings (Western League) 3–4, 10, 11–14, 19, 25–26, 32, 38, 41, 44, 45–47, 55, 60, 65, 67–68, 69–70, 78–79, 81–84, 85–86, 109, 111–116, 127, 130, 146, 170, 174, 176, 178, 181–184, 186–189, 197, 199
Kansas City Blues (American Association) 8–9, 12, 18, 22, 23, 32, 33–34, 38, 41, 43–44, 46–47, 55, 57, 67, 73, 74, 76, 83–84, 86, 90, 96, 100–101, 109, 111–116, 127, 147, 152, 154, 162, 165, 168, 176–177, 191, 194
Katoll, Jack 73
Kavanaugh, William 114, 152
Kebler, J.A. 109
Keith, Buchanan 17
Kelley, Michael 23, 42–43, 53, 91–92, 100, 118, 119, 145–146, 158, 166–167, 194, 195
Kellum, Win 57, 69, 193, 194, 196
Kelly (umpire) 98–99
Kenna, Ed 72, 79, 80, 183, 198, 200
Kerwin, Dan 97, 192, 194
Ketcham, Fred 46, 197
Killen, Frank 193
Killilea, Henry 29
Kilm, George 53, 192, 194
Kleinow, John 194
Knoll, Julius 192, 193
Kostal, Joseph 55
Kuhns, Charlie 193
Kundegraber, Ed 73, 95, 100, 170

Ladendorf, George 30
Lafayette, Indiana 138
Lake View grounds (Peoria) 79, 81
Lally, Dan 68, 193, 195
Lanigan, Ernest J. 13
LaPorte (Indianapolis patrolman) 101
Lennon, George 8, 16, 17, 23, 40, 42, 52, 86, 115, 118–126, 154, 166, 177, 179, 185
Leonard, Frank J. 144, 145, 150, 158, 162
Lewee, Ed 43, 49, 97, 104, 165, 193, 195
Lexington Park (St. Paul) 61, 63, 90, 118–119, 126–127
Lincoln (Western Association) 8
Lincoln (Western League) 180, 182, 184, 187, 189

Little Rock (Southern League) 71, 154
Lockhart, W.E. 184
Logansport, Indiana 138
Lohbeck, Joe 198
Los Angeles (Pacific National League) 157
Louisville (Western Association) 17, 22, 23
Louisville baseball parks 58–59
Louisville Colonels (American Association) 8, 35, 39, 41, 44, 50, 53, 67, 68–69, 73, 74–77, 86, 144–145, 147–149–152, 154, 167, 177–178, 185, 191, 194
Lowe, Bobby 171–172, 180
Lucas, William 114
Lucia, Fred 174, 186, 199
Lumley, Harry 43, 76
Lundbom, Jack 48
Lynch, Billy 53
Lyrics of the Hills 72

Mack, Connie 29, 43, 53, 54, 149
Mack, Edward 114, 116
Maney, Vincent 192
Manhattan, Kansas 169
Manhattan Gold and Silver Mining Co. 19
Manning, James 8, 10, 11–15, 19, 23, 25, 26, 47, 65, 110, 128, 130
Marion, Indiana 60, 67, 137
Marsh, Arthur M. 20
Martin, Frank 154
mascots 70
Maupin, Harry 78
McBride, George 55, 193, 200
McCarthy (umpire) 174
McCloskey, Charles 71, 199
McConnell, Jack 70, 199
McCreery, Tom 161, 194
McFadden, Barney 94
McFarland, Claude 69, 192
McGill, Willie 70, 105
McGowan, Hugh 24
McGraw, John 7
McHale, Bob 55
McIntyre, Charles 195
McKibben, Bryon 25, 36, 43, 49, 65, 94, 129, 147
McKinnon, James 110, 129
McMackin, Sam 52–53
McMakin, John 160
McNeely, Harris 80, 200
McPherson, John 66, 82, 200
Memphis (Southern League) 53, 74, 109
Meredith, Elmer 103, 104, 154, 196
Merrill, H.G. 51, 151
Messitt, Tom 46, 70, 198
Methodist ministers of Indianapolis 138
Meyer, William 4–5
Millard Hotel (Omaha) 65
Miller, Frank 83
Miller, Ralph 39
Milwaukee Baseball Park 15, 20–21, 25, 67, 170–171

Index 215

Milwaukee Brewers (American Association) 8, 15, 23, 27, 32, 34, 37, 43, 50, 57, 62, 67, 72–74, 77, 84, 86–87, 96, 99, 101, 103–104, 106–107, 109–112, 114–115, 121, 123, 131–137, 141–143, 147–149, 154, 157, 162–163, 168, 175–176, 180, 189, 191, 194
Milwaukee Brewers (American League) 3, 4, 11, 14, 29
Milwaukee Creams (Western League) 14–15, 19–21, 24, 25–26, 28, 30, 32, 40, 55, 65–68, 71–74, 78–80, 82–84, 85–87, 93, 97, 99, 108, 109–115, 127, 130, 146, 168–170, 172–176, 178, 182, 184, 186–187, 189, 197, 199
Minneapolis (Western League) 3–4, 8, 10, 11, 16, 20, 108
Minneapolis Millers (American Association) 8–9, 20, 23, 34, 38, 41, 45, 61, 67, 73, 75–77, 109, 117, 127, 141, 147–148, 154, 157, 160, 168, 176, 179–180, 191, 194
Minnehaha Driving Park (Minneapolis) 16, 20, 38
Missouri University 14
Mitchell, W.W. 81
Mitchell Hotel (Peoria) 81
Mock, Homer 36–37
Mohler, E.F. 55
Montreal (Eastern League) 54
Moran, August 80, 82–83, 93, 95, 103
Morrison, Bill 171, 200
Motz, Frank 37
Mud Hens nickname 6
Mulford, Ren 179
Mullane, Tony 100–101, 105
Muncie, Indiana 138, 140
Murnane, Thomas 151, 179
Myers, Bill 192
Myrick, C.H. 128–129, 189

Nance, Kid 55, 97, 106, 192, 194, 195
Nashville (Southern League) 109, 152
Nashville, Tennessee 74
Nation, W.R. 184, 189
National Agreement 3, 6, 30, 34, 148–149, 177
National Association of Professional Baseball Leagues 6, 8–9, 10, 11, 31, 33, 35, 38, 55, 74, 85, 111–117, 124, 128, 150–155, 158, 172, 175, 177, 180–182, 186
National League 3, 8, 10, 33, 42, 53, 57, 117, 125, 127, 147
Nattress, Billy 54, 193
Neil, Charles 59
Neil, Thomas 59
Neil Park (Columbus) 59, 163
New York (American League) 129, 146, 149
New York Giants (National League) 42–43, 53, 63, 172
Newmeyer, Harry 80
Nichols, Charles "Kid" 12–14, 25, 26, 36, 46, 49, 70, 86, 127, 128, 130, 146, 183, 198, 200

Nicollet Park (Minneapolis) 16, 20, 38
Nill, George 199

Oakland (California League) 99
O'Brien (Indiana Senator) 138
O'Brien, Jack 198
O'Brien, John 49, 91, 197
O'Connor, Patrick 153
Odell, Fred 54, 105, 194, 195
Ogden (Inter-Mountain League) 42–43
O'Hara, William 153
O'Leary, Charles 78, 95, 198, 199, 200
Olmsted, Hank 69
Omaha (American Association) 8, 17–19, 21, 180
Omaha baseball grounds 19, 68, 82
Omaha Indians (Western League) 3, 8, 10, 11, 14, 17–19, 25, 36, 55, 63, 65, 66, 68, 70, 78–84, 85, 147, 154, 174, 178, 182, 189, 197, 199
Omaha Railway Company 125–126
O'Neill, John 199
Order of Base Ball Rooters (St. Paul) 61
O'Rourke, James 114
Owen, Frank 65, 78, 80, 82, 149, 198
Owens, Red 160
Owens, Tom 54, 195
Oyler, Andy 157

Pacific Hotel (Chicago) 113
Pacific Northwest League 115
Packard, Durand C. 11, 15, 19–20, 25, 30, 33, 41, 63, 70, 71, 92, 94, 108, 110, 114–117, 122, 127, 130, 149, 172, 175, 181, 183, 186–188
Pardee, Al 37
Parvin, Frank 66, 79, 198
Peoria Distillers (Western League) 14, 20, 24–26, 35, 42, 55–56, 78–79, 81, 83, 85, 90, 95, 98, 108, 128–129, 146, 169, 173–174, 178, 182, 184, 186, 189, 197, 199
Perini, Louis 189
Phelon, W.A., Jr. 121, 124
Philadelphia Athletics 43–44, 53, 72, 153–154
Philadelphia Phillies 183
Phillips, Bill 179–180
Phyle, Bill 55, 103, 141
Pierce, Elmer 154
Players' Protective Association 23, 38
playing rules 23, 24
Portland (Pacific Northwest League) 153
Postal, Fred 12
Power, Charles B. 6
Powers, Pat 112–114, 125, 181
Powers' plan 112–115
Preston, Walter 70–71
Providence (Eastern League) 42, 53, 125, 150
Pueblo, Colorado 109
Pueblo (Western League) 3, 20, 108–109, 180, 182, 189
Pulliam, Harry 149, 188

216 Index

Quick, Edwin 153
Quin, Harry D. 4, 8, 15, 18, 23, 27, 32, 39, 50, 54, 61–62, 72, 74, 84, 86, 87, 109, 131–137, 141–143
Quinn, Bobby 74, 140, 162
Quinn, Joe 25, 56, 66, 78, 147, 157, 174, 198, 199

Radcliff, C.E. 70, 71, 93
Raymer, Fred 160, 195
Reach, Al 72
Reach baseball 32
Reilly, Charles J. 11
Reisling, Frank "Doc" 144, 145, 158, 160, 166, 196
Retail Liquor Dealers' Association (Indianapolis) 138
Richter, Francis 175
Roach, Mike 161
Robinson, Clyde 43–44, 46, 55
Rock Island, Illinois 31
Rockford, Illinois 14
Roe (umpire) 95
Rohe, George 147, 198, 200
Roth, Frank 50
Rothfuss, Jack 101, 192, 195
Rourke, William 8, 17–19, 22, 25, 26, 38, 64, 65, 68, 94–95, 110, 128, 147, 175, 180, 184, 188–189
rowdyism 82–83, 87–107
Ruschaupt, Charles 8, 179
Ryan, Jimmy 4, 118

Sacramento (California League) 55, 148
St. Joseph Saints (Western League) 3, 9, 11, 14, 19, 25, 36, 41, 55, 70, 78, 83, 85, 108–109, 129–130, 147, 174, 178, 180, 182, 189, 197, 199
St. Louis (American League) 3, 11
St. Louis (National League) 25, 51, 56, 60, 147, 149
St. Paul (Western League) 3–4, 10, 11, 108, 127
St. Paul Commercial Club 119–120
St. Paul Saints (American Association) 8, 16, 23, 34, 39, 40, 42–44, 52–53, 56, 57, 61, 67, 75–77, 91–92, 105, 109, 115, 117–126, 141–143, 145–146, 147, 160–161, 163, 165, 167–168, 177, 191, 194
Sanborn, Cy 73
San Francisco Baseball team 42, 52, 53, 55, 141, 153
Saugston (Indianapolis patrolman) 101
Saunders, P.H. 183, 185
Schaefer, Herman 42, 195
Schafstall, Bob 95
Schaub, Bob 50, 148, 166, 193, 195
Schlafly, Larry 103, 195
Schmidt, Henry 55, 149
Schriver, Bill 192
Sears, W.W. 128, 175

Seattle (Pacific Coast League) 147, 155
Sexton, Michael 30–31, 64, 71, 73, 83, 85, 86, 89, 93, 95, 97, 99, 110–111, 114, 127–128, 170–171, 174–175, 179–181, 184–185, 187–189
Shannon, William "Spike" 100, 115, 119, 165–166, 167, 191, 194, 195
Shaw, Al 43
Shay, Danny 52
Sheibeck, Frank 193
Shively, Doc 10, 23
Simmons, George 128–129
Sioux City, Iowa 109, 170, 173
Sioux City (Western League) 3, 9, 14, 20, 24, 60, 180, 182, 184, 187, 189
Sioux Falls baseball team 154
Slattery, Jack 143
Smith, Jud 193
Smith, Mike 192, 194
Smith, Robert A. 126
Somers, Charles W. 48
South Side Park (Chicago) 118–122
Southern Hotel (St. Louis) 181
Southern League 52, 53, 74, 109
Spalding baseball 24, 32
Speer, Kid 43, 146, 192, 195
Spies, Harry 192
Spokane (Northwestern League) 55, 153
Springfield (Connecticut State League) 153
Springfield (New England League) 54
Stallings, George 39–40
Stearns, Dan 90, 93, 95, 198
Stevens, Charley 110
Stewart, Ace 35, 198
Stewart, Joe 166, 167, 196
Stimmel, Archie 42, 91, 141
Stone, George 197, 198
Stratton, William Scott 64, 81
Strauss, Jake 96
Streib, Julius 199
Strobel, Charles J. 4–6, 8, 23, 34, 36–37, 47–48, 57, 60, 62, 110, 123, 142, 145, 152–154, 164–166, 180
Sullivan, Frank L. 129–130
Sullivan, Sutor 148, 194, 195
Sunday baseball 16, 24, 58, 59–60, 67–68, 119, 121, 126, 137–140, 182, 184, 185
Sutthoff, Jack 193
Swigert (umpire) 93–94
Swormstead, Len 200
Syracuse (Eastern League) 40, 43, 153

Tacoma (Pacific Northwest League) 147
Tannehill, Lee 69, 75, 77, 149, 191, 193
Tebeau, George 8, 9, 10–12, 14, 15, 20, 22–23, 26, 33–36, 41, 43, 47, 50, 58–59, 74, 86, 89, 109, 111, 119, 123, 127, 130, 140, 145, 157, 159, 161, 179, 183–189
Tebeau, Oliver "Patsy" 10
Thiel, John 199
Thoney, Jack 143

Index 217

Thornton, John 83, 93, 99
Tibald, Peter 200
Tindell, Charles 75, 90–92, 97
Toft, Jack 150
Toledo (Interstate League) 5
Toledo (Western Association) 3, 5–6, 10, 47
Toledo Mud Hens (American Association) 8–9, 23, 24, 34, 36, 47–48, 52, 57, 68, 77–78, 97, 105, 109–110, 123, 141–142, 144, 147, 153–154, 160, 164–166, 168, 177–178, 180, 185, 189, 191, 194
Toronto (Eastern League) 39, 45, 50, 150, 185
Torrence, Cy 76
Towne, Jay 199
Troop A First Cavalry 15
Truby, Harry 35
Tucker, Terry 63
Turner, Dan 192, 194
Turner, James H. 135–136
Turner, Joseph 21, 22
Turner, Terry 143, 193, 194, 195
Turner, W.J. 132–136

umpires 24, 29, 75–76, 89–107
Unglaub, Bob 104–105, 148, 161–162, 195
uniforms 18, 62, 65, 159
union activities 61–62, 86, 164
Union Park (Denver) 16, 20
University of Kansas 14, 146
Utah League 51

Van Brunt, John H. 130
Van Brunt, W.T. 7, 15, 19, 21, 23, 24, 25–26, 28, 30, 50, 67, 73, 85, 110–112, 114–116, 122, 128–130, 182
Vaughn, Harry "Farmer" 56, 81
Victor, Colorado 182
Victor baseball 32, 124
Viox, Roney 69, 193, 195

Wagner, Ivor 62–63
Waldron, Irv 197, 199
Walker, Tom 195

Wall, Joe 70–71
Walton, Thomas 95–96
The Wardrobe 179
Warner, Frank 42
Washington, D.C. (American League) 12, 14, 152, 157, 171–172
Washington Park (Indianapolis) 137, 139
Watkins, William H. 8, 23–24, 36, 52, 59–61, 67, 76, 103, 109, 111–112, 114, 119, 123, 137–140, 145–146, 158, 179–181, 185
Weimer, Jake 46–47, 55, 78, 80, 95, 199
Werden, Perry 148
West Virginia University 72
Western Association 4–6, 8, 17
Western League 3–4, 7, 8–9, 11, 15–16, 19–21, 23–25, 27–28, 30, 32, 33, 35, 41–42, 44, 49–50, 55–56, 66–68, 69–71, 73, 78–88, 89–90, 92–94, 104, 110–117, 122, 127–130, 133, 149, 168–175, 178, 180–189
Wheeling (Western Association) 45, 72
White, Charles D. 30
White, Harry 195
Whitfield, James 11–12, 14–16, 17, 24, 29–30, 34, 38
Whitridge, Al 41, 198
Williams, Tom 75, 193
Wilmot, Walter 16–17, 20, 23, 34, 38, 45, 50, 52, 77, 100, 121, 127, 143, 145–146, 148, 157, 158, 160–161
Wilson, Bill 42, 146, 174, 199
Wilson, Parke 25, 41, 70–71, 90, 92–94, 147
Winslow, H.A. 23
Wolf, Billy 55
Wolfe, Barney 49
Wonderland Amusement Park 137
Wood, Bob 157, 161, 163, 194, 195
Wood, George B. 184
Worcester (Eastern League) 148
Wright, Joe 82, 174, 186
Wylie, Harvey 165

Yeager, George 100, 105–106, 161, 194

Zalusky, Jack 45